James Boyd Brady

The Sängerfest Sermons

James Boyd Brady

The Sängerfest Sermons

ISBN/EAN: 9783743331174

Manufactured in Europe, USA, Canada, Australia, Japa

Cover: Foto ©Thomas Meinert / pixelio.de

Manufactured and distributed by brebook publishing software
(www.brebook.com)

James Boyd Brady

The Sängerfest Sermons

The Sængerfest Sermons.

THE

SÆNGERFEST SERMONS

BY

JAMES BOYD BRADY, B.D., D.D.

PASTOR OF FRANKLIN STREET METHODIST EPISCOPAL

CHURCH, NEWARK, N. J.

———————

NEWARK, N. J.

ADVERTISER PRINTING HOUSE,

1891

To

THE GERMAN PEOPLE WHO CAUSED THEM:

THE CONGREGATIONS WHO LISTENED TO THEM:

THE PEOPLE OF NEWARK WHO ENCOURAGED THEM:

AND ALL CITIZENS INTERESTED IN

THE WELFARE OF THIS REPUBLIC,

AND OF THE WORLD THROUGH THE

PROPAGATION OF ITS FUNDAMENTAL INSTITUTION,

THESE DISCOURSES

ARE RESPECTFULLY COMMITTED.

CONTENTS.

PREFACE.

THE preaching of these sermons was unexpected till a week before their utterance was begun. Their publication in present form was as unanticipated as their expression from the pulpit. Circumstances were the factors that called for them from without; conviction the power that generated them within. The following were the circumstances:

The officials of the "Great German Sængerfest" decided to hold their "grand" quadrennial in Newark, N. J. Five thousand selected singers (it is said), from the leading capitals of America, came to sing, and one hundred thousand to hear, on the various days of the feast. The singers were booked to sing on Friday 3rd, Saturday 4th, Sunday 5th, and Monday 6th of July, 1891. But the 5th of July was the Sabbath, and great anxiety and curiosity were felt in Newark, as to what the Germans would sing on Sunday, and also as to how they would otherwise keep the Sabbath.

As soon as the programmes were printed, it was evident; no more regard had been paid to the Lord's Day than to any other day. Instead of showing the customary courtesy to hosts, the Germans actually determined, to defiantly violate our Sabbath laws on the largest scale, notwithstanding the fact that they were the guests of a Christian city. So when the Holy Day came, it was trampled ruthlessly in the dust by two hundred thousand German feet in the city of Newark—a city noted for its churches, charities, and "fair humanities."

It was then I determined to lift up my voice in protestation, whether any man stood by me or not. I knew the Lord was with me, and that was enough. The first sermon so much excited, not only Newark, but America, and the English and German speaking world, that many specimens of comments and criticisms were sent me from all over the commonwealth, containing aspersions of the most violent type. Seeing that the arrow had entered "between the joints of the harness," after due meditation and prayer, I deemed it my duty to follow up the attack, till the enemy either fled or surrendered. I knew I was not going to surrender or flee, and I knew, also, that God Almighty's Word was sufficient to make any enemy do both.

This has been achieved, and this volume contains the truth that accomplished it. The design of publication is two-fold. First, to correct the scurrilities of a large part of the secular press. Certain powerful papers have had the nobility to stand by the truth, and to them I return sincerest thanks; but in the majority of papers I have been half-quoted, mis-quoted and substituted. I have been mis-represented and mal-represented. Represented dancing, represented swearing, represented raving madly, represented sane as Solomon and savage as the Demoniac of Gadara, represented as the most despicable reptile and the most divine among men. No name of vulgarity that could be thought of but has been applied, and no threat of barbarity that could be conceived but has been hurled.

Under these circumstances, I thought it would be but just to all who have favored me with either human or inhuman attention, to apprise them of what I did say and what I did not say; where I stand and where I do not stand, and I found there was no way of doing this but by supervising my own stenographer and printer.

The second part of my motive in permitting the following pages to be printed is to do some good to my fellow men. "I never passed this way before. * * * I never may again." And therefore I need to do what good I can while passing Though small, the book contains good news enough, I trust, to float multitudes away, from the foaming cataract of Sabbath Secularization, out into the safe, serene sea, of Sabbath Spiritualization.

It would be immodest and perhaps super-egotistical to say anything about the audiences that waited on these discourses during delivery. Still, I cannot refrain from here recording my high appreciation of, and gratitude to, the great numbers of intelligent men and women who, time after time, accumulatively to the end, filled the house to overflowing, on warm Summer evenings, to hear the truth of God concerning His Holy Sabbath and His Sacred Son.

Honesty compels me to say, that for continuity, appreciation, intelligence and sustained enthusiasm, I have at no time seen such congregations anywhere, except during great religious awakenings.

In addition to expressing my appreciation of these congregations, I mention this fact, to demonstrate to the lethargic and discouraged how the masses of intelligent people, in the Church and out of it, are hungry for an authoritative solution of the Sabbath question. It is an issue that comes into powerful touch with their weekly life, and they want to know what to do with it, and if we, the preachers, do not tell them, the devil and his deputies won't be slow to show their way of solving it.

Many talk as though Sabbath spoliation and its associate evils, were confirmed invasions we must accept, as direful evolutions of our times and place. With such cowardly mincing no Christian can have sympathy, much less alliance. Whatever may be the pandering sentiment touching this matter in other large cities, it certainly does not flourish in Newark, and by God's help it is proposed it shall not.

To demonstrate how the people of Newark stand with reference to whether the sacred character of religion through Sabbatic ministrations shall be sustained or not, the unrestrainable expressions from the audiences during the delivery of the following discourses have been retained. This is my apology for what, under ordinary circumstances, would be an unchaste and indelicate retention. As things stand, however, we run the gauntlet of even this accusation, in order to let all readers see how dear God's Word, Son, Services and Day are to the best people of New Jersey.

These sermons lay no claim to literary merit, or rhetorical finish. These feats of pulpit acrobats were no part of their design. They were delivered each Sabbath morning and evening, like rugged salvos of artillery, against a great, menacing, living, curse. They were given hot from the pulpit by the aid of a stenographer immediately to the press; and there was neither time nor desire to refine and polish them. They do claim, however, to contain important truths, drawn forth from the shrouded sum of beings and of things, flung with a fearless hand, to defeat the rampant outrages of our place and times. If they shall subserve in large measure this living purpose, then the author will be jubilant ; if in small measure, grateful; if in no apparent measure, he will still be satisfied, as he has the inward consciousness of having done his duty.

Furthermore, these discourses lay no claim to sermonic style, exegetical display or modality of structure. The enemy was present. The main object was his attack and defeat, and therefore, but little regard has been paid to homiletical pruderies.

THE AUTHOR.

The Sabbath Sængerfest of the German and of the Christian Contrasted.

Sunday Evening, July 12, 1891.

Amos v, 23; viii, 10.—" Take thou away from me the noise of thy music for I will not hear the melody of thy viols," (violins.) * * * " I will turn your feasts into mourning and your songs into lamentations, and I will bring up sackcloth upon all loins and baldness upon every head and I will make it as the mourning for an only son, and the end thereof as a bitter day."

BUT

Isaiah xxxiv, 10.—" The ransomed of the Lord shall return and come to Zion with songs and everlasting joys upon their heads. They shall obtain joy and gladness, and sorrow and sighing shall flee away."

THAT we may see something of the scope, and feel somewhat the force of this Sabbath theme, it is necessary to remember a few historic facts. The Hebrew nation was a great object lesson, set in the midst of the earth, and of the ages for all mankind to read. The facts recorded of that chosen race, are for our instruction and inspiration, upon whom in these latter days the " ends of the world have come." The text in Amos represents the way the Almighty dealt with the Hebrews when they departed from His commandments, and adopted the habits which their own evil hearts prompted or the aberrant customs of the Sabbath iconoclasts around them suggested.

The text from Isaiah, portrays with songful imagery how, gathering from hill and plain, they should exultingly repair, first to the Zion below, and next to the Zion above, when they were true to the Sabbath day, and to the commands which Jehovah, grouped around it, and taught during its hallowed hours by his servants.

The Hebrew race has in part fulfilled its mission. The obedient have gone up.   The disobedient down.   A new race in these times hath God chosen to pioneer his cause.   All observation proves this to be the Aryan race.   Settled originally in Central Asia on the banks of the Oxus, one branch diverged southeastward over the Himalayas, into the fertile delta of India ; the other branch spread westward, swept into Europe and there formed the various nations that have made that continent the most progressive and powerful of the Old World.   Large deportations of that Aryan race have during the last two centuries crossed the ocean, and settled in this New World, which God had kept hidden till the rest of the earth was ripe for the accomplishment, of His benevolent designs, in heaving America out of the midst of the floods.

These Aryan people, whether on this or the other side of the Atlantic, are the chosen people of these times to diffuse civility, knowledge, humanity, industry, progress, peace and salvation throughout the earth.

We belong to this chosen race. Amos defines how the Almighty will spurn the songs, and blight the feasts and persons of those of us who are faithless to our high commission. Isaiah describes the march of sorrowless, and gladsome triumph of those who are faithful to their great vocation.

It is in this condition of affairs that "the burden of the word of the Lord," that pressed upon Malachi, has been pressing upon me for the last week. A burden which I cannot throw off if I would, and would not if I could. Duty, "stern daughter of the voice of God," I must follow thee wherever thou dost lead, for thou dost weave life's truest pattern, and he who is "false to thee, breaks a thread in the loom and will find the flaw when he has forgotten its cause." Therefore, popularity, fame, honor, promotion aside; duty, as I see it, I must and will follow, though I lose all. [Amens.] Aye, more; threats, executions, flagellations and coarse criticisms I shall welcome, rather than diverge an inch from what I conceive after prayer and faith, study and examination to be duty. [Amens, many.]

And now that duty, however painful, I must begin. Would that some one else were charged with the solemn mission! But woe unto me if I am not dutiful. A branch of our Aryan brothers, commissioned as are we, to show the love and lustre of God to all the world, played false to Him and us, in this city on last Lord's Day. The breach was too extensive and influential to pass unnoticed by any clear-eyed, single-hearted, "watchman" on the walls of Zion.

A large number of our young men and women, graduates of our Sabbath-schools, were tempted to participate in the desecrations of last Sabbath in Caledonian Park. Like a bewitching glamour the great Sængerfest drew them from their homes, their churches, and their God. Of the forty-five thousand present, twenty per cent. are said to have been our people. And so delighted were they with its specious charms that an observer said to me: "The young American Newarkers took to it like ducks to water." Who, with any soul of evangelic love, can contemplate such a Sunday holocaust with either equanimity or hope? Who, that has a voice and place to stand, can survey such pollution of our youth through violation of the Sabbath, without lifting up a voice "like a trumpet" against it. [Amens many.]

I hate to stir up strife among the citizens of this "no mean city," and as for our German fellow citizens, there are many elements of excellence in them which even Christians can afford to follow.

Their superior industry, patience, economy, integrity, cohesiveness, fortitude, culture, and fidelity to secular trusts are pleasantly conspicuous among us. Many of them, too, are liberal, progressive and religious. They have their churches in our midst, and a German Christian is, as a rule, a good Christian. Our most benevolent Methodist churches are composed of German members. Of these I have nothing but good to say. They set us an example and we should follow their steps. But there are others of this Aryan German-American stock who have forced me, as a " watchman " of God, to pronounce against them eight counts of heinous guilt committed in this city last Lord's Day. Some of you, before I conclude, will be tempted to say : " He hits rather hard, and with too sharp and strong a weapon." But let me remind you there is no use of striking an elephant with common stripes.

When in Ajmeer of Rajpootana the Rajah sent two elephants, caparisoned in royal style, to bear me from the new city of the British to the old city of the far-famed Rajpoots. While on the elephant I noticed my escort carried a heavy long pole with a pointed end, and inquired (half suspectingly) its use. He told me it was to drive the elephants. I inquired why he did not use a whip? and received for reply: " Elephants care nothing for whips; it takes goads to guide them." The application is plain.

The charges I make are as follows. My warrant
is in my commission: "Them that sin rebuke before
all, that others also may fear."—Tim. v, 20.

First—The Germans sold and bought beer, not
only by the glass but by the barrel, and drank, in
many instances, to intoxication, on the Lord's day.

Second—They gambled at the cane-ring, rifle galleries and wheel of fortune, till many found their
purses rather depleted, for full enjoyment the rest
of the holy day.

Third—They engaged in a *singing match* for a
Schubert bust; and it would have been less offensive
to have engaged in a horse race, since a horse is
less valuable than a man. This, too, they did on
the most sacred day of God.

Fourth—They sang secular songs and ballads
and played ballad music until it seemed all the gorgons of gloom, and griffins of doom laughed and
cried. "We have taken the city; Newark henceforth shall be ours, since it has become so neglect-
ful of its interests as to sanction such defamation
of its most holy time."

Fifth—They paid no regard to the requirements
of the American Sabbath, and no respect to the
customs of the American people, any more than if
we were all dead.

Sixth—They cast out as evil the counsel of the
Most High, and trampled one of the most important commandments that ever thundered from His
throne, heedlessly under their feet.

Seventh—They wantonly and unblushingly violated the spirit and letter, of those great principles of *equal obedience before the law*, which have made this commonwealth so good, great and prosperous.

Eighth—They not only shockingly shattered the laws of this State, but they wilfully, knowingly and flagrantly outraged the laws of this City, in which they were treated with great hospitality and deference by people of all creeds and classes. See page 304 and Sections 647 and 648 of our City Ordinances.

But some may say the Germans should be indulged a little for what they did during the Civil War. No matter how much citizens have done for the State, it does not justify them in breaking the laws of the State. This is an axiom in jurisprudence to which all statesmen assent. No man has a right even by extraordinary services, to the State to claim exemption from the rightful laws of the State. And if such a right of fracture cannot be procured by service, how much less by foreign birth and ancestry. The claim is put in by many on behalf of the Germans, " Oh well, it's the custom of their country to infract the Sabbath, and therefore we must let them do it in this country."

It's the custom of Brahmans and Mohammedans to shiver to atoms the dishes from which Christians have eaten. I have had mine so shattered. They can do that if they please in their own country, but as sure as the sun shines, they cannot come into my house and smash my dishes. [Laughter.]

But, supposing men could, by meritorious service, acquire the right to rise superior to, and lord it over the laws of the State, what have our German brethren achieved for the formation and integration of this Republic, that should lead them to indulge such pretentious assumptions? How can they have the cool effrontery, to come here and appear by their actions to say, "We are superior to your Sunday laws. We come from Germany, where they don't care anything about Sunday any more than any other day, and we are going to have our way here, law or no law." Who are these, that they can afford to defy the mission of American law? I acknowledge they did something during the late Civil War; but, is not that offset by the mercenary Hessians, who fought against Washington for the sake of British gold? But, that aside, what have the German brethren done for the founding and development of this great commonwealth? It was the colonists of English ancestry who, first of all, threw off the British yoke. It was the Irishmen of Pennsylvania, that supported Washington in many of his hard campaigns. It was the French who, when despair hovered over all the land from Maine to Georgia, came to the rescue and lavishly supplied both money and troops, till they enabled the Commander-in-Chief to invest and then capture Cornwallis at Yorktown. [Applause, that was suppressed by the preacher.] It was the Spaniards who somewhat seconded the efforts of the French, and it was an Italian (Columbus, of Genoa), who with the aid of Ferdinand and Isabella discovered the land. But what conspicuous achievements have the Germans accomplished?

Supposing, however, they had done great things; if they had even discovered the country; if they had wrenched it from the avaricious clutch of Britons; if they had framed the constitution; if they had fought the battles of 1812; if they had shone in military resplendence in the Mexican campaign; if they had been the pioneer corps, that moved in the van of westward wending empire, opening up the land; if they had developed our agricultural and mining resources; if they had established our educational system, and our humanitarian charities; if they had even established our churches, schools, colleges and been the life and soul of our mechanical contrivances. Even had they accomplished all these and many more valuable achievements, nevertheless, I stand here in the name of this country, and in the name of Almighty God, to declare that they have no more right to prostitute the Sabbath laws of this Republic, State and City than they have to go to Washington and blow up the Capitol. [Applause that could not be suppressed.]

It is deplorable to see so exalted and responsible an American citizen as his Honor, Leon Abbett, the Governor of this State, figure as the friend of a society which prostitutes the holy Sabbath, an institution which it is his duty to · support and defend. It is distressing to see his Honor, Joseph E. Haynes, the Mayor of this great and growing city (renowned for the multiplicity of its manufactures), presented as in the pocket of President Brewer Krueger, favoring a convocation which, during its visit as our guest, shattered every Sabbath law on our statute book. It is very startling to find so good a man as George A. Halsey, Esq., acting as Honorary President. And it is almost equally shocking to find Allan L. Bassett, Esq., President of our Board of Trade, and P. T. Quinn, Esq., Secretary of that Board, appearing physiognomically on a programme of an assembly that was conspicuous above all things, for its violation of that day, whose observance has made possible such an excellent Board of Trade. [Applause.]

But it is claimed that our German citizens are mighty in music. Granted. But where did their music come from? Did it come from the old thunder-god Thor of the ancient Teuton? Did it evolve from any of the gods of the Scaldic Sagas, or from any other idolatrous and barbaric source? I can assure you nay! It has been my duty in order to become prepared for the mission

which I feel God has for me in this world, to
visit and examine nearly every heathen country on
the globe. My ears were ever on the alert for
music. But in no land unpermeated to quite an
extent with Christianity, through Sabbath services, did I hear anything worthy of the name of
song. Starting on the minor key, all unchristian
lands croon out a weird, plaintive, piteous wail
that makes one distressingly sad, who has been
swept with the triumphant symphonies of Christendom.

No, there is little or no symphony outside of
Sabbath-keeping lands. The heart, man's great
melodist, has not been made melodic, and how can
the people sing? The Divine Harmonist, through
Sabbath ministries, has not re-strung their cardiac
chords to the lyre of heaven, and hence there can
be no melody.

This being a historic fact, I return to my question. Where did our German citizens obtain their
superior soul-swelling music? A child can answer;
from the Church of God. It began with Miriam
and Moses, in response to divine deliverance; it
was continued by David and his musicians through
the tabernacle Sabbath services; it flowed on in
ever refining strains, through the long-drawn aisles
of Solomon's temple; it received a new impetus
that flooded to the full, human beings with Sabbatic and divine emotions, when the Great Messiah

came, and just before His final battle He with His
disciples "sang an hymn."

Then, the goddess of music, which had long
been trammeled, was set free. She took her way
through Asia Minor, Thessalonica and Italia; on
over white-hooded Alps into the forests of Thurin-
gia; on along the banks of the limpid Rhine and
arrowy Rhone, subduing the savage breasts of
aboriginal Germanic tribes; and though restricted
for a time by the arrogant abuses of the Papacy,
during the "Dark Ages," yet Savonarola in Italy,
Huss in Bohemia, Calvin in Switzerland, and
Luther and Melancthon in Germany, once more
set her free. On she took her course, with brighter
sheen and calmer features and more melodic voice
than ever, over France, across the British channel,
and charmed with her Sabbatic strains the then
disrupted Isle of Britain.

Nor stayed she on the other side the sea, but
from the Mayflower, of precious memory, spread
her Sabbath sonnets far and wide over this new
asylum of the free. But it was on her course
hither, as the symphonic chieftainess of the new
world, that she was caught by the ancestors of our
German citizens in Europe, and afterward Handel,
Gluck, Haydn, Mozart, Beethoven, Schubert, Cho-
pin, Mendelssohn, Wagner, and all other great
composers drew not only many of their themes, but
all of their lofty inspirational moods from her Sab-

batic presence. Sabbatic, I say, for had it not been for the Sabbath she never should have been born. This is demonstrated by the fact, that she has not appeared in Sabbathless lands, except as carried there in Christian hearts.

Now, then, since the Gospel Sabbath, through the Church, is the mother of all inspiring song, and since that Sabbath is the day consecrated by Jehovah, dedicated by the Church, and appointed by the American State for the contemplation and the praise of our Creator and Preserver, I take this stand, fearlessly and firmly, as a minister of God and an American citizen that this holy day should not, and by the help of heaven shall not, be polluted by profane songs, even if they are the degenerate progeny of an apostatized section of God's Holy Church. [Amens and hallelujahs.]

Now I come to the Sængerfest proper, which is said to have captured Newark and set her wild with joy. As an aged maiden, long neglected, approached by a jovial suitor, forgets her wrinkles, puts on her powdered lavender, with her gayest attire, and tries simperingly to look smart and young ; so Newark at the approach of the Sænger-festites, supplied herself abundantly with her most odoriferous and gummy fluid; tricked in her most variegated finery, and flaunting in her red, white and blue bunting presented herself to dance obedi-ence to the Sabbath befouling sackbuts of the

2

Sabbath defiling Teuton. I pronounce it a desecration of the stars and stripes (those symbols of
our National light, liberty, purity and God-given
power), to hang them out in honor of a convention
that came here to pollute our Holy Sabbath day.
[Shouts of applause that could not longer be restrained.] But then as to the music; they say it
was grand. Yes, grand atheistic wind. I have
been informed from a source that I have no reason
to doubt, that the Sængerfestites and the Turners
are the atheistic wings of the German-American
people, and that is one reason why I call their
music atheistic wind.

Let us now contrast this Godless storm on the
Lord's night with some of the hallowed strains of
Zion, sung in the churches on the same evening.
There were nine pieces on the Sængerfest programme. First the prelude "The Meistersinger of
Nuernberg;" this was executed by the orchestra.
Mr. Frank Van der Stucken mounts the dais and
waves the baton. The great instrumental band
strikes in at his signal. The waves of artful
sound swell through the great auditorium.
There are masterful science and art displayed on
the great occasion. But where is the God who has
not even been acknowledged on His own Sabbath
night. He doubtless heard the prayerless prelude and if He said anything, it must have been
some such words as those of our text, " Take thou

away from me the noise of thy music, for I will not hear the melody of thy viols (violins)." Contrast this with Handel's Oratorio of the Messiah, Haydn's Creation, Mendelssohn's Elijah, and many other sacred classic compositions, which they might have played and sung and which were presented in the churches. Human structures of Holy Symphony which angels might well fold their wings to hear. Oratorios which remind us of our second text, "And the ransomed of the Lord shall return and come to Zion with songs and everlasting joy upon their heads; they shall obtain joy and gladness, and sorrow and sighing shall flee away."

The second piece was "Weihe des Liedes," signifying the consecration of song, and it would have pleased many exceedingly, if that consecration of song suggested by the title, had been carried out during that Sabbath evening; alas, this was not done, for the next piece was a "violin concerto", and the one after it was a grand chorus called "The Songs," but there was no worship, no God, in these secular performances, and it was not intended there should be. More suitably, indeed, might that vast assemblage of God-defying and Sabbath-breaking singers have sung :

> " Plunged in a gulf of dark despair
> We wretched sinners *lie*,
> Without one cheering gleam of hope
> *We're unprepared to die.*"

And it would have been pleasing to have found them following this up with the additional un-paraphrased stanza of that majestic Hymn of Isaac Watts:

> " With pitying eyes the Prince of grace
> Beheld our helpless grief:
> He saw, and, O amazing love!
> He ran to our relief."

[Amens and Hallelujahs.]

The fifth piece was the aria from " Samson and Delilah." No doubt this was artistically superior for it was sung by a competent diva of the opera, who could put into it all the grotesque good humor of Samson Agonistes, on the one hand, and the radiant charms of Delilah Deception on the other. But it is a wholly un-Sabbatic production, utterly unfitted to waft the souls of men upward, in befitting gratitude toward God. Contrast this with the adoring strains of Addison, and consider how infinitely superior they are for a Sabbath evening.

> " When all Thy mercies, O my God,
> My rising soul surveys,
> Transported with the view, I'm lost
> In wonder, love, and praise," etc.

[Amens and Hallelujahs.]

The next was ballad music by the orchestra and the one after that was " Heather Rose," by the

Cappella. But they played and sang with a mere eye to art on the Lord's night, instead of a profound emotion of adoration and love. And on account of this profanation, they ought to have heard the repelling words of Jehovah the Almighty in thunder crashing over them, " Take thou away from me the noise of thy music," etc. How differently we felt here in this Church, with the spiritual singing on the same evening, of—

> " Come, ye disconsolate, where'er ye languish;
>   Come to the mercy-seat, fervently kneel;
>   Here bring your wounded hearts, here tell your anguish;
>   Earth has no sorrow that Heaven cannot heal," etc.

[Hallelujahs and glories.]

The eighth was a double, (*a*) " Murmeludes Lueftchen," and (*b*) " Fruchlingslied," which respectively mean, " Murmuring Zephyr," and " Spring Song." These were no doubt highly artistic, sentimental and realistic. But amid it all, the thunder of the word of an incensed God on account of His outraged Sabbath, was breaking over them in repelling disapproval, "take thou away from before me the noise of thy music," etc. How infinitely better we are in our churches on Sunday nights, my friends, singing such soul-soothing sonnets as—

> " Sun of my soul, thou Saviour dear,
>   It is not night if thou be near," etc.

[Amens.]

The closing piece was the "Festival Hymn." There may have been friendship, sociality and sentiment in it.   But how much superior that great band of men would have been, if they had sung soberly, appreciatively, and appropriatingly that Sabbath evening—

"Abide with me, fast falls the eventide;
The darkness deepens. Lord, with me abide.
When other helpers fail and comforts flee,
Help of the helpless, O, abide with me," etc.

[Amens many.]

The Lord loves the Germans as He has loved us. He died for them as for us.   They are as dear to Him as any other nation, and His cry of pity over them is, "How shall I give thee up?" [Tears.] Oh, that they would turn unto Him and live. They are physically and intellectually a great people, and if they will accept the salvation, the very Son of God died to procure for them, they shall be equally great spiritually.   O, for a hundred spiritual regiments of these men, whose military war cry is, "Forward, ever forward," to join the advanced thinkers, and workers in America, in fusing the various nationalities into one great, sympathetic, homogeneous, harmonic whole.   This would aid greatly the work of national assimilation of our commonwealth.   And why not?   The glory of the Germanic confederation, the grandeur of the German throne, have been built up and made cohesive, by the religious life of the best people in Germany. The beer and balderdash of infidelity and Atheism would soon disintegrate this lovely structure, the result of ages, if they were to become the ruling elements. And as these evil elements would ruin Germany, so they would America. Let us pray and work for the evangelization of the German people. Their safety, and the safety of this Republic are dependent upon their conversion to God the Almighty. [Cries, "That's so."]

The young Kaiser, I see, has lately been visiting England, and has had a regal welcome, and I am very glad of it. When last in Berlin I was constantly impressed, not so much with the statesmanship of Bismarck, and the military genius of Von Moltke, as by the humanitarian, democratic and religious characteristics of the royal family of Germany. The evidences of these are on every hand. These, after all, more than all else, under God, have made united Germany; and I am, therefore, glad to see that Britons have received the young and manly Emperor so cordially. Now there is a Prince whom that young German Emperor seeks and serves, and He is our Jesus, the " Prince of peace." [Amens and hallelujahs.] Let us pray that Our German citizens may speedily receive Him who proves the glorious Saviour, of the

Kaiser of the land of their nativity. Then, in this
land of their adoption, with flags intertwined and
hearts interwoven we shall together " Return and
come to Zion with songs and everlasting joy upon
our heads, and we shall obtain joy and gladnesss
and sorrow and sighing shall flee away." [Amens,
hallelujahs, and deep feeling.]

Note.—Such were the criticism, clamor and demands for im-
mediate apology for the preceding discourse, that the preacher
delivered the following on the next Sabbath morning.

My Apology to the German People.

SUNDAY MORNING, JULY 19, 1891.

I. Cor., ix, 3.—"Mine answer to them that do examine me is this:"

Acts 20:24.—"But none of these things move me, neither count I my life dear unto myself, so that I might finish my course with joy, and the ministry which I have received of the Lord Jesus, to testify the gospel of the grace of God."

ST. PAUL, like his Master, was a plain speaker, especially when he attacked living systems of error. He never attacked any other kind of error. You do not read of Paul wasting his time striking at the Antediluvians. Whenever he spoke he struck a living thing. Hence he attacked the Jewish sinners and the Gentile sins. He had no time to waste in preaching at cemeteries; nor have I! My mission is to living men. It was so with Jesus, Elijah; with Savonarola, Knox, Huss, Luther, Whitefield and Wesley. They all attacked with vigor the sins of their times. I received letters during the past week saying I was personal. I admit that I have been personal. I can not help being personal if I do my duty. Elijah was a very personal man. When King Ahab came to him after the drought of three years and six months and said, "Art thou he that troubleth Israel?" Elijah answered and said, "I have not troubled Israel, but *thou* and *thy* Father's house." He aimed at his man and brought him down. The same thing was true of Nathan when David fell into sin with Bathsheba. Nathan did not go about saying some one had done wrong. He came out before the King and said, "Thou art the man." And David repented and was saved. Jesus was as personal as either Elijah or Nathan. He did not go round talking of past events, but about the needs of his times. Hence when He speaks, He speaks to living men. He had words of sympathy and help for the needy and penitent, but for the self-sufficient Pharisees He had words of warning and tones of thunder. He said: "Ye Pharisees, hypocrites"—direct personal address. "How can ye escape the damnation of hell?" Rousing appeal!

Therefore, I do not care how prominent a name may be, if it is associated with grave public wrong I am going to mention it.

That kind of preaching brought upon Paul

persecutions, by "stripes and imprisonments." Moreover, "Thrice he was beaten with rods, once stoned."
Notwithstanding all this he was strong to rise up
and say, " None of these things move me, neither
count I my life dear unto myself." They have been
able to mutilate my body; those stripes and stones
distressed my flesh, but "me," Paul the spirit, "none
of these things move me." There are persecutions
just as heavy now as then—different kind of course.
But whenever a mighty mountain of sin, is energetically and fearlessly attacked now, there will be
as strong upheavals, as there were at Lystra and
Philippi or any other place where Paul preached the
Gospel. This is seen from the simple fact, that last
Sunday night, I stood in this place and preached
on the condition, of certain of my fellow citizens
with most benevolent design. Yet such is the
storm raised that one church is known, and one
preacher traduced from ocean to ocean. Comments and criticisms, of the most scurrilous kind
have been made upon me, in thousands of papers
throughout the land. Names from the meanest
insect to the highest fiend have been conferred upon
me. But "mine answer to them that examine me
is this": "none of these things move me, neither
could I my life dear unto myself, that I might
finish my course with joy, and the ministry which I
have received of the Lord Jesus, to testify the Gospel of the grace of God." [Amens and hallelujahs.]

If I were to burden you with the number of threats, that have come to me you would be appalled. "If found in any German community in the Union I should be torn limb from limb. If I ever go to Hoboken or New York, I am to be thrown into the Hudson, turned into a fish and then devoured by the devil; my ministerial reputation is gone; I shall never get another church; my former church was glad to get rid of me, and my present one would be glad to get me out." Well, this is bad enough. But "None of these things move me, neither count I my life dear unto myself, so that I might finish my course with joy, and the ministry which I have received of the Lord Jesus, to testify the Gospel of the grace of God." [Amens and hallelujahs all over the house.]

I have not time or desire to take special notice of newspaper scandals, further than to say, that an expert in this regard in New York said, there had been sent from many newspapers and periodicals multitudes of clippings to various parts of the world, so that Franklin Street is known all over the earth by this time, or will be when the ships get around with the notices. If people from Canton and Singapore, come to see what kind of people you are, you will understand it. Most of this has been done for scandalization, but God will surely work it all out for His glory, and the good of His cause, therefore not even cosmopolitan newspaper scandalization moves me. This is the old attack on the nation, in the new form of breaking down the Sabbath, the most sacred institution we have. Who are the men that do this shameful work? They are not all of any one nationality. But they are all imbued with the same lawless and perverse spirit.

They are possessed of the same spirit of the old-time rebels, who said to the South, "go out," and to the North, " keep back," and let there be a disruption of these states. These are the men who favor Sabbath-breaking. You see in the newspapers the same old disintegrating force at work. They gather around the fair tree of the Church as so many poisonous worms beset the palm of the Orient. When Orientals wish to deprive these worms of their destructiveness, they take a species of tar and about six feet up the tree paint a girdle round it. My friends let us girdle the Sabbath with heroic protests, before the vipers get up and destroy the flowers, and fruit of a century's cultivation. God grant that the church may become earnest in this matter, and so by heaven's help keep the Sabbath Day inviolate. [Amens all over.]

I do not care what happens me if the Sabbath is kept holy, and my German brethren saved. If I could save our German brethren in this city, I

would lay down my body in the street and let them
walk over it to salvation. Albeit, my German
friends, are as a rule, possessed of a large share of
adipose tissue, which I do not now care to diagnose.
My ministry has been received from the Lord Jesus.
My business is to testify the Gospel of the grace of
God.   Jesus the Jehovah is the Being from whom
I received my commission.   I have received it from
the Newark Conference, only as a form of ratifica-.
tion.   My real commission comes from the King.
If all the Conferences in the world, stood between
my King and me, I would walk over them and say,
" Master, what wouldst thou have me to do?"   I
have little business with what man says, but I have
very important business, with what my Lord and
Master says. [Amens and hallelujahs.]   What is the
business of a minister?   To testify the Gospel of
the grace of God.   Yes, says some one, then you
are to preach *love?*   Certainly, my dear friend, from
whom I received that letter about love.   I know
that love is the beautiful grace and " God is love,"
but when he made the moral universe, there had
to be many other virtues with love.   There must
be *justice* and *temperance* and *patience* and *fortitude*,
for these graces are all important, and the Gospel
includes them all.   The Gospel is full of love, but
implies everything else that is right in the moral
world.   Hence the Gospel is of a corrective nature

and it must denounce all public wrong. *We* have seen that in what we have said, concerning Elijah and Jesus and St. Paul. This, therefore, is a part of the Gospel, and if you will look to your own history you will have an illustration. You remember when you were a boy, going out after your mother had told you to stay in. She began to lay on the rod energetically for a lady. You hopped around and didn't like it, but when you grew up to know your mother, you blessed her for every time she restrained you. Every man here who has had a faithful mother and father knows that justice, is as necessary in the household as love.

What is true in the family circle, is true in the State, for the State is only an extended family. If one of the members persist in breaking an important law, what is to be done? Somebody ought to do the correcting. The State ought to do it. But the State often does not live up to its duty, and this city sometimes winks at sin, and there seemed no one else to do it, and hence it was left to me. What I have said and what I shall say is because I love the German people, and because I love the Newark people. There is no man, woman or child in this city whom I can not take to my heart and love, whether German, French, Irish, Chinese or Japanese. My Master loved and died for them all, and should not I?

I have an apology to make, but before making that apology, I want to say, furthermore, that I am debtor to every man, woman and child in this city.   Paul was a debtor to the Jew, the Greek, the bond and free, and the commission under which I labor makes me a debtor to every man and woman in this city.   I owe every citizen of this city, the glorious Gospel of the grace of God.   I have shown my sense of debt and love, to the people, by standing in the front of the storm.   I surmised that none of the other ministers in town, would speak on this subject of Sabbath desecration.   I feared they were afraid to touch it.   Therefore all the more need for me, or some one, to come out and speak against the breaking of the law, the trampling on the Holy Bible, and the desecration of the Sabbath Day.   I am willing to show that I love my German brethren as I love myself ; "though the more I love the less I be loved."   I did not use all the terms attributed to me by the multitude of reporters.   When these sermons are published, my fellow citizens will see this.   Reporters in the back seats, please take note of that.   These reporters — God help them — who write for a penny a line, must write spicy, sharp articles to make their productions acceptable in competition with several others at the office, and

so, you see, they have strong temptation to make a
speaker appear ridiculous. Well, there are some
of you here this morning, and I see you and know
you. We will all have our day, and truth and honesty will be crowned, and falsity and dishonesty
will be damned. I have nothing to take back of
what I did say, and I do not feel disposed to apologize for what reporters said. Luther, before the
Diet of Worms, could not help himself for the
stand which he took. He would gladly have com-
plied with the persistent entreaties of his friends, if
there had been no God, but looking to God he
said:

"Hier stehe Ich, Id kann niche anders; Gott helf mir."

That sentence has gone through all German history—a sentence of glory working its way into
many a German heart and making it triumph over
sin. I take my stand by the side of Luther, and
say: "Here I stand, I cannot do otherwise, *God
help me!*" I say more; that just as Luther overturned the Papacy in Europe, as he overturned
systems of indulgence, the sins of proscrip-
tion and persecution and made Europe free by
taking this stand, so, my dear German friends,
would to God that we might go up into your beer
gardens, and turn them into Christian camp grounds,

and take worldly songs out of your mouths; and put spiritual songs into your hearts. [A flood of amens and hallelujahs.]

Now if you will permit us, we will do it. I have the best band of Christian workers in this church I ever saw, and we are ready to go up. How different would be conditions after we had been there awhile. How happy you would grow on the new wine of the Kingdom of God. There would not be any need of beer. We get gloriously happy without the article.. No more Sabbath violation; no more sinful pleasures, unbelief, doubt, rationalism, atheism. We would ·turn Caledonian Park into a hallelujah meeting that would bless city, and State, country, and world. [Many amens and glories.]

Now I have an apology to make to you. I have this apology to make, because I received a bushel of letters and newspapers, all demanding an apology. Some of the newspapers have said that if Brady doesn't get down on Newark streets, and apologize to the German people, he is no Christian. Now I have an apology to make.

First—I apologize to you, my German friends, *because I did not sooner declare to you* the evils, of the Sunday habits in which you have been indulging before you became so confirmed in them. When pastor of Central church I should have lifted up

my voice in such tones that you would have heard
on the "hill," as you hear now. [Amens, hallelujahs and great feeling.]

Second—I apologize, my German brethren, because I did not sooner show you the appalling
end, of the evils in which you are in the habit
of indulging every Sabbath of your lives.

Third—I apologize to you, my German brethren,
on behalf of all the Christians in all the churches
who have not had sufficient Christianity, to lift up
their voices against your desecration of God's
holy day and so save your precious souls.

Fourth—I apologize to you, my German brethren (I would to God it were Christian brethren),
on behalf of the ministry of Newark, that, (although you were in the garden of our Sabbath,
trampling on the choicest spiritual plants of a
century's growth and culture), lifted not up
its voice strong enough, for you to hear a tone.
Get that all down, ye reporters. [Amens over
the house.]

Fifth—I apologize, my German brethren, because the Christians in this land, have not suf-
ficiently appreciated you, so as to bring you
up into the church of the living God, and util-
ize all your symphonic powers, in spreading the
gospel of Jesus Christ, and so save your own souls,
those of your families and of many around you.

Sixth—I apologize to you, my German brethren, not because we do not appreciate Handel's " Messiah," Beethoven's " Pastoral," and Mendelssohn's " Elijah," for these we do appreciate, but I do apologize because we have not made you familiar with the melodies of Watts, and the magnificence of Charles Wesley, and of other sweet Hymnists, who have helped Faith to sway her sceptre over the world for the last hundred years.

For these things I apologize, but I have no apology to make for one single jot or tittle, of anything that I said, and I have no reason to apologize for reporters, for saying I said things I didn't say. God bless the reporters. He can bless even them— pretty hard business. [Laughter.]

Your reformation, my German fellow citizens, under Luther, has made us acquainted with the great doctrines of the Scriptures. Indeed, it has made us acquainted with the Scriptures themselves, for before that, the Bible was for centuries a sealed book. And all through the vicissitudes of that great man's life there came to the Church a glorious force of victory. That hidden force is the fortress in which I hide myself on all occasions of storm. Dr. Talmage says, when he gets up a storm in Brooklyn, he goes to Coney Island. When I get up a storm in Newark, I go to my knees and pray until I get the victory. Then I say let the storm sweep. Your great reformer who gave to Methodism its possibilities, used to sing his storm-swept soul into strength by chanting—

> " Ein feste Burg is unser Gott,
> Ein gute wehr und waffen," etc.

We all need this strong, this Almighty Fortress of which Luther sings — And we have it, too, thank God. But we need to do something. The commission of our Master is, "Go ye into all the world and preach the Gospel to every creature beginning at Jerusalem." (I want you to get this down, gentlemen of the press.) Don't take the whey and leave the cream as you usually do. I say that as Methodists our mission is to "go." All good goes by method. The bad alone is methodless. And so we are to go and save others methodically. Our mission is an unintermittent progression, from conversion to world-wide evangelization. We dare not stop, our march is onward. There are people who believe in staying at home, and having a good social time, and letting the devil get the people. We don't believe in any such treason. [Amens like a flood.] We believe in having a good spiritual time, by going out into the world, and stretching out a helping hand to the helpless, and lifting up men who have fallen. We go forth with the cry:

" O for a thousand tongues to sing
    My great Redeemer's praise ;
The glories of my God and King,
    The triumphs of his grace !

My gracious Master and my God,
    Assist me to proclaim,
To spread through all the earth abroad,
    The honors of thy name.

Jesus ! the name that charms our fears,
    That bids our sorrows cease ;
'Tis music in the sinner's ears,
    'Tis life, and health, and peace.

He breaks the power of canceled sin,
    He sets the prisoner free ;
His blood can make the foulest ciean ;
    His blood availed for me.

He speaks, and, listening to His voice,
    New life the dead receive ;
The mournful, broken hearts rejoice :
    The humble poor believe.

Hear Him, ye deaf : His praise, ye dumb,
    Your loosened tongues employ ;
Ye blind, behold your Saviour come ;
    And leap, ye lame, for joy."

[Great feeling and hallelujahs.]

Now my German brethern, I have only one illustration to draw that will enable you to see where I stand. You have no better friend in Newark than you have in me. I am willing to do or say anything that is right, for your welfare. I said a good many things that nobody else dare say. Herein I have proved my love for you.

Supposing on the Niagara River there is a beautiful flotilla coming down; charming music, flags flying, beer passing round and down; most glorious time for a beer bibber; many people on shore, all saying, "Ha, ha! what magnificent music, what a beautiful flotilla." But all this time that float is drifting toward the circle of the great Niagara plunge. One man on shore sees it and lifts his voice like a trumpet over the river and cries: "The rapids are before you; steer for the shore!" The captain hears the warning, turns shoreward and the people are saved. Now I ask whether those flattering admirers of the flotilla, on shore or the man who had the love, to lift up his voice and give the warning cry, is the flotilla's friend. You have been using Sunday as the stream of time, to drift you toward the great Niagara of destruction, instead of toward the glorious goal of Heaven, and I again lift up my voice and say: Brethren, *cease making Sun-*

day a drinking day, and use it as a Divine day and God will bless you now and forever. [Amens like a sea.]

NOTE.—The interest excited by the apology, was even more intense than that resulting from the charge, and so the succeeding sermons were preached according to the demands of the hours as they arose.

Sabbath Secularization.

SABBATH EVENING, JULY 19, 1891.

Ex. xx, 8—" Remember the Sabbath Day to keep it holy;"
Mal. iv, 6—" Lest I come and smite the earth with a curse."

THERE was not time on last Sunday night to
say all that should be said at this time on
Sabbath Desecration. I therefore resume the
theme to-night, for the purpose of shedding much
needed light upon this all-important theme.

I shall treat the subject under two simple heads,
which will be easily by you remembered:

I.—THE CAUSES OF SABBATH VIOLATION.
II.—THE CURSES THAT FOLLOW IT.

I.—THE CAUSES.

First — Among these I place a misconcep-
tion of the high and authoritative origin of the
Sabbath Day. In that vast natural cathedral of
Arabia, spired and turreted with its battlements
of reddish rock, whither the Children of Israel,
under the leadership of Moses, had gone to receive
the Law of God for all mankind, the thunder of
the Divine Voice first was heard by man. That

3

Voice commanded Moses to come up to a loftier granitic shrine, and there receive that code of morals which was a transcript of the Eternal Mind for all nations and all times. Moses obeyed, and tells us that upon two tables of stone, with His own finger, God wrote out the Ten Commandments. The fourth of these was: "Remember the Sabbath Day to keep it holy." This command, therefore, is not of common origin. It is not a temporary ordinance, which may be put off with impunity, like an inconvenient robe. It is a part of the infinite fitness of this universe, therefore of equal force, authority and importance with "Thou shalt not kill," "Thou shalt not steal," and all the others. It is as immutable in its nature, and as exacting in its claims, as any one of the ten, and, indeed, there are reasons which, as I proceed, shall show why, in some weighty regards, it is most important of all the others.

Wherefore, "Remember the Sabbath Day to keep it holy," "lest I come and smite the earth with a curse."

Second — The prostitution of the Sabbath is caused by a misunderstanding of the meaning of this day. It had a peculiar significance, all its own, then; it has an exclusive sanctity peculiar to itself still. It was to be a sign, a signal, a standard of inviolate covenant between God and His chosen people, and hence Jehovah said:

"Verily my Sabbaths ye shall keep, for it is a sign between me and you throughout your generations."

Idolatrous nations were to be around the Israelites on every hand—the Phœnicians, the Moabites, the Midianites, the Syrians, the Arabians—practicing their idolatries, of Moloch, and Ashtaroth and Baal, gods of their own vile invention. They had turned, as most nations of the earth, from the real spiritual Almighty Being, who made the sea, the sky, the stars, the hills, and all things. And now there was danger of the Israelites becoming contaminated by the customs of their neighbors, and so here was one-seventh of time lifted up to sanctity and eminence among them, to remind them every week of Him who had brought them up out of the land of Egypt "with an high hand and an outstretched arm." And so long as they kept the Sabbath holy they never fell into idolatry; but when they prostituted it to visiting the carnivals of the heathen, they speedily lapsed into the horrible moral condition of the idolaters about them. History repeats itself. And whenever our American Sabbath is permitted to degenerate from its high and holy significance, and we break it down and trample over its ruins into the camp of the enemy, there is nothing in our modern progress, nor in earth, nor in heaven, to prevent us from becoming a nation of heathenish

idolaters, subject to all the desolations that overtook the Hebrews.

Wherefore, "Remember the Sabbath Day to
keep it holy," "lest I come and smite the earth
with a curse."

Third—Another cause of Sabbath breaking is a
misapprehension of the mission of the Sabbath.
This mission is by far the most important to us of
any portion of time. The other six days of the
week are to be used in physical labor for the food
we eat, the clothing we wear, the homes we live
in. In these days we are to "labor and do all our
work," but the seventh has a most merciful and
mighty mission. It is the time when the body of
man is to rest, recuperate, and so gain resiliency
for future effort. It is a time when the mind of
man is to have a complete change of occupation
from the secular to the sacred, from the low to the
lofty, from the sordid to the saving, from the
contracting to the expanding, from the degrading
to the elevating and ennobling forces of this life.
The Sabbath, too, is the time especially and delib-
erately set for the still loftier purpose of refining
the spirit of man. This spirit, which is so sinful
and so gross that Paul, who knew human nature
well, and was also inspired by the Spirit of God,
characterized it as "being filled with all unright-
eousness, fornication, wickedness, covetousness,
maliciousness, full of envy, murder, debate, deceit,

malignity." And then, becoming more personal, he called the Gentiles "whisperers, backbiters, haters of God; despiteful, proud boasters, inventors of evil things, disobedient to parents, without understanding; covenant breakers, without natural affection; implacable, unmerciful." And of the Jews he also said: "There is none righteous; no, not one," and then writes a dark catalogue of crimes against them, which grew largely out of their imperfect knowledge of the mission of the Sabbath, which by its ministries is to lift man nearer God, and man nearer man.

The mission of the Sabbath, then, is quite unique and peculiar. It is to give rest and recuperation to man's body and mind, 'tis true; but the highest, holiest, and most important function of the Sabbath is to refine, exalt, inspire and cultivate man's spirit, till it is free from the weeds of woe, and full of "love, joy, peace, gentleness, goodness, meekness, temperance, faith and charity." In other words, the mission of the Sabbath is to renovate, educate, illuminate and refine crude, gross, sinful human nature till in its sublimity it rises by the very law of spiritual coherence and affinity into perfect compatibility with the nature of the Lord God Almighty; so as to become a crown jewel of Him in immortal youth, beauty and strength.

Wherefore, "Remember the Sabbath Day to

keep it holy," "lest I come and smite the earth with a curse."

Fourth—Another cause of the fracture of the Sabbath is the persistent vandalism of sensuous men. There are in these times, in this land, and in this city, many who wish to treat themselves and others as if they were only animals instead of men. They clamor for what only pleases for time, and in their effort to gain present pleasure forget their real nature and their God. They grow impatient of restraint, and decry all interference with their wishes as illiberal restrictions and infringements.

> " They howl for freedom in their senseless mood,
> And still revolt when truth would set them free ;
> License, they mean, when they cry liberty."

They want freedom for their physical nature, regardless of customs, laws and principles. They clamor for license, to get away from the loving designs God their Father has for them, and cry for secular recreations instead of Divine realizations. Sordid amusements that embase, instead of holy amusements that ennoble. Debauching dissipations that defile, degrade and damn, in place of those exalting aspirations that purify and enthrone.

This I call the vandalistic use of the Sabbath. And the leaders of this vandalism are not to the American manner born. They are, for the most part, adopted · fellow citizens, who, when badly enough off at home, came here and settled down. You opened your ports and privileges to them. You opened up your virgin soil, your factories, schools, superior business advantages, and your hard-earned, blood-bought governmental equities to them. You practically said: "You, although foreign born, can have all the immunities and opportunities of our own people. You can have the liberty for which our fathers fought and died. You can have your full share of the blessings that have been won at the outlay of incalculable suffering, blood and treasure. You can freely and fully have all the bonus and benefits of our code of equal and impartial laws. Over you shall wave the illuming stars and the protecting stripes. Before you lies the fertile soil; around the possibilities of unprecedented success."

They have accepted these proffered and liberal favors. They have thriven on them. They have grown numerous and rich, as Jacob in the house of Laban; and, now, after all this, they turn round and claim the prostitution to their own secularizing practices of the most sacred institution we have in our land—the institution of the American Sabbath.

They want to take this day, through whose ministries this nation has been integrated; this day, solemnized and dignified by the memories of Sinai; this day, sacred with the Sabbatic splendors of the Pilgrim Fathers; this day, which has been employed in educating, inspiring and molding our people into the greatest homogeneous nation of patriots, philanthropists, philosophers and Christians that is now or ever was on the planet.

These men, of whatever name and of whatever nation makes now to me no difference, who work to deform this Christian Sabbath from a holy day into a holiday, from a sacred day into a sensuous day, from a praying day into a play day, from a praise day into a carousing day, from a divine day into a drinking day, I pronounce are the worst enemies of this Republic, and the vandals of modern society, and baleful and barbaric will be the results if they are not driven back within the laws, where we and they belong. And if they will not go inside the laws of this commonwealth, why, instead of paltering for their votes, frame laws that will drive them from under the folds of our flag. This is my policy, because I believe that it is the diplomacy of God. [Amens and hallelujahs.]

This Republic has the highest, widest mission ever delegated to any nation. This Republic is designated by heaven, in these later times, to rip up the old forms of human bondage that have been bandaging men all over the earth. This Republic, therefore, in heaven's name, must be kept inviolate. [Applause.]

But history demonstrates and experience proves, that it cannot be so kept unless its Sabbaths are protected from desecration. This foul fiend of Sabbath desecration must be expatriated. [Amens.] If not, it will stop our progress, spoil our civilization, de-Christianize our institutions, increase debauchery, augment drunkenness, devastate our churches, disrupt our government, and spread vice, crime and desolation on every hand, and will make us a by-word and a hissing before the eyes of all nations, and of the Almighty, forever. [God forbids.]

Wherefore, " Remember the Sabbath Day to keep it holy," " lest I come and smite the earth with a curse."

Fifth—Another cause of Sabbath breaking is the compromising spirit of time-serving apologists. [Voices—" True."]

These, following the precepts of Frederick W. Robertson and the Roman Catholic Church in her practices, say : " Let us compromise a little with the sinner ; let us go half way with him, and change the Sabbath into a half holiday instead of an entire holy day. Throw the art galleries, the public libraries, the parks, the railroads, the steamboats, the museums, all open, and wink with the corner of your left eye if the saloons open a side or back door on Sunday. This is the plush-clad velvet claw which grows great with covered talons of venomous steel, and which, whenever the time comes, will strike out and tear the American Sabbath to pieces.

Why? Because as when a lion gets a taste of blood his whole nature becomes voracious for gory victims, so when our rising race gets a few drops of the deceptive sweetness of Sabbath violation they will rush in and slaughter the entire day.

But these semi-vandals of the Sabbath say our Saviour recognized the need of secularities on the Sabbath. The ox fallen into the pit may be lifted out; the beast in need of drink may be led to watering, and His own defence of His disciples shows that corn ears may be plucked and dislodged from their husks on Sunday. As for ox accidentally in the pit, no sane Sabbatarian would object to the merciful act of pulling him out. As for the watering of the stall-fed animals, every Christian would on the Sabbath give them water. And as for the corn husking, the historic setting needs but to be understood to enable us to see it was an act of merciful necessity. The Saviour and His disciples were hungry from long fasting and weary with protracted toils around Capernaum. They were on their way to another town when a sense of famishing overtook them. To relieve their dire necessity, as David ate the shewbread, under stress of circumstances, they rubbed the corn heads in their hands and ate the kernels. But you will observe the mission on which they were. Were they on a pleasure excursion? Were they going to a musical fandango? Were they bound for a beer

garden carousal? Were they heading for a bac-
chanalian scene of frolic, dissipation and revelry?
Nay, verily; but on their way to the synagogue
(church), where Jesus preached the Gospel in His
love, and healed in His pity, a man who had a withered hand. Truly by this we get a key to the
whole situation. The Sabbath, indeed, was for
man. Aye, was man's healing day. It was to be
man's restoration day. It was to be the day set
apart for his leisure, his culture, his education, his
inspiration. It was to be the day for good works,
for good places, for great glories.

It was to be the day when the strong might help
the weak, the rich the poor, the virtuous the
vicious. It was to be the day when that divine
love that floods the universe and pours itself out
in healing balm upon the open wounds of a bleeding world should be recognized, and appreciated,
and appropriated. [Amens, hallelujahs and glories
over the house.]

It was to be the day when the sacred teachers sent
by God should stand up in their holy places and
teach, and impress, and inspire the multitudes of
the sinful, careworn and needy. It was to be the day
when the masses would lay down their burdens
and come, free from care and fear, and commune
with the truth and with the intelligent fountain of
benevolence and love, till they, breaking out into a
jubilee of song, should be lifted up into spiritual

exultation. It was to be a day in which the life
and love of God should become so regnant in the
masses of human souls that they would swell with
joy divine and need no other comforter. In a
word, it was to be a day in which mankind were to
break away from the woes of earth and lay hold of
the joys of Heaven. [Hallelujahs.] Thus the Sabbath was made for man, and not man for the
Sabbath.

Wherefore, "Remember the Sabbath Day to
keep it holy," "lest I come and smite the earth
with a curse."

There is just one more cause of the prevalence
of Sabbath breaking in these times I shall mention.
That is the effeminate and apologetic way in
which some ministers preach on the subject, and the
shabby, evasive way in which others avoid it. Such
watchmen are over politic and under polemic, over
diplomatic and under heroic. They might offend
some half Sabbath breaker ; they might displease
some rich or influential Sabbath desecrating official,
and so they sound tiny whistles, when they ought to
blow rams horns, and fill the world with the sound
of trumpets. Ezekiel was troubled for want of
these in his day :

1. Again the word of the LORD came unto me, saying,
2. Son of man, speak to the children of thy people, and say
unto them, When I bring the sword upon a land, if the people of
the land take a man of their coasts, and set him for their watchman :

3. If when he seeth the sword come upon the land, he blow the trumpet, and warn the people ;

4. Then, whosoever heareth the sound of the trumpet, and taketh not warning ; if the sword come and take him away, his blood shall be upon his own head.

5. He heard the sound of the trumpet, and took not warning ; his blood shall be upon him. But he that taketh warning shall deliver his soul.

6. But if the watchman see the sword come, and blow not the trumpet, and the people be not warned ; if the sword come and take *any* person from among them, he is taken away in his iniquity ; but his blood will I require at the watchman's hand.

7. So thou, O son of man, I have set thee a watchman unto the house of Israel ; therefore thou shalt hear the word at my mouth, and warn them from me.

8. When I say unto the wicked, O wicked *man*, thou shalt surely die ; if thou dost not speak to warn the wicked from his way, that wicked *man* shall die in his iniquity ; but his blood will I require at thine hand.

9. Nevertheless, if thou warn the wicked of his way to turn from it ; if he do not turn from his way, he shall die in his iniquity ; but thou hast delivered thy soul.

Away then, with all this mincing, man-fearing spirit. Away, eternally away, with every policy that would muzzle you as a messenger of God.

Sinai is behind you ; let it again thunder through you. Jehovah is within you ; let His lightnings play from your eyes, your hands, your feet, your voice, until as full a blaze of glory flames in your pulpit from your presence as flamed from the face of Moses when he came down from the mount with the Law. [Amens many.] Then, when with commanding mien you exclaim: "Remember the Sabbath Day to keep it holy," the people will heed and obey, lest Jehovah come again "and smite the earth with a curse."

II.—But little time is left me to treat of the curses that follow Sabbath breaking. They are many and great. Sabbath Prostitution is the old Virago of all the ages. I see her, with bleared eye and cracked voice, rise up among the nations, and gradually grow grimy and gray; grimy with the blood of her victims, gray with the weight of her woes. Her mouth is full of cursing and bitterness; she pours forth ignorance like a flood, and vice like a sea. Her course is marked with a trail of poverty, tears, blood, agony and death. Her alliance is with the Devil, and her commission is to go forth and slaughter the King's innocents on every hand. She is to do this by making vice pleasing, the saloon attractive, the beer garden inviting, the secular Sunday concert classical and grand. She has room for the millions; room for all. Wherever she is admitted the bugles of the Church sound everywhere a retreat. Retreat at home, retreat abroad. Retreat for the unite, retreat for the aggregate. Retreat down the declivities of a pleasure park toward the Styx of damnation. She has curses for every person and every thing that is good. She has curses for the Church and curses for the Sunday-school. She has curses for the honest min ister and the faithful member. She has curses for the prayer meeting and the praise meeting. She has curses for the class meeting and the Epworth League. She has curses for the Word of God and the upright sermon. She has curses for the missionary societies, and all benevolent and philanthropic societies. Let her loose and she will pull down our church spires, demolish our cathedrals, desolate our colleges, ruin our public schools. Let her loose, and she will break up our charities, overturn our philanthropies and damn our humanities. Give her full sway, and she will pollute that part of our press she has not already polluted ; she will invade our Senate halls, climb up the walls and tear down our Capitol. Let her have full swing, and she will sterilize our fields, curtail our commerce, paralyze our trade, stifle our improvements, strangle our industries. Give her her way, and she will fill the land with poverty, " lamentation, and mourning, and woe," and the earth will have all its healing wounds opened afresh.

Oh, my God, we want to have a funeral, and we want the corpse to be this Sabbath Prostitute. [Amens and hallelujahs.] Dig deep and wide the grave, ye men of God. Make secure the ready coffin ; and now, ye undertakers of the Church, put her in. Come, ye pall-bearers of the Lord, bear her not to any cemetery on earth, but bear her to the rim of the earth and throw her off.

[Amens and great sensation.] Down let her fall ten hundred million miles and twice ten hundred more, till she plunges into the red billows of the bottomless pit, and sends splashes of fire and brimstone against the roof hell. [Volleys of amens.] There let her lie; till this world, including our German brethren, through Sabbath keeping shall have been redeemed, and taken home to that delightsome land where

> " Congregations ne'er break up
> And Sabbath has no end."

"Remember the Sabbath Day to keep it holy" here, if you would acquire the real homogeneity for enjoying its eternal antitype hereafter.

Amens.

Sabbath Spiritualization.

SUNDAY EVENING, JULY 26, 1891.

Isaiah lviii, 13-14.—"If thou turn away thy foot from (trampling on) the Sabbath, from doing thy pleasure on my holy day, and call the Sabbath a delight; the holy of the LORD, honourable; and shalt honour him, not doing thine own ways, nor finding thine own pleasure, nor speaking thine own (worldly) words : Then shalt thou delight thyself in the LORD; and I will cause thee to ride upon the high places of the earth, and feed thee with the heritage of Jacob thy father; for the mouth of the LORD hath spoken it."

ON last Lord's night I spoke to you on the Causes and Curses of Sabbath Seculariza-tion. To-night I shall present to you the manner and blessing of Sabbath Spiritualization.

First, then, the manner in which we are to keep the Sabbath. This is portrayed in our text. Hold back—"turn away thy foot"—from trampling on the Sabbath. It is sacred. Feet walking on secular errands; feet carrying on worldly business; feet running for personal amusement; feet flying for scenes of revelry and dissipation, are to be kept off the holy hours of the Sabbath. When we are tempted by example, by impulse, by interest, or by anything else under heaven to desecrate the Sabbath on any of these or kindred errands, we are to stop, hold back, and turn ourselves in the opposite direction, find more exalted and spiritual business, and so turn away our " feet from treading down the Sabbath."

The manner in which the day is to be spiritualized by us is seen furthermore in the next clause: " From doing thy pleasure on my holy day." This means worldly pleasure, of course. The pleasures of the dance, the saloon, the theatre, the ball match, the excursion, the beer garden, the gaming table, the convivial carousal, the business pursuit. These, and many more are included in "thy pleasure." From them and all their kin we are on God's day to turn away—as from the thunder of a Vesuvius or the crash of a Niagara.

The manner in which we are to keep the Sabbath is further seen in the words "And call the Sabbath a delight." It is to be no irksome, dull, monotonous day. It is to be no sad, somber, plaintive time. It is not to be a time of restless ennui; a period whose hours drag oppressively along. It is to be by us made a delightsome day, the most delightful by far of all the week, the most precious and rapturous of all the seven. Those who must needs " thrust their necks into a yoke, wear the print of it and sigh away Sundays," miss the sweet and subtle spell, the holy thoughtful calm that a truly-kept Sabbath weaves within the souls who know how to keep Sunday. These make it a " delight." They make it a delight by reflecting on all the goodness of their Heavenly Father till breaking out with bliss-swelling spirits they sing, meditating on his marvelous goodness.

> " Bless the Lord, Oh my soul,
>   And forget not all His benefits," etc.

They further make it a delight by contemplating the glories and graces of nature, the majesty and magnificence of law, the sweep and strength and sweetness of Scripture, the evident fitness of praise, the glorious privileges of prayer, and the illustrious opportunities of hearing and seeing the divinely appointed and inspired messengers of God.

It was some such appreciative contemplation as this which led Longfellow in his Christus to exclaim : .

> " O day of rest, how beautiful, how fair,
>   How welcome to the weary and the old,
>   Day of the Lord and truce to earthly care,
>   Day of the Lord as all our days should be."

Then too it may be made a great delight by the opportunities its holy hours afford for doing

good to those who need. To a soul that has
caught march with the evolution God, this is the
greatest luxury of all. Teaching some budding
mind how to leaf and blossom. Some eager,
passionate heart what and how to feel. Some
wandering wild life how to return to the Father's
fold. Some orphaned outcast how to come back
to an all endearing love. These and similar
activities bring us into the majestic sweep and
trend of our Master's principal purpose. A
Master omnipotent, whose prime purpose in this
universe is to pardon, purify, instruct, inspire and
mold the children of men until they become fit to
be the children of God. The enrapt Sabbath-
keeper sympathetically sings with Henry Carey:

> " Of all the days that's in the week
> I dearly love but one day,
> And that's the day that comes betwixt
> A Saturday and Monday."

Another way we are to spiritualize the Sabbath
according to our text is by honoring the Lord in
honoring its holy laws.

"And call the Sabbath the holy of the Lord
honorable, and shall honor it." The Sabbath is an
arc of time which God himself has sanctified for
the purpose of being felt and seen. This is its
primordial and final design. By honoring this
sacred time we acknowledge and honor Him. It

is like an observatory, in which the telescope is hung. That telescope would be useless without the structural setting of the architect. The sacred Sabbath hours are the time-setting of the revealing word of God, and that word is He. The proof of this is seen in the fact that where there is no Sabbath there is no authentic revelation. The Parsee has his Avesta, the Brahman his Veda, and the Buddhist his Dharma, but they are all at best but gropings after Deity. The Christian, however, has his Bible and it comes with such an authoritative and objective presentation of the Almighty in His natural and moral attributes, that while looking through its pages as through focussed lenses, the honest spiritual soul perceives the awful, yet loving outline of its Lord. It is by honoring the Sabbath in reading, hearing, believing and obeying this word that this universal Lord comes near to human nature and transforming it, embraces it as an Almighty Father. [Amens.] It is this close relation between the day of God, and the word of God and the word of God and the Lord, that makes the spiritualization of the Sabbath of such momentous import to the human race. The man who lifts his hand to war upon the Sabbath, lifts it up also to attack the word. The man who raises his voice against the word raises it against the Lord. The three are indissolubly joined by Jehovah—what He has joined together let no man dare to sunder.

Desecrate the day, bury the word, and we shroud God from the world and are back to barbarism as bleak as that which blights either China or Japan. Honor the Lord in the day by doing the will of the word, which is God, and our march is forward till this earth rolls in an atmosphere of heavenly sweetness and glows like a globe of holy light. [Hallelujahs.]

It is by thus honoring the Lord on the day by the word that we are elevated to such a rapture and character that we find it pleasant to observe the concluding part of the manner of keeping the Sabbath expressed in our text : " Not doing thine own ways nor finding thine own pleasure nor speaking thine own (secular) words."

To persons who live on a low spiritual plane such deprivations as these are meaningless and insipid and even repellant.

To persons who keep the Sabbath from mere family custom, who have at best but blunt spiritual perceptions, made still duller by ever increasing deteriorations, the import of such commands are utterly unintelligible. Such disintegrating formalists

> " Eat and drink and scheme and plan,
> And go to church on Sunday,
> And are *somewhat afraid of God*,
> But *more* of Mrs. Grundy."

But to persons in an exalted and thorough state

of consecration these words come welcome as the bugle notes of battle to the impatient warrior. Such warrior cheerfully exclaims: My "own ways" I forsake, my "own pleasures" I resign, my "own words" I abandon for infinitely better, "for Thine, for Thine." To such there is a charmful beauty in the poetic imagery of Charles Swain when he sings in " Sabbath Chimes."

> " There's music in the morning air,
>   A holy voice and sweet,
> Far calling to the house of prayer,
>   The humblest peasant's feet.
> From hill and dale and distant moor,
>   Long as the chime is heard,
> Each cottage sends its tenants poor,
>   For God's enriching word.
>
> The warrior from his armèd tent,
>   The seaman from his tide,
> Far as the Sabbath chimes are sent
>   In Christian nations wide,
> Thousands and tens of thousands bring
>   Their sorrows to his shrine,
> And taste the never failing spring
>   Of Jesus love divine."

Having seen we are to keep the Sabbath by turning from selfish and secular pursuits and pleasures by making it a day of holy delights and honorable joys, we next come to examine the blessings of such Sabbath spiritualization.

These blessings are exceedingly suitable, minute

and extensive. The promise accorded in the text
to those who attain to this real manner of Sabbath
keeping is most cheering.

" Then shalt thou delight thyself in the Lord,
and I (God) will cause thee to ride upon the high
places of the earth and feed thee with the heritage
of Jacob thy father ; for the mouth of the Lord
hath spoken it."

I—There are blessings here for the individual. The
unit of society needs and wants to be blessed. As
social factors of the great fabric of human integration, we need blessings so as to fill well our
appointed place in the great ever evolving organism.

As the units are, so will the composite be. This ·
is a law no integration can subvert. God, therefore, proposes to bless us by the proper use of the
holy day as composite factors of society, first
singly, then as a whole. There are many springs
of blessings, no doubt, and they are all to be
used in their places. There is physical culture,
educational development, artistic acquirement,
scientific attainment, humanitarian excellence,
philosophic achievement, logical acumen, patriotic
zeal, moral rectitude and polite urbanity. These
are all blessings of which every person should if
possible be possessed. But though they are all
valuable and important, yet apart from the
inspirational element they are comparatively
valueless. This inspirational force which being

personally absorbed diffuses itself through the
whole gambit of personal attainments and utilizes
and conserves them, is promised to such an
extent as to be delightsome.

" Then shall thou delight thyself in the Lord."
When? When thou callest the Sabbath a delight
by spiritualizing it. This delight in the Lord All-
Loving and Almighty, is the loftiest attainment
offered anywhere to man. But money cannot buy
it, position cannot claim it, learning may be void
of it, moral excellence cannot acquire it, and no
natural or acquired quality in man can attain unto
it except that self-sacrificing, self-denying element
which comes forth before the Lord and cries : " Thy
Sabbaths I will keep." Why should obedience to
this command, " Remember the Sabbath day to keep
it holy," so far outstrip all others, even of the deca-
logue, in importance. Because by its observance
a disposition to keep all the other commands is
acquired and developed. Because it is the Divine
insulator for man. We have seen bodies to be
charged with electricity insulated from sordid sub-
stances by glass lest the electric element should
escape the object to be electrified. In like manner
man must be insulated from the gross things of the
world before he can experience the divine electriza-
tion. The Sabbath is the Time Insulator. The
All-Loving and All-Wise has chosen it with which

4

to elevate man so high that he is capable of divine receptions and delights.   [Hallelujah.]

Two men show the antipodal results.   One of these when Saturday evening comes prepares for a gala day on Sunday.   He packs his purse with wages his family should have.   He rises early, eats and hies away without thought of good or God, to meet his boon companions, bound for the revel or excursion, or some similar recreation.   The eating, drinking, joking, story telling, swearing and lying, are abundant.   The joviality of the men is enhanced by intoxicating fluid.   His thoughts, feelings, motives and emotions are all "of the earth earthy."   He returns at night a weary, impoverished, fretted, half or wholly drunken man and requires a day or two of special care before he is himself again.   Such a man may spend a thousand such Sabbaths and each one makes him worse than he was before, till finally he becomes only fit to be " punished with everlasting destruction from the presence of the Lord, and the glory of His power."

He has infracted and polluted the Time insulator and it has become a curse to him instead of a blessing.

But here is another man who, when Saturday evening comes, begins to prepare for the Sabbath.   He bids adieu to worldly care.   His mellow mind contemplates the approach of the Holy day with the tranquility of a happy hope.

The sweet Sabbath dawn stirs within him holy texts and hymns of love and praise. His mental mood is molded by the serenity of delightful meditation on the word and works, the laws and the love of God. The hours fly sweetly by and find him still in the happiest of moods He is delighting himself in the Lord. He lives and breathes in the Ever-Living and All-Loving One. So sacred, so sweet, so strong are his thoughts and feelings of fidelity to Him that he has no time, no desire to let the trudging and defiling train of worldly thought or sentiment enter his being. He spiritualizes the Sabbath by sanctifying himself to its sacred insulating design. He shuts out the distracting world. He shuts in the becalming God. His life warms. His affections burn. His admiration kindles. His delight knows no bounds as he communes with and contemplates his Father's person with all its glorious attributes of wisdom, justice, truth, power and love, and his Father's domain, of which by filial homogeneity he has become an heir. The night comes on and as wending his way from church, he looks up at the girdling galaxies of glorious and innumerable worlds, he delights in the fact that his Father made them all. Thus to rest he goes, having woven into his life new patterns of loveliness, by fresh thoughts and frequent baptisms, till finally having been fitted by frequent fidelities and conformations, he is taken

home above the stars to " glory, honor, immortality
and eternal life." [Praise the Lord.]

Surely then Sabbath spiritualization is the greatest blessing to the individual, since it enables him
to delight himself in the Lord and ride upon the
high places of earth to heaven.

II—I further affirm that Sabbath spiritualization is the greatest blessing that can come
to the family. Indeed, the Christian Sabbath has been one of the great factors that
has formed family life. The promiscuity of
primitive peoples for long wild ages was far and
wide diffused. The exogamy of the clans succeeded sometimes in establishing a little more
humanity, such as was involved in the the treatment of the wife as a captured chattel and cherished
booty. Endogamy or marriage within the tribe
was a step still farther forward in the socialistic
tendency toward a better state of things. Polyan-
dry, too, was practiced in several quarters of the
world as a strange convenience. Simultaneously
with these sad socialistic relations, polygamy pre-
vailed in all nations. Even the Hebrews were not
exempt from its distresses and corruptions. But
when the Christ came and the Christian Sabbath
was instituted ; and the doctrines of monogamy,
caught up from the lips of the Christ, rang from
the tongues of Apostolic orators, then monogamy,
the flower and the fruit of all other socialistic forms

began to take on vitality and coherence, and so during the last 1800 years has been lifting our race to the highest phase of social development yet discovered, or discoverable. This latest and best form of sexual relationship was not only born of Christianity, but it is to the utmost fostered by the sacred influences of a well kept Sabbath day. The tendency of Sabbath violation is toward family dissipation and disruption. The tendency of Sabbath spiritualization is toward family purity and coherence. Indeed it may be said that to find true types of monogamic family life, we are confined by facts to Christendom. The other peoples of mankind retain most of the barbaric abuses of the family relation. Women still are disfranchised and depressed, children treated with cruelty and passionate rigor, and even infanticide is practiced with legal impunity in many parts.

As a rule there is no noble family life where the Sabbath is violated. But where it is kept sacredly the nobility and inviolate sacredness of the family relation are conspicuous features of society.

Observe how the Sabbath is made a blessing to the family. The father who has for six days been toiling is now free from drudgery, at home. The mother feels a weight of responsibility lifted from her heart because he is there. The children " climb his knees, the envied kiss to share." The beauty of fatherhood, the glory of motherhood and the

promise of childhood all garland with strength
and sweetness, the little band. Mutual respect,
love and admiration are prevalent. The feeling
with each is :

> " Mid pleasures and palaces though we may roam,
> Be it ever so humble there's no place like home.
> A charm from the sky seems to hallow us there,
> Which seek through the world is ne'er met with elsewhere."

This is the natural sentiment that accompanies a
pure home life, but when we come to add the
spiritual feelings, then the spectacle becomes sublime. These feelings the Sabbath gives the best
opportunity of planting and maturing. The close
relations into which the members of the household
are drawn, the teachings of the father, the love
of the mother, the responsiveness of the children,
all coalesce to make a divine group through the
ministrations of a divine day.

Thus the hours sweetly pass, each leaving some
brilliant precipitant of truth or grace in the units
of the home, till finally the evening shades prevail.
A quiet, peaceful, restful charm abides on every
heart. The father, who is still in a sense the
high priest of the Sabbatic circle, prepares his mind
for leading his little band to the throne of grace.
The mother encourages this seemly and important
service by patient queenliness and helping love.

The scene is set forth with inimitable beauty by the popular Scottish bard :

" The cheerfu' supper done, wi' serious face
    They round the ingle form a circle wide ;
The sire turns o'er wi' patriarchal grace
    The big ha-bible, once his father's pride.
    His bonnet rev'rently is laid aside,
His lyart haffets wearin' thin and bare
    These strains that once did sweet in Zion glide.
He wales a portion with judicious care,
And ' Let us worship God,' he says with solemn air.

" They chant their artless notes in simple guise,
    They tune their hearts, by far the noblest aim ;
Perhaps Dundee's wild warbling measures rise ;
    Or plaintive martyrs, worthy o' the name ;
    Or noble Elgin beets the heavenward flame—
The sweetest far o' Scotia's holy lays ;
  *Compared with these, Italian trills are tame,
The tickled ears no heartfelt rapture raise,
Nae unison ha'e they wi' our Creator's praise.

" The priest-like father reads the sacred page :
    How Abraham was the friend of God on high ;
Or Moses bade eternal warfare wage
    With Amalek's ungracious progeny ;
    Or how the royal bard did groaning lie
Beneath the stroke of heaven's avenging ire ;
    Or Job's pathetic plaint and wailing cry ;
    Or rapt Isaiah's wild seraphic fire ;
Or other holy seers that tune the sacred lyre.

" Perhaps the Christian volume is the theme :
    How guiltless blood for guilty man was shed ;

How he who bore in heaven the sacred name
    Had not on earth whereon to lay His head ;
    How His first followers and servants sped
The precepts sage they wrote to many a land ;
    How he who lone on Patmos banished
Saw in the sun a mighty angel stand,
And heard great Babylon's doom pronounced
        by heaven's command.

" Then, kneeling down to heaven's Eternal King,
    The saint, the father, and the husband prays ;
Hope ' springs exulting on triumphant wing,'
    That thus they all may meet in future days,
No more to sigh or raise the bitter tear ;
    Together hymning their Creator's praise,
In such society, yet still more dear,
While circling time moves round in an eternal sphere."

    [Hallelujahs.]

Thus, by spiritualizing the Sabbath, "They delight themselves in the Lord, and He causes them to ride upon the high places of the earth, and feeds them with the heritage of Jacob their father; for the mouth of the Lord hath spoken it."

Again, I announce that Sabbath spiritualization is the greatest blessing of the Church. Money, influence, eloquence, music, ritual, learning, all depend upon it for success. When these spiritualized families gather into the larger assembly, how blissful and powerful that assembly becomes. De-vitalize the unit and you de-vitalize the family. De-vitalize the families and you de-vitalize the

Church. But when the smaller family groups
come together, all radiant with joy and hope, faith
and love, how easy and how beautiful are preaching, prayer and praise.   ◆

The whole church is at once afloat, bathing in
glory, swimming in bliss. The minister himself
feels the uplifting power, and inspiring spell of the
congregated factors around him. His mind and
heart, already aflame with truth, now catch new
torches of light, fresh forces of love; and like a
workman who needeth not to be ashamed, rightly
dividing the word of truth, he easily goes " into
the treasure house and brings forth things both
new and old." The vast congregation catches
again the reflex of its own flame and rises, stage
by stage, to truth after truth, and grace upon
grace, till the presence of the Lord is as sensibly
felt as when it shook Sinai, filled Solomon's temple, or swept with a storm of delight the souls
of men at Pentecost.   [Chorus of hallelujahs.]

Where is the Sabbath spiritualizing community
that does not now enjoy such superior glories?
And everything else is made rapturous by the
exalted unity and love of such experiences. It is
delightful to conduct such church services; it is
delightful to enjoy them. It is delightful to conduct the Sunday-school. It is delightful to manage
the finance. It is delightful to assemble in the
weekly prayer meeting. It is delightful to come

together in the love feast and class. It is delightful to carry such recollections and inspirations
through the hours of the work-day world.
[Amens.]

Truly to such Sabbath keepers God fulfills his
promise. " Then shalt thou delight thyself in the
Lord, and I will make thee to ride upon the high
places of the earth, and feed thee with the heritage
of Jacob thy father; for the mouth of the Lord
hath spoken it."

Again, I proclaim that Sabbath spiritualization
is the best blessing of the State. It has been my
good fortune to travel in many lands on all the
continents of the globe. While doing so I kept
my eye steadily on this particular subject. I everywhere observed the accompaniments of, and effects
produced by the non-Sabbatic nations, the semi-
Sabbatic and the wholly Sabbatic peoples. In the
non-Sabbatic nations I found humanity in its most
baleful, fierce and deplorable state—wretched beyond expression; stagnant, repulsive, fiendish, and
abominable. Instance the aborigines of New Zea-
land, the black fellows of Australia, the Malayans
of the Eastern Archipelago; the Chinese, who are
civilized by Confucius and religionized by Laotze
and Gautama; the Japanese, who are civilized by
Buddhism and religionized somewhat by Shintoism; the Hindoos, who are civilized by the Brahmans, and are being now evangelized by Chris-

tianity. All these and many other Sabbathless
peoples whom I have visited, are exclusive, cruel,
unfraternal, unprogressive and debased beyond all
conception, much less expression.

As we come westward, the first semi-Sabbatic
people we meet are the Mohammedans, who keep
Friday, instead of Sunday. Then the Greeks,
the Italians, the Portuguese, the Spaniards, the
French and the Germans, all of whom, largely
through the laxity and indulgence of the papacy,
are semi-Sabbatic nations. If you go to church in
the morning and keep Sunday till twelve o'clock
you may play fiddle, dance, drink and dissipate all
the rest of the day, and be a good Christian. Letting down the gates so far has deluged continental
Europe so much with Sabbath desecration that in
many places few people aim at keeping any part of
the sacred day.

Now, if Sabbath secularization be a natural and
good thing, and if semi-Sabbatic secularization be a
better thing, as is claimed by the Roman Catholic
clergy and by the European vandal immigrants,
why has no nation that has adopted either the one
or the other as its custom leaped to the front and
became the leading nation of the earth? And it is
a notorious fact, well worthy of the stateman's
study, as it is worthy of every man's attention,
that since Christianity was born no Sabbathless
nation, and no semi-Sabbatic nation has come for-

ward in commercial, in educational, in financial, in
progressive splendor and potency, and become the
acknowledged leader of all the other nations of the
earth.

There are but two nations on the earth to-day
that aim at wholly Sabbatic spiritualization. These
are Great Britain and the United States of America. And is it not a striking fact, that when we
come to look for commercial supremacy, educational supremacy, industrial supremacy, mechanical
supremacy, financial supremacy, naval and military
supremacy, philanthropic, patriotic and progressive
supremacy, we have to turn to some one of these
wholly Sabbatic nations? The great leading forces
that are molding the present and mapping out the
future, are not preëminent in any of the semi-Sabbatic or non-Sabbatic nations. And is not this proof
patent to the reasoning faculties of any sane mind
of the fact, that the wholly spiritualized Sabbath is
better for nations than a half-kept Sabbath? As, of
course, I will acknowledge that a half-sanctified
Sabbath is better than no Sabbath at all.

And is it not presumptive proof—aye, more;
demonstrative proof—that God is still working the
world toward its goal through the spiritualization
of His day, and that the nations who keep it as He
directs "shall delight themselves in the Lord," and
that He does cause "them to ride upon the high
places of the earth," and does "feed them with the

heritage of Jacob"? (which was to be an ever-augmenting heritage); "for the mouth of the Lord hath spoken it."

I need not now detain you to show the relation of Sabbath keeping to personal liberty, to the universal extension of the franchise in this and other lands, although the task would be an easy and an interesting one ; nor need I detain you to describe how the bleeding wounds of this erring world can only be stanched and healed by Sabbatic ministries, and how human bondage can be broken, and human woe assuaged alone by the sacred setting apart of one-seventh of time for the purpose. Nor need I keep you on this warm Summer night in this immense audience to portray to you the glories that at death shall break upon the ecstatic vision of the sons and daughters of God, who have stood bravely forth against the tides of infidelity, that now threaten to engulf our American Christian Sabbath.

If God were not over the floods, amid the shadows, keeping watch-guard o'er His own, we might reasonably despair. But He is there, and there to stay, till the arrows of His light have smitten to the dust every hand and head lifted against His day, and till all the people of this earth shall delight in the Lord and ride on the high places, first of earth and then of heaven. O Sabbath day ! sweet queen of time. Behold her! She has come down the centuries with voices pure and sweet, face and form angelic and beautiful. She with seraphic hand has strewn the ages with clusters of human graces and celestial hopes. She shines in thousands of pulpits beside the messengers of God, wafting their glad tidings of redemption to myriads of despoiled and sin-sold souls. [Showers of Amens.]

She pillows on her bosom the fevered brain of the student young, and draws the coy and gentle maiden up to noblest life. She blesses the stalwart man, bearing his weight of woes, and shows him he may cast his heavy burdens on the Lord. [Hallelujah.]

She smooths the ruffled brow of careworn age, and strokes with virgin palm the hairs all hoary grown; she blesses the dying sick and with up-lifted finger rends the veil of gloom that hangs between here and home, and bids the departing view the glories of the other shore. She pours balm over the poor man's brow and rest over his weary heart and limbs.

She grasps the fretted steed of the work-day world and bandages up its bruises, and washes away its swelter and its foam. She inspires the lover of his race to visit the cottages of the for-saken and turns him into a ministering angel to the sick and poor. She has visited millions of mankind and gives them a code of honor which higher is than law.

She enters barbaric lands, stacks the bloody spear and stays the red rivulets of savage gore. [Praise the Lord.] She marches forward with gracious step into landscape, villa, town and city, and makes the hearts of millions glad by the music of church bells and ascending psalm. Thus she blesses this wearied, stricken world; and who shall recall her from her high mission of help? Who shall dare pollute her unsullied robes? Where is the man that shall dare insult her by trampling on one of her sacred hours? Where are the men that arrogantly presume to debauch and defile one moment of her sacred time? Paralyzed be the foot that shall tread on her. Withered be the hand that shall stretch itself out against her. Consumed be the eye that shall corrupt her; torn out by the root be the tongue that shall speak against her, and damned must be the soul that spurns her services of love. Go on then, thou sweet Queen of heaven, go; sent out of eternity from the everlasting Father, by the Redeeming Son. Go on scattering weekly thy blessing over every land. [Amens, many.] Go on blessing persons, families, churches, nations, with thy heavenly, refining, spiritualizing joys.

A hundred million Christian voices, a hundred million Christian hearts from all parts of this redeemed world join mine to-night in saying, go

on, stately, silent, pure, in thy heavenly mission
till the belated sons of this great transitional
century, shall, re-born, flood thy hours with redemption songs. Go on, till thy clear, clean, crystal
moments shall be used by all human eyes to look
at Him thou dost enshrine. Then shall all mankind delight themselves in God and "ride upon the
high places of the earth" to the higher places of
the heavens. [Many Amens.]

The Sabbatarian Prince.

SUNDAY MORNING, JULY 26, 1891.

Mark ii, 28—"Therefore the Son of Man is Lord also of the Sabbath."

IF the Son of Man were Lord *only* of the Sabbath His Lordship would be of little account to us. But it is because He is "Lord also" of the Sabbath this declaration from His own lips becomes of infinite import to every thoughtful mind.

It is His Lordship over the great internal and external factors of all being that gives infinite and focussed force to his declaration of Lordship over the Sabbath.

In order that we may see the pith and point of this, look at the commanding supremacy mighty men achieve, when it is known they have immense personal resources and demonstrated practical ability accorded them.

To illustrate—When a great man towers up above his fellows afar and leads them on to treasures and triumph, there is a sense in which he becomes to them sovereign.

When Alexander the Great rose like a military flame, conquering all before him at Issus, Granicus and Arbela, and leading on his troops to oriental riches, he became prince of commanders to the Greeks.

When Julius Cæsar rose like a lustrous star, subduing the brawny hordes of Belgia, Gaul and Britain; crossing the Alps and the Rubicon, leading his cohorts down upon the rich Italian plains, he became kingly to his soldiery.

And when Napoleon of Corsica rose like an ensanguined sun bathing in the blood of nations, rising in resplendence over Montenote, Rivoli and Lodi; glowing with a dazzling brilliancy round Marengo, Austerlitz and Jena, and raising France to unequalled military splendor, he became all commanding to his countrymen.

And so when the Chieftain of the armies of heaven sped from His high command down to this realm of sin and shame, assumed humanity by His birth in Bethlehem, evinced divinity by His life in Palestine, atoned for sin by His death on Calvary, conquered death by His resurrection from Joseph's tomb, opened heaven by His victorious entrance into paradise, and clove by the cleavage of His own right-hand, a course to eternal conquest to every obedient son of Adam. Thus in a higher, deeper, broader sense does He become kingly to His followers. Let us seek a comprehensive view of this most illustrious Sabbatic Prince, for none have every truly seen Him but to love and to adore.

If this view we obtain, we must "launch out into the deep" of His divinity, for as they who stand in a narrow bay watching wavelets ebb and flow upon the shaly strand have a puny image of the ocean, so they who gaze upon some mere inlet of our Sabbatic Chieftain's power must have a meagre conception of his amplitude of glory. But as they who go out upon the mighty bosom of the ocean to study its kind and potent properties, feel and see its ever active swell, swayed by moon and sun, refreshing the world, so they who go out into the boundless expanse of their Saviour's power will feel they have found Him, of whom Moses in the law and the prophets did write, "the Immanuel, which being interpreted is, 'God with us.'"

I.—Our Sabbatarian Prince is the Chieftain of nature as well as of the Sabbath. It was He who molded the mountains and formed the valleys; He fashioned the rivers and sent them through the landscape like strands of molten silver, shimmering and singing to the sea. He laid the foundations of our world; set it on its axle with needed pose and poise. He rules its volcanoes, earthquakes, whirlwinds, typhoons, thunders, lightnings and canopies of cloud. He holds the oceans and the seas in the hollow of His spiritual hand and orders the intricate laws of cohesive life and motion. He has formed the fish, fowl, beasts and man, and favors them with those manifold provisions on which they daily feed.

He also arched the deep dome of distant blue and pillared it with a light which streams from two and a quarter octillion tons of fire by day, and gemmed it with those gentle rays which rain from an immeasurable abyss of stars by night.

He wheels on this great golden galaxy of girdling worlds so smoothly we never feel the motion; so securely there is no collision; so punctually they are always on time; so swiftly a cannon ball is slow compared with their rapidity; so noiselessly there is heard no thunder of wheels or horn of engineer, save as they in passing strike a vibrant chord of that amazing harp hanging from His own great throne, swelling forth the grand sub-bass of that excelling song, " Worthy is the Lamb that was slain to receive power, and riches, and wisdom, and strength, and honor, and glory, and blessing," and echoing forth in eternal melody the supreme refrain, " For by Him were all things created that are created, whether they be thrones, or dominions, or principalities, or powers, all things were created by Him and for Him, and He is before all things, and by Him all things consist "(cohere), * * "that in all things He might have the preëminence."

On, then, ye explorers of nature, on! Set your eyed batteries against the sunny day and starlit night. Unfold sun after sun, law after law, space after space! Display the order, magnitude, multitude, magnificence of these heavenly worlds! I claim them all as fitting brilliants for that brow which once was diademed with thorns, for "on His head are many crowns," and "it pleased the Father that in Him should all fullness dwell." Oh, Sabbath-keeping disciple of Jesus, how inspiring is this illustrious truth to you? Who shall lay anything to your charge? What shall successfully assail you? Let tribulation, distress, persecution, famine, exposure, peril and sword come on! Let the powers of life, the forces of death, adverse angels, assaulting principalities, storming powers, foes from the present, foes from the future, foes from the past, foes from the height, foes from the depth, foes however grotesque, grizzly, horrible, from unknown regions send forth their long lines to the charge. Defended by the Almighty Maker and Governor of all the regions and forces of the universe, you are tranquilly secure.

Your adversaries may drive you far down into deeps of sorrow, into meshes of temptation, or they may drag you abroad into expanses of bewilderment. But I see Him coming down with many crowns upon His head through the gloom-drift of the ages, crying, as He approaches, "these are my jewels," and so you can confidently sing, Oh, Sabbath Saint,

" I know not where His islands lift
Their fronded palms in air,
But this I know I cannot drift
Beyond His love and care."

But whilst this supremacy of our Sabbatic
Prince is the most charming truth to the Christian, it is the most alarming to the sinner. Unsaved one there is no escape from this omnipresent
and Almighty Saviour. If you will not receive
Him as pierced for your sin, you must receive Him
as pierced by your sin. If you will not come to
Him; then He must come to you. If you will
not receive Him as your deliverer, you must
receive Him as your judge. If you hide at the
roots of the mountains it will be to meet His presence there. If you nest among the stars His
hand will pluck thee thence. If you take the wings
of the morning and fly avast over the awful rim
into the region of nothingness, even there shall
His hand hold thee, for the darkness hideth not
from Him, the night shineth as the day; the darkness and the light are both alike to Him. Since
then you cannot flee from Him, I pray, I beseech,
I implore you fly to Him and be by Him forever saved. Then freed from sin and suffering,
danger and despair, and fixed upon one that has
strangely become all in all to you, your song
shall be :

" Lord of earth Thy forming hand, well this beauteous globe
  hath planned,
Woods that wave, and hills that tower, oceans rolling in their
  power,
All that strikes the gaze unsought, all that charms the lonely
  thought;
Yet, amid this scene so fair, oh, if Thou wert absent there
What were all these joys to me, whom have I on earth but
  Thee?"

And when admitted into Heaven again you can
sing :

" Lord of Heaven before my sight, rolls a world of purest light
Where, in love's unclouded reign, parted hands are clasped
  again;
Martyrs there and seraphs high, blest and glorious company,
While immortal music rings from unnumbered seraph strings;
Oh, this scene is passing fair, yet if Thou wert absent there,
What were all these joys to me, whom have I in Heaven but
  Thee?"

Keepers of the Sabbath cheer, for "the Son of
man who is Lord of the Sabbath" is Lord also of
the vast and varied resources of fathomless nature
and all the riches of the earth, and all the wealth
of the sea, and all the glories of the sky and all the
laws of time, and all the treasures of eternity belong to you who shrine Him in your hearts during
the ministries of His sweet Sabbath days. [Amens
and Hallelujahs.] "For all are yours since ye are
Christ's and Christ is God's."

II.—Again, this Sabbath Prince is the great Grand Marshal of history. History is more than a "barbarous dissonance" of gory ages, slowly setting into seas of blood. It is more than a procession of blind beings coming up out of mystery, marching through suffering and going into mystery.

History is a divine epic, Christ is the poet and humanity the theme. Mankind, therefore, need not be borne on a " wailing wake of wandering foam " through a dreadful drama to a tragic end. For as Clio was Chief of the Muses, so Christ is the Chief of History, moving on through all its discordant eras with steady aim in view.

The nations He has woven into the sublime constituency of His plan, and the harp which appears wet with tears of time, jangled with the throbs of sorrow, still beateth out its melody above the sky. The dissonances of passing events are but the babble of the orchestra getting into tune. There is a viewless, voiceless presence, mingling everywhere with the toiling throng. This presence is our Sabbath Prince. He lifts His hand and the human tide divides—the evil to the left, the good to the right. Neither policy nor pleading can alter the historic law. Like gravitation, it never yields.

"He who is morally right cannot be politically wrong. He who is morally wrong cannot be politically right." This principle is fundamental.

Trace a few nations and this irrevocable law will appear. Babylon, founded by the hunter Nimrod, rose to surpassing splendor in the valley of the Euphrates. Her youth were vigorous, her women virtuous, her men prosperous. But with prosperity came luxury, ignorance, arrogance and pride. Her youth grew dissolute, her men shameful, her women shameless, her senators obsequious, her princes imperious, till in all the haughty inflation of a despot Nebuchadnezzar, the conqueror of Syria and Palestine, exclaimed from the summit of her hanging gardens, " Is not this great Babylon that I have built for the house of the Kingdom by the might of my power?" There was a voiceless presence watching the vain-glorious speaker and Nebuchadnezzar was driven from his palace and the abodes of men among the beasts of the field till he had recognized the God of Heaven. And a few years later under his son Belshazzar, Babylon, which rose "like a lovely pearl in a setting of emerald," fell fated, for the cup of her iniquity was full.

Her walls, eighty-seven feet thick, towering three hundred and fifty feet in air, could not protect her. Her hundred brazen gates, designed to roll back the waves of war, could not defend her. Her two hundred and fifty towers of chiselled marble were unable to shield her. And even a Daniel, with all his divine dreaming and interpreting, could not roll back the

5

ruinous tide.   She had captured the Hebrew nation ; shackled the people of God ; rifled the temple
of Jehovah ; fostered the black broods of corruption. and so the *mene* and the *tekel* and the *upharsin*
which are finally inscribed on incorrigible nations
glared fatefully from her walls.   The hidden heavy
hand which striketh out of Zion smote her by the
troops of Cyrus.   She expired beneath the blow,
gasping a dread death agony, and over her heaps of
ruins, which hide not her guilty gore, scarcely will
a Bedouin pitch his tent; and so the sites of magni-
fical palaces are given up to the hooting owl, the
howling hyena the screeching satyr, the serpent and the wild beast; and over the expanse of
weird desolation the hidden hand that marshals
history, has inscribed before the eyes of reflecting
nations and of men: " He that exalteth himself
shall be abased." " Beware of covetousness, which
is idolatry."

To show that our Sabbatic Prince is in secular
history, moving among the nations with steady
aim in view, look upon the splendid but sad scenes
of Grecian story ; the brevity, "the brilliancy, the
exquisite ideal beauty of the Athenian race," " the
grace and supremacy of their art," " the splendor
and perfection of their literature," the courage
and exploits of their heroes, the glory and beauty
of their temples—enwreathe them with world-wide
admiration.

And oh! had Athens learned the lesson of obedience, "how gracious and beautiful had been her righteousness." But beautiful Athens at the base of her unequalled Acropolis perversely sinned, and so ninety short years after her warriors had routed the countless hosts of Hystaspes and Xerxes on a "sleepless September night," the baleful wail rang down the walls of the Piræus which announced that the famous fleet of Athens had been captured at Aegospotami. The deeds of Marathon and of Salamis under another Epaminondas could not be repeated, and "even-handed justice placed the chalice of mingled poison to her lips which she had forced the unfortunate to drink." And the Prince of the Sabbath, who hears His Father say: "Rule thou in the midst of thine enemies," "Judge thou among the heathen," "Wound the heads (of treason and tyranny) over many countries," struck her polished pollutions, inscribing on her classic ruins in letters of scorching fire, before the eyes of all mankind, that "beauty without purity, that intellect without holiness, that eloquence without conscience, that art without religion, that insight without love, are but blossoms whose roots are in the corruption of the grave."

Take but one more example to prove that our Prince is in secular history, making it sacred, too, and molding and supervising it for the final overthrow of all great evils.

Rome rudely snatched the sceptre from the palsied hands of Greece, and so long as Rome was pure she was strong. So long as she was the Rome of the Camilli, the Cincinnati, the Fabii and the elder Scipios; so long as her Senators came from the "honest labor of the farm," and her Consuls from the "hardy labor of the plough," she advanced, till her eagles fluttered over one-third the globe. But when the "dregs of every iniquity poured into the Tiber;" "when the old iron discipline yielded to abounding iniquity and veneered vice; when her trade became imposture and her literature a seething cynic scum, then Rome, whom mightiest nations curtesied to, fell, fatally wounded before a hated cross held in the bleeding hands of the world's true King," and the Sabbath Prince wrote in letters of warning flame over her dismantled Coliseum, her crumbling palaces, her wrecked and forsaken Forum, the burning sentences for all mankind to read, that it is "self-denial and not luxury, humility and not insolence, charity and not violence, justice and not ambition," divinity and not humanity, that are to elevate nations as well as men.

Thus my friends when you sweep away the superficial shadows and penetrate beneath the surface of events to their cause, you find one there marching through the chaotic gulf of human history. His presence is divinely terrible and

divinely beautiful, moving with a mute majesty
that everywhere sends overwhelming ruin upon
the unimprovable peoples of mankind. The great
Isaiah caught prophetic glimpses of Him trampling
nations in his fury till their life blood besprent his
raiment, because the day of vengeance was in his
heart and the year of his redeemed was come. The
persiflage of journalism and the vaporing of
infidelity shrivel up before His face as trees to
tinder, turn before the shafts of lightning torn.
And my hearers this avenging, ameliorating Immanuel is going on by line upon line, warning
upon warning, disaster upon disaster, evolution
upon evolution, mercy upon mercy, till all the
world submit gracefully to his sweet pacific sway.

Look at the condition of affairs to-day as they
appear on the political map of the world.

Resting in northeastern Atlantic lies an Isle not
larger than our York and Jersey, whose war drum
in every clime salutes the rising sun. She has her
hand on dominions, on our own continent many
times larger than herself. The great Pacific is
mottled with her colonies, and the best parts of
Africa are under her control. She holds the keys
of the Gates of Hercules ; and the Mediterranean,
with all its classic memories, is studded with her
possessions. Syria, Persia, Turkey, are hanging
on her golden girdle, and she sways her sceptre
from the high crests of Afghanistan to the shores

of Ceylon over a population eight times her own.
In response to her call the hermit nations of China
and Japan have opened up their ports. Why this
world wide power of that isle of the Northern Sea?
Does the secret lie in her insular position, in the
prowess of her army and navy, or in the bravery of
her people? No, but in the empowering, hidden
hand of Him who loves her open Bible, who is
adored in her free churches, who is preached on
her kept Sabbath, who is exalted and revered by
the masses of her people, who is honored and
acknowledged generally from the humblest hut to
highest palace of the nation, and so long as this
divine Jesus of the Sabbath is the keeper of Great
Britain's seals, so long as He is worshipped by the
parliament and by the people, so long as he vitalizes
her throngs and her thrones, in vain will Lord
Macauley's prophetic New Zealander come to
gaze from London bridge upon the ruins of St.
Paul's. But this inviolate protection will cease if
ever Great Britain's Sabbath is deluged with dissipation, secular songs and drinking carousals.

  And what is the real cause of the prosperity of
these United States? Is it because we have
3,000,000 square miles of territory? South America
has more, 12,000 miles of ocean frontage. Africa
has more, 24,000 miles of river navigation. China
excels us. Is it because our lakes, rivers, cataracts
and prairies are most expansive and our annual

products most abundant? Is it because our territory, garnished with grain and flecked with fruits and flowers, stretches through thirty degrees of latitude and like a variegated virgin bathes her feet in the warm waters of the South, and pillows her cool, quiet head amid the iceberg palaces of the North?

Is it because our troops fought so bravely at Bunker Hill, Trenton and Yorktown during the Revolution? At Monterey, Palo Alto and Contreras in the Mexican campaign? At Vicksburg, Antietam, Gettysburg and Wilderness during the Rebellion? With all due appreciation of territorial magnificence, and with all patriotic thanks to the soldiers of this commonwealth, I must, in justice to the truth of God, declare that the prosperity and perpetuity of this republic rest, not altogether on geographic splendors, agricultural glories, commercial superiorities, nor even upon brilliant military achievements. But in the last analysis, the mission and magnificence of this country for their perpetuation depend, upon the Almighty and All Loving Redeemer of mankind, the Sabbatic Prince whom we adore. He is the infallible Magna Charta of all important privileges.

And so long as He is adored by our people,

"The star-bangled banner in triumph shall wave
    O'er the land of the free and the home of the brave,"

So long as His Sabbaths are kept,

> " Will freedom from her mountain height
> Unfurl her standard to the air,
> And break the murky spell of night,
> And set the stars of glory there."

[Shower of amens.]

And furthermore, so long as His church is true in England and America, will He march on among the nations, overthrowing the bad, establishing the good, expelling cruelty, curbing passion, branding suicide, repressing murder, driving the shameful impurities of paganism into congenial darkness. He will go on overthrowing tyrants, foiling pluto-crats, freeing slaves, nursing the sick, restoring the fallen, sheltering the orphan, elevating women, shrouding in a halo of innocence the tender years of the child. He will go on changing pity into a virtue, elevating poverty into a blessing, ennobling labor into a dignity. He will go on revealing the beauty of purity, the glory of meekness, the grandeur of charity, the eternal nobility of man and the transcending goodness of God. Nor will He be stayed by sceptics, rationalists, free thinkers, nihilists, agnostics, deists or atheists, till rum, rowdyism, rascality and every species of wrong be turned into tophet together. And He will use steamships, railroads, telegraphs, telephones and all other inventions flowing from the fertile brain of His church, to ride into the uttermost parts of the earth. In this time of the end foreseen by the prophet Daniel, when "many run to and fro, and knowledge shall be increased," the presence of our Prince is increasingly immanent on the field, moving forward with steady purpose, preparing the wide world for salvation as He has prepared salvation for the world. [Hallelujahs.]

He has abolished Egyptianism and out of its wreckage evolved the sacredness of the human body. He has overcome Zoroasterism and out of its system portrayed in sharp contrast the battle between good and evil. He has overcome Grecianism and out of the wreck brought forth ideal beauty. He has overthrown imperial Romanism and out of the disaster established the authority of law. He has overthrown Thorism and on the ruins raised up a resplendent freedom.

Elusive as electricity, greater than gravity, silent and steady as the motion of the spheres. He has already moved into the hermetic nations of the East, nor will He leave them till the Taoism, Confucianism and ancestralism of China have fallen before His gospel, and the Buddhism, Shintoism and evils of Japan have been abolished by His truth, and the Brahmanism, Vishnuism and Sevaism of India have fled into oblivion before the glow of His heavenly spirit, and into every other idolatrous segment of the earth will He move till all idolatries He shall have buried in the same grave in which He

has already entombed the mythical idols of Babylon, Greece and Rome, Egypt, Persia and Teu-
tonia. Then the redeemed race, entranced in
ecstacy, will sing from pole to pole as they fix their
affections upon the Great Deliverer,

> " Welcome, sweet day of rest,
>   That saw the Lord arise;
> Welcome to this reviving breast,
>   And these rejoicing eyes !
>
> The King himself comes near,
>   And feasts his saints to-day;
> Here we may sit, and see him here,
>   And love, and praise and pray.
>
> One day in such a place,
>   Where thou, my God, art seen,
> Is sweeter than ten thousand days
>   Of pleasurable sin.
>
> My willing soul would stay
>   In such a frame as this,
> And sit and sing herself away
>   To everlasting bliss."

Amens and hallelujahs!

How consoling must these great facts be to you
to-day? Oh! followers of our Sabbath prince.
He has by his Father been delegated vicegerent
of this universe. "All power is given unto Him
in heaven and on earth." His resources are illimitable, His purpose is eternal and His love is infinite.

He has undertaken the greatest and most loving contract that ever was projected. " He will not fail or be discouraged " till he brings forth victory. [Amens.]

The Sabbath is His great field day of action. He has appointed it as the time when men, free from the siren charms of the earth, shall be fascinated and redeemed with the ever evolving themes of heaven.

It would be easy to go on and show the grand reasons why the Son of Man is Lord of the Sabbath. Because on it he rose, because on it he specially sends out his messengers and forth His spirit. Because by it He will instruct, inspire, mould and elevate the teeming millions of mankind so that all eternity shall become Sabbatic and all redeemed humanity serene.

Like fragments of eternity He has set His Sabbaths in the midst of these toiling, sweltering days of time, that all who are weary and heavy laden might hear of Him and come to Him for rest. [Chorus of hallelujahs.] He has launched the Sacred Seventh like a rescue barque and sent it out in the midst of the foaming billows. He is the captain; His ministers the crew; His church members the passengers : rescue of all the race the object.

> " Awake ye saints, awake, and hail the Sacred Day.
> In loftiest songs of praise your joyful homage pay,
> Come bless the day that God hath blest,
> The type of Heaven's eternal rest."

If then this day is the world's life-boat, framed of twenty-four glorious beams of time, what shall we say to the pirates who want to defile its hours and pollute its moments, and take it down with them-selves through the gugling billows of damnation? That is the vital question now agitating the whole earth. What would you do with other pirates but attack them with shot and shell, and make it so hot for them that they either retreat or surrender. This is the only remedy for these Sabbath scuttlers. There is nothing else to be done. They will encroach and encroach, and seize and seize, and intrude and intrude, till they have turned the fair ship of heaven into a charnel house of beer kegs, fermentations, dissipation and licentious abominations. Out upon them, oh! ye Deborahs in Israel, and as the brave Barbara Heck, when through Sabbath card playing Philip Embury, was disgracing this day of the Lord, went up and threw the whole pack into the fire and ordered him up from his back sliding to preaching the word of God, and so became the first foundress of Methodism in New York, if not indeed America. [Hallelujahs.] So approach these Sabbath prostituting sinners and like Saint Barbara, lay violent hands on the desecrating utensils, and summon them with a storm of earnestness to duty " for the Kingdom of Heaven suffereth violence and the violent take it by force."

And ye Nehemiahs who are building the crystal

walls of the new Jerusalem in the hearts and minds
of the people, shut down the gates on Sabbath
defilement.

Out upon the defilers with the double forces of
love and law, and let them know that you will "lay
hands on them." Hands of faith and love and
prayer, if need be, if they depart not from dissipating and defiling the Holy Day.

And as you go on this duty do not look to man.
" Vain is the help of man." Look to God for help
and Jesus Christ will come again and demonstrate
to the people of Newark from the meadows to the
hill that the Son of Man is preëminently fitted for
Lordship of the Sabbath, since He is the active
Prince of nature and of history.

The Sabbatarian Prince—Continued.

SUNDAY MORNING, JULY 26, 1891.

Luke vi, 5—"And he said unto them that the Son of Man is Lord also of the Sabbath."

ON last Lord's Day we observed that our Saviour is the appointed Mediator between God the Father and man the sinner. That this high station and His own Divine nature constitute Him Creator of man's physical sphere and Conductor of man's historic evolutions. That this illustrious Vice-gerency gives pith, point and power to His own declaration that He is "Lord of the Sabbath." Because being in possession of all the forces of nature and resources of history, He is well able to maintain the sacred majesty of that Holy Day against all obtruders.

This morning we shall go two steps further and portray our Sabbatic Prince as Lord also of sacred Revelation and Christian experience, and demonstrate therefrom that He is peculiarly fitted to be "Lord of the Sabbath."

I.—He is the Lord of sacred Scripture :   He is
the central figure of redemption's story.   It was
the Prince of the Sabbath that appeared to the first
human pair after the sad scenes that forfeited Paradise, giving them hope by promise that " the seed
of the woman should bruise the serpent's head,"
and warning by circling sword of flaming Seraphim, which guarded the way of the tree of life.

It was the Prince of the Sabbath that commanded
Noah to preach to the early sinning giants, to build
the Ark, and from the floods to save, by his own
family, the human nucleus from which races of
smaller statue, but larger virtue, might spring.

It was this Lord of the Sabbath commissioned
Abraham to go forth from his ancestral home to
the land he knew not of, but from whence he would
make his children as the sand on the seashore for
multitude, and as the lustrous globes which nightly
gleam in an oriental sky for beauty.

It was this Lord of the Sabbath guarded from
harm the tender years of Moses, conducted him to
Arabian solitudes and there gave him high communion, commanded him from burning bush to
rescue Israel from Egypt's thrall; sustained him
by mighty miracle and august presage, in the presence of earth's greatest king ; opened the Red Sea
that he and his might pass unharmed ; whelm'd
his royal foes in its closing billows ; gave him, mid
thunders that shook Sinai, the moral law ; fed

his nation of delivered slaves with manna miraculously provided; slaked the thirst of itinerating millions with a river which strangely followed them; guided the march for forty years, and finally swept with the sword of Josiah the land of Canaan, so that the Chosen could settle amid its verdant valleys flowing with milk, and its vine-clad hills exuding honey.

It was this Lord of the Sabbath who appeared to Job amid his crashing fortunes and inspired him to cry through all disaster and recrimination, as if strung upon a Divine diapason, " Though He slay me yet will I trust in Him," * * * " for I know that my Redeemer liveth."

It was this Lord of the Sabbath annotated those lyric and didatic odes of the poetic king and royal prophet, which, after having cheered David and his mighty men amid the fastnesses of Engedi, around the court of Achish, in the caverns of Adullam, in the forest of Hareth, in the wild wilderness of Ziph, around the cliffs of Carmel, in the ancestral home of Hebron, throughout the wars against Philistine, Moabite, Ammonite, Syrian and Rabbah, are yet to float on till they swell God's praise from the ponderous peaks of the Andes to the crystal crests of the Himalayas.

It was this Sabbath Lord appeared to the lofty-souled Isaiah as the Mighty Comer in the bright but tragic future, ensanguined with an atoning

gore, which wrung from him the cry from his
watch-tower, " Who is this that cometh from Eden
with dyed garments from Bozra, this that is glorious in his apparel, traveling in the greatness of his
strength," and gave him for answer, " I that speak
in righteousness, mighty to save."

It was this Sabbath Lord appeared on the lonely
banks of Chebar, kindled the keen vision of exiled
Ezekiel, to see those eyed wheels white with heat
flying round their dreadful rings, rolling forth
might and mercy on mankind.

It was this Sabbath Lord stood before the eyes
of Jeremiah, the weeping lion, turning his tears
into eternal crystals, which enabled him to discern
in the gloom-clad distance the world's adorable
Deliverer coming as Jehovah Tsidkenu, " the Lord
our righteousness."

It was the Lord of the Sabbath enabled the
minor prophets to catch those fine touches, of fan-
tasy and flame, that heralded the morning's dawn
in the approaching person of the Son of God Himself coming to dwell among and die for men.

At length that sacred Person came, of maiden
mother and virgin wife so appropriately born, in
Bethlehem, fulfilling the old-time prophecy, " But
thou, Bethlehem Ephratah, though thou be little
among the thousands of Judah, yet out of thee shall
He come forth unto me that is to be Ruler in
Israel ; whose goings forth have been of old,

from everlasting."—Micah v, 2. No royal babe
had ever such wondrous and majestic natal con-
voy. The stars deputed one of their number to
hover with lustrous rays over the manger cradle
of the baby King. The angels sent the brightest
choir they could furnish to sing in shepherd ears
His advent—"Glory to God in the highest;
peace on earth, good will toward men." The sages
from the East deputed three of their number
(Balthar, Gaspar and Melchior) to present Him worship, accompanied with gold, frankincense and
myrrh. And on His great inaugural day, from the
riven heavens the Eternal Father cried to the
crowds on the Jordan: "This is my beloved Son,
hear ye Him."

The commissioned forerunner was already standing in his track, with heroic soul beating under
rugged robe of camel's hair, with emaciated ascetic
form, that had issued from the caves of communion,
girt with leathern girdle, living on locusts and wild
honey, drinking water from the brook and making
the whole land echo with the strange cry. "There
cometh one after me who is preferred before me
for he was before me." "There standeth one among
you whom ye know not, whose shoes latched I am
not worthy to unloose. He shall baptize you with
the Holy Ghost and fire. "Behold (in Him), the
Lamb of God which taketh away the sin of the
world."

And as soon as that Surpassing Stranger appeared his whole life was elevated with a startling sublimity. Nature reversed her laws at his will. The "unconscious water saw its Lord and blushed." The lame leaped as harts, the eyes of blind men saw, the tongues of dumb men spake, the spirits of demons shrieked and fled, paralysis, leprosy and all manner of diseases passed away. Death itself, gave up its dead. Hypocrites and incorrigible sinners chafed with dread; the devil was vanquished in the wilderness; hell and all its host were overcome in Gethsemane; death was doomed by death on Calvary and nature's loftiest law gave way before that omnipotence, which became the ascending chariot of the Mediatorial and Victorious Conqueror from Olivet. [Many glories.]

Oh, classic grounds of the patriarchs, upon your acres have pressed the sacred feet of Him who was nailed upon the bitter cross for our advantage. He has finished the Redemption; He has laid the foundations of the new spiritual world; He has gone to execute his plan; gone to send down the fires of the Pentecost through all human ages; gone to inspire the spirits of His people with power from on high; gone to reappear in a blinding glory on the high road to Damascus, which shall fling from His saddle the Arch inquisitor and change Saul the slaughterer into Paul the preacher. [Hallelujahs.]

It was this Sabbath Lord, who, by His spirit,

appeared in the tender remonstrances to the Corinthians; in the exalted arguments to the Romans; in the burning logic of the Hebrews; the heavenly joy of the Philippians; the divine fulness of the Colossians; the peans of the heavenlies to the Ephesians in the liberating epistle of Philemon, in the pastoral manuals to Timothy, in the faith and work epistle of James and love letters of John.

It was this same Sabbath Lord reappeared to those aged eyes of Patmos (which often glanced lovingly into His face from His bosom), standing in the midst of creation's sevenfold lights, head white with antiquity : eyes flaming with command ; " voice as sound of many waters ; " " countenance as the sun shining in its strength ; " moving with natural grace and beauty mid heaven's mightiest mysteries; opening seals of history ; sounding trumpets of destiny ; pouring wrath-vials of doom ; hurling thunderheads of ruin and lightnings of withering vengeance upon sin and giving those gorgeous gleamings of the New Jerusalem with which the Great Book ends.   [Hallelujahs.]

Thus, though this volume was written in sixty-six parts, by forty-one authors in the uplands of Armenia, in the lowlands of the Nile, in the solitudes of Arabia, in the landscapes of Canaan, on the distant banks of the Euphrates, and in many an unknown nook of the Mediterranean, yet each fits all, all fits each, for there is no part of which the Sabbath Prince is not the unifying and Immanent Soul.

He is in its prophecies, making them sure; in its history, making it majestic; in its poetry, making it sublime; in its types, making them significant; in its arguments, rendering them unanswerable; in its promises, rendering them valid; in its threatenings, rendering them terrible. Over the surface of this book there runs a broken record of sin. Under the surface of this book there runs an unbroken swell of love. These two lap and tie in the first sentence of Genesis and the last of Revelations, and the whole volume quivers with the tremor of an Almighty kindness, which lives till it consumes the world's woes and carries the devoted reader to eternal ecstacy; because the Sabbath Lord, who is the expression of that love, lives in every jot and tittle, so that even a significant vowel point cannot pass away till all be fulfilled. Oh, Blessed Book! My father's guide, my mother's joy! No wonder the sceptics could not stab thee, nor rationalists rend thee, nor atheists and infidels bury thee, nor even papists burn thee, since in thee He lives who gives all worlds their life; since by thee He moves who marches among the nations, overthrowing their towering evils as very little things. [Praise the Lord and amens.]

Blessed Book! Thou hast shone into the brawny breasts of our savage ancestors and of them hast made men; thou hast set the moral canopy of the

benighted world with many hopeful stars; thou
dost send thy auroral rays over the dales of Asia,
the glades of Europe, and the virgin landscapes of
this young land.   Shine on! oh, venerable volume;
shine, till all men brothers be, and Christ is worshipped as the Sabbath Lord by all.   [Amens.]

Oh, Blessed Sabbath King!   I will stay my soul
on Thy triumphs when in the midst of life's fiercest
battles; I will pillow my head on Thy promises
when I come to lay me down in the gloom of the
grave; I will fly to heaven on Thy word when my
body lies in the cold embraces of the tomb.   For
the Son of Man is Lord also of the sacred Scripture as He is of the Sabbath.   And this is another
fact that gives such solemn majesty and sublime
meaning to that Holy Day. Oh, Blessed Septenary,
appointed and governed by our Redeeming Lord,
may thy sacred ministries sweep us weekly nearer
home.   [A rain of amens.]

And as the Lord of the Sabbath is also Lord
of Creation, History and Sacred Scripture, so He
is Lord of the highest and best human experiences.   It is said that Mercury made the three-
chorded lyre of the Greeks, by which men's hearts
were cheered with song.   But the Lord of this
sacred seventh of time has framed the triple-chorded
harp of Redemption of a vibrant note from nature,
a long resounding tone from history, and a recon-

ciling chime from Scripture. From these, with
wounded hands, he beateth out regenerating symphonies the whole world round. And this great
and glorious change comes upon the sons of sin
by personal experience.

Experiment is the order of the day in art and
science. It is fitting it should be the stirring question of the hour in the soul's salvation.

> " What we have felt and seen
> With confidence we tell."

> " He who has felt the power of the Highest
> Cannot confound or doubt Him, or deny ;
> Yea, with one voice, oh world, though thou repliest,
> Stand thou on that side, for on this am I."

In this experience seen by faith and felt by love,
the Lord of the Sabbath is the All-Surpassing Central Figure. His administrative force transforms
the whole ; this our own experience verifies.
When our sins rose up like appalling monsters from
the deep past of our life, armed with thunderheads
of desolation, and charged with lightnings of equitable wrath, and our remorse was quivering with
demons and laden with despair, and our baleful
eyes could scantily make way for the contrite tears
that welled up from our crushed and wounded
heart ; then, when thus transfixed, we wept our
way toward the cross in our plea for pity, there
appeared this strangely wounded form ; over his

head an aureole like a nimbus hung; from his hands
and feet, and side, and brow, there dripped from
opened wounds the blood, and he strangely whis-
pered in our heart, "I suffered this for you," and
then in answer to that inly-speaking voice, dire
depression as if by magic fled. The hectic fever
of our hearts was stilled; the thunders ceased; the
lurid lightnings passed; the clouds rolled away;
the demons disappeared as with that right bleeding
hand, He rolled up the accusing scroll, of our dark
volumed crimes and threw it into oblivion forever,
saying "I was wounded for your transgressions; I
was bruised for your iniquities and the chastisement
of your peace was laid on me, and by My stripes ye
are healed." But though thus pardoned we found
ourselves out on the arid mountains of error still
orphaned and far from home, with souls that were
needy, helpless, ready to die, famished and eager
to appease our heart hunger with the husks which
no man gave. There was no one to take us in, no
one to save us from the pitiless storm, and no home
before us but the grave. Lo, we descried through
the tear dimmed eye of our faith that same form
again, but now transfigured, wafturing us home,
and saying with all the tenderness of a heavenly
shepherd's voice: "Come unto me all ye that labor
and are heavy laden and I will give you rest."
"In my Father's house are many mansions," etc.

These were gladdening words, and we leaped to

obey them; we left the far country of sorrow and sin; we followed the great but gentle voice within, till finally we found ourselves safely and serenely in our Heavenly Father's Church of love, of praise, of prayer below, and so we are here to-day. [Hallelujahs.] "No more strangers and foreigners, but fellow citizens with the saints in light, and of the household of God," expecting our native heaven. But though thus beneficently forgiven and adopted, there was still another great work to be accomplished. We felt at times in us the wolf of sin, the leopard of passion, and the lion of leasing, making a ghastly charnel house of our very hearts. Then again we lifted up our prayer. He listened to our pitiful cry; He looked with eyes of refining fire upon their malignity and malice; He entered our souls, crimsoned as He was with regenerating love. The savage menagerie felt the withering spell of his taming presence; the wolf slunk down beside the lamb of love, the leopard crouched meekly beside the kid of peace, the lion became harmless and docile as the patient ox, and there was no destructive power left in all the realm of our souls. And ever since our graces sleep as sweetly on the tamed passions' necks as did Daniel on the lion's mane. [Hallelujah.]

World, flesh and Satan have since rushed upon us like maddening floods; but our Deliverer has

6

always lifted up a standard against them ; and we feel, as He stands between us and our adversaries,

> " What though a thousand worlds engage
> Ten thousand hosts our souls to shake,
> We have a shield, shall quell their rage,
> And drive the alien armies back ;
> Portrayed, it bears a bleeding Lamb ;
> I dare believe in Jesus' name."

[Showers of amens.]

There was but one more blessing which we needed to enable us to pursue our way like conquerors filled with the joy of conquest ; and this was the great gift of the Holy Ghost. Nor was our Sabbath Lord slow nor scant in conferring this high rich blessing. Tenderly he breathed upon us, as of old, saying : " Receive ye the Holy Ghost," and that Divine Comforter came in when we heeded the voice of Christ and opened wide our hearts.

He came as the promised representative of our Lord, teaching us all things ; bringing all things to our remembrance that Jesus said to us ; turning sorrow into joy ; adversity into prosperity ; pain into pleasure ; darkness into light ; weakness into strength ; poverty into riches, and death into life. He comforts us by this Blessed Holy Ghost in all our perplexities ; teaches us the plans of Providence, the meaning of mystery, the mission of pain. [Praise the Lord.] He gives us those wisely meted measures of light which gradually dawn upon us as our eyes can bear, till finally now we see—

" That God is love, and love creation's final law,
  Though nature, red in beak and claw
  In ravine, shriek against the creed,"

He shows us that though we are now traveling through the middle of the nightshades of time, yet we are traveling toward the eternal morning; that though—

" Down below a sad, mysterious music,
    Wailing from the woods and on the shore,
  Burdened with a grand, majestic secret,
    Which keeps sweeping from us evermore,"

" Up above a music that entwineth
    In eternal chords of golden sound
  The great poem of this strange existence,
    All whose wondrous meaning hath been found."

———

Oh, the gracious grandeur of that morning
  When the Christ shall come to take us home,
And from sighs and tears and death returning,
  We shall gather in our Father's home.

Brethren, the glory of the Greeks was Alexander, because of Granicus; of the Carthagenians, Hannibal, because of · Cannæ; of the French, Napoleon, because of Austerlitz. But our glory is

the Lord of the Sabbath, because of Calvary and
Pentecost. It is through Him, riven here, we see
the stars of hope.

Indeed, 'tis through Him we see the universe set
in harmony to the music of man's redemption. It
is through Him we perceive the coherence of the
parts of life's strange drama, and look out with wonder on the perfection and harmony of God's great
living temple. [Hallelujahs.]

When wandering round St. Peters, Rome, the
greatest cathedral and most complex of any on the
planet, a temple on which the Raphaels, Angelos
and Berninis have exhausted their artistic skill, you
come upon a plain small door along the building's
side. It seemed an entrance to the poorest part of
the temple, but in a moment after passing through
this narrow door the interior of this mighty fabric
rose in proportionate grandeur before the view.
The awful dome of Angelo, where flew giant
prophets wielding pens large as men ; the marble
pillars to find which the bones of the world had
been disjointed and polished; the superb paint-
ings by angel artists and rarest statues streaming
gracefully from the gods of sculpture; the exquis-
itely fitted mosaics which dazzled the eye and impressed the memory ; the entrancing music pealing
now as from afar off tubes of thunder, and then as
from near divine abodes. What that unpretentious
door is to the greatest cathredral of earth, the Lord

of the Sabbath is to the great living temple of this universe. When you enter and look through Him contradictions become harmonized, disproportions proportionate. [Hallelujahs.]

Nature is so transformed that every bush is aflame with God. History is so transposed that every event shines with the potent purpose of an eternal Lover. Scripture becomes so important that it appears as the literary fabric, on which is displayed the divinely focused lens of the Son of Man, through whom we look on the Fatherliness of God.

Experience becomes so saintly and so satisfying that the soul swells in an ecstacy of exultation at the recollection of the divine goodness and mercy. [Amens.] Oh, men and women bound for eternity through inextricable mazes, draw up all your forces and with heaven storming prayer enter that door, for " the kingdom of heaven suffereth violence and the violent take it by force," and the Lord of the Sabbath is Lord also of salvation to the backslider. Some of you may be backsliders, and you have lost the door in threading your way through the dark and dismal labyrinths of this world.

In 1877 I was passing along the Appian Way to inspect the catacombs. Arriving at the St. Sebastian chapel a serge clad and sandaled monk with tiny taper led the way into these deep far reaching recesses of the historic Christian dead. Here were cups russet with the martyrs' blood, here little chapels where they prayed, and there dungeons where they died, but there was one crypt which for a time became a living tomb. A ventursome young archæologist dared alone these complex and illimitable alleys, and tied a cord at the entrance, unwinding it as he proceeded, hoping it would lead him safely out. But while flushed with excitement over some new discoveries, he unconsciously let slip that cord on which his life was suspended. Discovering his loss, terror struck him through and through, anguish fevered heart and brain, transfixed with half despair he searched vainly for his treasure, baffled at every avenue, foiled by every device, he finally swooned away in a paroxysm of despair, recovering just a little sensibility he felt something familiar had been touched by his hand. He felt for it again, and found it to be his long lost cord. His half departing soul flew back into his body, he sprang to his feet intoxicated with hope, and folding up his cord as he walked found the exit and the day.

Backsliden brother, you are that man. I place in your hand the lost clue. Fold it round your heart and follow it, and it will lead you to the only entrance to eternal life; to every blessing in the life that now is; to every glory in the life to come.

And let the whole world know, especially let this city from centre to suburbs understand that this

Jesus, the Christ, the Logos, the Almighty Chieftain of the mighty powers of nature, of the great evolutions of history, of the illuming powers of Revelation, of the best and highest human experiences, is the Lord of the Sabbath Day, and that, therefore, He is amply able to level the resistless artillery of heaven, and sweep into abysmal ruin all persistent desecrators of this His sanctified septenary of time. Therefore, Sabbath violator of whatever nationality thou art, fly from the pollution of the Holy Sabbath as from an earthquake, and set it apart as the appointed time to prepare for the Sabbath without end. [Amens.]

The Sabbatic Knight in Complete Armor

SUNDAY EVENING, AUGUST 2, 1891.

I. Samuel, xxi, 9.—"If thou wilt take that take it, for there is
none other save that here. And David said, There is none
like that ; give it me."

Ephesians v, 10-14.—"Finally, my brethren, be strong in the
Lord, and in the power of his might. Put on the whole
armour of God, that ye may be able to stand against the
wiles of the devil. For we wrestle not against flesh and
blood, but against principalities, against powers, against the
rulers of the darkness of this world, against spiritual wickedness in high places. Wherefore take unto you the whole
armour of God, that ye may be able to withstand in the evil
day and having done all, to stand. Stand, therefore, having
your loins girt about with truth, and having on the breastplate of righteousness."

DAVID was fleeing from the dark-souled, sus-
picious Saul, unarmed and unprepared for
battle. In the precipitancy of his flight he rushed
into the tabernacle at Nob alone (the House of God
is the best place to go in trouble), and asked Ahimelech, the high priest, for spear or sword. The priest
replied: "The sword of Goliath, the Philistine,
whom thou slewest in the valley of Elah, behold it

is here wrapped in a cloth behind the ephod. If thou wilt take that take it, for there is no other save that here." David, with the curt, prompt decision of a warrior, said: "There is none like that; give it me." This is the history of our Old Testament text; now for the history of our New. St. Paul had been ranging, as the first great Missionary warrior of the infant Church among the Gentiles. He had swept like an all-observing eagle over Bithynia, Galatia, Troas, Macedonia, Greece, and many other places subdued by Roman arms, and at length had entered Rome itself, where he was guarded as a prisoner by relays of the far-famed legions. He had ample opportunity of observing the armature of the world-conquering cohorts of the capital. He was just closing an important letter on "The Heavenlies" to the Ephesian troops whom he had in a three years hard fought campaign banded into the Army of the Church at Ephesus; with a heroic soul, glowing with supernal militancy, he seized upon the imagery of the secular armor before him to symbolize the spiritual armory within him, and so through his pen he exclaims: "Finally, my brethren, be strong in the Lord and in the power of his might. Put on the whole armor of God, that ye may be able to stand against the wiles of the devil, for we wrestle not against flesh and blood, but against principalities, against powers, against the rulers of the darkness of this world, against spiritual wickedness in high places; wherefore take unto you the whole armour of God, that ye may be able to stand in the evil day, and having done all to stand." He then proceeds to present the various pieces of the Armature which would render the Christian Sabbatic host invulnerable, invincible and victorious. As we to-night survey this panoply donned by the real Sabbatic knight we trust all of you will see " There is none like that," and exclaim, with David, " Give it me." [Amens.] There have been many calls to arms, but there never was and never will be so important a call as this, for we have the greatest battle in all this universe to fight, and yet of all creatures we by nature are least defended.

The bee has her poisonous poniard; the eagle his beak, wing and claw; the hart his halberts of horn; the wolf and seal their robes of fur; but nature, alas, has left us weaponless and costumeless. Born without natural armature, we are physically exposed to the wild fury of the elements. We have had to organize into societies of farmers, builders and weavers against starvation, and notwithstanding all protective policies a host of pangs sweeps us on to the grave. This physical destitution is emblematical of our intellectual deficiencies. For our bodies are not only undefended; our minds are also wofully exposed. The bird surpasses us in sagacity; the beast in instinct; whilst there is scarcely any great law of life concerning which we have not erred. We have been deceived about the earth beneath us, the stars above us, the elements around us. We have erred concerning gravity, chemistry and history. We have blundered in regard to social order and civil government. We have misconceived the structure of our own being and the conservation of our existence, while the great questions of life, death and destiny wrap us in an endless maze of mysteries.

Our bodies and minds are not only endangered, but our spirits are utterly defenceless and insecure. The discontent, the restlessness, the anxieties, the sins, the insanities, the suicides and murders prove this abundantly. It is not life that men lead—it is anguish, and mankind would not

> " Grunt and sweat under such weary life
> But that the dread of something after death;
> The undiscovered country from whose bourn
> No traveler returns, puzzles the will,
> And makes us rather bear those ills we have
> Than fly to others that we know not of."

We are powerfully attacked as well as fearfully exposed. Terrible powers are set in relentless battle against us. The onset has been raging along all human ages. There is no acre but is strewn with the dust of the dead. The slaughter still goes on with an awful vigor.

Each day presents scenes of conspiracy, violence, looting and assassination. We lift up our voices and denounce misrule, Sabbath breaking, lying, thieving, tyranny, imposture, villainy, anarchy, socialism, nihilism, infidelity, and go home sighing out: "Man's inhumanity to man makes countless thousands mourn." But it is man's attack by the devil and his armies that "makes countless thousands mourn." We are attacked by a deeper and more tremendous enemy than that of man. We are attacked by crafty, cruel fiends, countless in number, measureless in strength and subtle in tactics. If the source of evil were in man alone, I would like to take a contract to evangelize this world, inside the limits of the present century.

But, beside every drunkard is an invisible fury, urging him on to drunkenness. At the ear of every thief is a viewless demon, whispering vile encouragement. At the right hand of every murderer is an unseen assassin, spurring him forward to blood. In every implement of vengeance is an imp of woe; in every dirk of death a demon.

These are the hidden marauders that have been on a raid round this world from the days of Adam. Now appearing as the accuser of good men as in Job: then as the tempter of the very Son of God; then as the deceiver, as in the Gospels; and murderer as in John; then as the "prince of the power of

the air," as in Ephesians, then as the great
red dragon, in Revelations. Notwithstanding
this, there are some who say satan is much
allayed of late. In the somewhat inelegant
though expressive language of a Western poet:

" They say he doesn't go round about as a roaring lion now,
But *whom* shall we hold responsible for the everlasting row?
Some one there ought to be to cast the blame upon;
For simple people want to know *who* carries his business on."

The devil still carries his own business on. He
and his hosts are invisible and immaterial, and
therefore less liable to repulse. The hosts against
whom Washington and Grant fought were beings
they could see and hear. These generals could
send out cavalry to reconnoiter the enemy. They
could shoot, sabre, bombard and cannonade them.
But here is a ghostly army, venerable in age, terrible in tactics, formidable, fierce, pitiless, whom, we
cannot see or hear. We feel the ever on-rolling
battle tides surging in stormful strife against our
breasts. But alas, we cannot without the telescope
of truth see the enemy's right, left nor centre. In
the light of our textual telescope glance at these
horrible hosts:

I—We wrestle with "principalities," "αρχας"
governments. Jesus himself called their chief "the
prince of this world," and this prince has his legions
grouped into the cohesive discipline of infernal

governments. Governments of great unity, efficiency and persistence; governments arranged to produce the greatest sin, suffering, disaster; governments that plan and fight night and day for the destruction of our race; governments so interlaced and interdependent that they strike together as one man. And how shall that offender escape on whose track are even human governments. What defaulter could escape the combined governments of Europe, Asia, Africa and America? Much less shall that man escape after whom are the governmental hosts of Apollyon the prince of pandemonium, who wears upon his gory belt the scalps of murdered millions. [Cries, God have mercy !]

II—But we are attacked not only by governments many but by " $\varepsilon\xi o\upsilon\sigma\iota\alpha\varsigma$ " "powers" mighty. In every nation it is the powers that give measure to governments. To measure the power of the American government you must measure the powers of the American people with all their modern improvements. The force of over 60,000,000 people is in every soldier's bayonet, policeman's baton and detective's badge. To measure the strength of the infernal legislations you must measure the strength of all Demondom. Originally of great power, indeed, next to God himself. They have practised on Egyptians, Jews and Christians. They made short work of Job's family and property, and by their modern improve-

ments of rum and rascality can make short work of
the best of you. As telegraph, telephone and
photograph in the hand of a nation speedily capture
a culprit, so the fine arts of modern fiendishness, in
the hand of our enemies speedily waylay the stout-
est saint and doom the most defiant sinner. For
it is powers working with governments against
which we have to contend.

III—But this is not all; these plundering powers
and governments are the *Kοσμοκρατορας του
σκότους του αιώνος τούτου* "*rulers* of the darkness
of this world." They have a monopoly of darkness;
they robe themselves in it; they fight furiously by it;
it is their chief instrumentality of success. If we are
going rightly they turn the darkness on to make us
believe we are going wrongly. If wrongly they
dissipate it to assure us we are going rightly.
If we are in the narrow path they fill it with gloom
and groans. If in the broad and downward, they
glaze it with the glare of a terrible fascination.
Darkness, dread and drear is the empire of Satan.
And if he could continue it he could make the
world void, lifeless, tenantless, a lump of death, a
chaos of hard clay, fit for the final conflagration.
Light is what we need; without it we cannot see
who, where, nor why, our enemies are. When
Greeks invaded Troy

> " The prayer of Ajax was for light
>   Through all that dark and desperate fight."

But demons, no light give to man. They soothe him under the dire night shade of sin; they sing him to quietude, under the Upas tree of asphyxiation, till dead in trespasses; blind to consequences; deaf to entreaties; oblivious to responsibilities; the fires of judgment are forced from the hands of an angry God; the black angels laugh; the doomed soul shrieks: "I am tormented in this flame." [Cries of God help.]

IV—These principalities, powers and rulers of the darkness not only slay in the realm of gloom, but they sally out and up to loftier places. Our text says we wrestle with " πνευματικὰ τῆς πονηρίας, ἐν τοῖς ἐπουρανίοις " "spiritual wickedness in high (heavenly) places." The high place of the successful merchant, and he is tempted to make all he can, keep all he may and leave all he must to ruin his offspring and appease the lawyers. The high place of the successful scholar, and he is urged to depart from "the old paths," criticise the Scriptures, discover some flaw in the word of God, and at length have the novelty of finding his soul lost forever. The high place of national and municipal government. These ambushed fiends crowd into Senators' seats and take possession of the very fountains of legislation. When Senators and Assemblymen vote for the modification of Sunday laws, so that God's Sabbath can be looted of its love. When they vote for the manufacture and sale of

liquid death till we have a saloon for every twenty
male adults; till we manufacture 120,000 prison
criminals yearly and make 200,000 children annually orphans and 80,000 victims yearly for drunk-
ards' graves; when our honorable Senators and
Congressmen legitimize these manufactures of misery, anguish, "lamentation and woe," let it be
known that they do it at the instigation of those infernal fiends, who came up from the darkness to
spread vice, violence, anarchy and desolation
throughout this republic. [Amens.]

These demonic hordes clamber also up into the
high places of the church. Having tamed the pulpit
they attack the pews and quote Scripture for their
purpose. Be calm, quiet and dispassionate, for "'it
is written, be ye temperate in all things;'" be mod-
erately righteous, for behold it is written, "Be not
righteous overmuch." And if there be those whom
they cannot soothe with the dulling opiates of indifference, then they set the stalwarts against each
other, and so neutralize their forces under the
specious plea of "contending for the faith delivered
unto the saints." Some are subsidized with promises
of fame; others hushed by pledges of pleasure;
others cajoled by appetite and avarice, and still
others tempted to forgo self-denial to enjoy the re-
laxing pleasures of floating with the current. A
detachment of skilful and trusted fiends, are sent
from the central government to watch the opera-

tions of this church. Before I get through with this sermon they shall have attacked many of you. Behold, then, the most exposed and defenceless race assailed by the greatest enemy that ever made an assault.

Thus you see the subtle, formidable and dangerous character of Satan and his hosts, the greatest, hellish army, led by the most skillful commander. Ghostly, invisible, mighty, numerous, drilled, armed with compacted governments shrined in a fierce array of pitiless powers, ambushed in deepest darkness, intrenched in the high places of the field and ever on the watch for victims. Busy were they in the days of Jesus. Out of Mary of Magdala he cast seven of their number, and from the wild man of Gadara, a legion. None of the giants of mankind unaided, have ever been able to stand up against their awful onset. What a formidable array of antagonists is this, to attack a world of disorganized, disordered, untrained, unarmed human beings: [Terrible !]

The man never has been born who in his own strength could stand before them. Even the Son of God appealed for reserves before his conflict in Gethsemane. Mere humanity is as chaff before the storm in their presence. None of you can hope to stand in your unsupported strength. The Devil and his hosts can throw you in either physical, mental or spiritual wrestling.. They can beat you in your business, your churches, your homes; anywhere, any way, any time. But, thank God, my hearers, there is a panoply here that I propose to present, that can make you the conquerors of these concentrated "principalities, powers, rulers of darkness and spiritual wickedness in high places," even though they were twice as virulent and victorious as they are. [Hallelujahs.]

But this is not the armor for the terrestrial tournament. It is not the finely devised visor and elegantly chased spear of the earthly warrior. It is not the foliated armor of the romantic knight, nor the embossed shield of the classic Greek; nor is it at all allied to the elaborately flowered and engraven sword and espadon of modern times. "For the weapons of our warfare are not carnal." But it is an armor which has descended from God out of heaven; it is an armor which was framed by the faculties of an Infinite Thinker, and tempered in the heart of an Infinite Lover; it is an armour in which none ever lost life or limb, and in which no one ever yet was wounded; it is an armour in which millions of human heroes have marched through the lines of the enemy; taken his trenches, driven him from his position and gone on to glory; it is an armour in which you can ensheen yourselves and follow the illustrious warriors who have gone before you. I now proceed to present a full-sized portrait of it in your presence.

There stands an exposed, defenceless and attacked hero, barbed with the fiery darts of the foe. Ah, my bleeding brother, let me put the Divine Armor on you piece by piece. Listen, he responds: "there is none like that—give it me."

I—And the first that comes to hand in the armory is the girdle of truth, "stand therefore having your loins girt about with truth." The belt of the ancient Greeks and Romans was a figure of this girdle. The belt was buckled round the loins where the upper and under pieces of armour met. In this position it gave the warrior solidity of military feeling, and strength and beauty of martial movement. And if that leathern girdle did so much for the ancients, how much more does the girdle of truth accomplish for the Christian? It was Lord Bacon who said:

" No pleasure is comparable to the standing within the vantage
ground of truth."

It was the immortal Bryant sang:

" Truth crushed to earth shall rise again,
The eternal years of God are hers."

It was Abraham Coles in his Evangel cried:

" 'The power to bind and loose to truth is given
The mouth that speaks it is the mouth of heaven."

And the illustrious Milton describes it as

" That golden key that ope's the palace of eternity."

But it remained for the Redeemer Himself to say :

" If the truth shall make you free ye shall be free indeed."

The truth of which this Christian hero's girdle is made is not mere historic, artistic or scientific truth. The belt may be embossed and adorned with these, but they never compose it. This belt is composed inside by truth of Divine doctrine, and outside by the truth of divine expression. The seeking penitent finds the truth of Divine doctrine in this Holy Word ;

First, God's creation of a special gem in His favorite creature, man ; then man's shameful fall by Satan ; then his encouragement by promise of salvation ; then his salvation sent in Christ ; then his personal baptism by the Holy Ghost ; then his conviction of personal sin ; then his repentance for sin ; next his pardon of sin ; next his regeneration of nature ; next his adoption from exile ; next his sanctification from sin to holiness ; next his victory over Satan ; next his soul's ascension to heaven ; next his resurrection from the tomb ; next his reunion of soul and body forever ; next his enthronement with God, his Father, Christ his Saviour and regenerate humanity on the throne of this universe forever.

This illustrious chain he discovers link by link, and as he unwarps one end from the georgeous heavens and the other from his heaving heart, it melts and fuses into a beautiful, powerful belt of expression, which he places round the joints of his action. See how it braces him! His head and heart were hanging like the weeping willows; now he feels himself a king, for he reads, and "hath made us kings unto God." And now this girdle begins to gleam on every side; out upon the path of duty, in upon the heart of love, up into the sky of hope, down into the abyss of woe, and in its light the skulking furies fly. [Praise the Lord.]

This is the kind of truth we need, my friends, at this time in this city. We need to gird ourselves with the truth, concerning affairs as they are. Let there be light upon the whole city government; upon the Board of Police, upon the Board of Fire Commissioners, the Board of Health, the Board of Education, the Board of Aldermen, and upon the Mayoralty. Let there be the light of truth upon the Monday laws, and *upon the Sunday laws* and *upon the saloon laws*, and upon the whole fabric of our municipality. [Amens.] Let it be known what public men are doing. Let every one be brought up under the burning truth of eternal justice, and equity, and honor, and every one of them who has lived up to duty, crown with the laurels of perpetuation; but every one who is besmeared with ignoble compromise and corruption, remand to privacy.

[Amens.] Let this girdle of truth swing into power the good, and out of power the bad. [Amens.]

The next piece of armor our Sabbatic Knight needs is a breastplate. The Emperor Julian, in his war with Sapor, was transfixed through the heart by a Persian javelin because he rashly rushed into the battle without his cuirass. And so would the Christian warrior; therefore, let me visit the armory again and get thee one. Here it is, the "breastplate of righteousness," This the Sabbatic soldier of Christ is to put on and keep on. "Ah!" he says, "There is none like that; give it me." [Amens.]

The Greeks and Romans esteemed their breastplates more important than the girdle. It protected the vitals, the heart, the lungs, the breast. But the Christian's breastplate is much more important to him. It is not formed of vincible and brittle steel, but woven inside with evangelic righteousness, which is love, and outside with legal righteousness, which is justice. It is Lord Byron sings in "Giaour":

> " Yes, love, indeed, is light from heaven,
>   A spark of that immortal fire,
> With angels shared, by Allah given,
>   To lift from earth our low desire."

It is the illustrious Schiller chants:

> " Love, only love, can guide the creature,
> Up to the Father, Fount of Nature ;
> What were the soul did love forsake her ?
> Love guides the mortal to his Maker."

And it is Scotland's greatest poet cries:

> " Love rules the court, the camp, the grove,
> And men below, and saints above ;
> For love is heaven and heaven is love."

Whilst St. Paul, St. John and Jesus yield it the palm. And if this love is the inside, justice is the outside of this wondrous breastplate. It was the broad-minded Burke who wrote, "Justice is itself the great standing policy of civil society." And it was the classic Addison who said, " There is no virtue so truly great and God-like as justice." Love and justice, blending on the hero's bosom, form a breastplate fit for any king. Not love and justice in books, not love and justice ringing from the legal forum, not love and justice fighting like furies, amid the thunderous roar of war; but love, sweet love, within the breast, and justice, " Δικαιοσύνης," glowing from the love-shrined heart, making man's vitality secure; love and justice flowing into a righteousness which lives and aches for duty, which enters the poor man's breast and sets him right with the rich, which covers the rich man's heart and sets him right with the poor,

which balances accounts with a manly grace between conservative capital and clamorous labor,
which is sterling, strong and true; but is sweet,
sympathizing, generous, which has a kindness in it
like that our Saviour ever bore, and a courage,
too, like that that David donned. This breastplate
demons cannot stand. It out dazzles the arch fiend
himself. He cannot pierce it nor hew it down;
he cannot reach it any more than a lizard can the
sun; it frightens him because he knows it is a
radiation of Almighty power; and this is the
kind of breastplate we need in which to keep the
Sabbath. When the breast is true and pure, when
the heart is clean, then are we so charmed with the
sights of God and good, that we have no time nor
taste for the sights of sinful pleasure. When Satan
comes with his black destroying broods, he does
not find our bosoms like houses prepared for him,
"empty, swept and garnished," but he finds them
full of Sabbath love, Sabbath joy, Sabbath sweetness, Sabbath glories. [Amens and hallelujahs.]
Seeing no chance, he retires and leaves us with
our happy families, our blessed Saviour, our beloved church, to go on our way rejoicing. On
with this breastplate, brothers; on with it fully.
On with it now, for "There is none like that;
give it me." [Amens.]

7

The Sabbatic Knight in Complete Armor—Continued.

I. Sam. xxi, 9.—"There is none like that; give it me."

Eph. vi, 15-20.—"And your feet shod with the preparation of the Gospel of peace; above all, taking the shield of faith, wherewith ye shall be able to quench all the fiery darts of the wicked. And take the helmet of salvation, and the sword of the Spirit, which is the word of God; praying always with all prayer and supplication in the Spirit, and watching thereunto with all perseverence and supplication for all saints; and for me, that utterance may be given unto me, that I may open my mouth boldly, to make known the mystery of the Gospel, for which I am an ambassador in bonds; that therein I may speak boldly, as I ought to speak."

IN our last discourse we saw that our Sabbatic Knight is naturally the most exposed of all God's creatures—that he is also more terribly attacked than any other being; but that there is provided for him an armor in which he is amply able to conquer all comers; and upon him we have placed two pieces—the girdle of truth and the breastplate of righteousness. And now he is so

confident he wishes to take the field; but we say:
"Nay, nay; not yet; for, lo, thy feet are undefended. Let us re-visit the Divine armory, and see
if we can find a suitable foot armature. Ah, yes;
here it is; the 'Gospel of Peace,' folded in the
words 'having your feet shod with the preparation of the Gospel of Peace.'"

When the Greek, with his heavy, hob-nailed
greaves, marched forth to the fray, full of Athenian
prowess, or Spartan pride, no spikes nor stones
could impede his way. No less important are
these strange war-shoes to the Christian. They
were long ages preparing. Infinite thought, plan,
purpose, broke through the heavens from time to
time; scintillated amid the rending scenes of
abandoned Paradise; shone amid the sublime
scenes of Egypt, Arabia, Palestine; broke forth
in burning bush, thundering law, mighty sage,
prefiguring priest and foretokening ceremony—till
at length, of virgin strangely born, the preparation
was made, ready for the will and work of man.
That will and work are to the soul what the feet
are to the body. Will and work are modes of the
Spirit's motion. These are the feet to be shod
with the preparation of the Gospel of Peace.
Hence the apostle says: "Put ye on the Lord
Jesus Christ." When so shod, the Christian hero
marches forward—over the ramparts of the scep-
tic, the shallow folly of the seducer, the fierce

stockades of the enemy. These shoes of peace
are like those of the Israelites in the Wilderness—
they wax not old, for peace is ever young. Peace
is the offspring of power; therefore, as said
Charles Sumner, in his "Grandeur of Nations,"
"Let the bugles sound the truce of God to the
whole world forever." But before those bugles
sound, the whole world shall hear and heed Christ
whispering peace from Galilee; peace to the feet
that have been dust-stained and far-traveled; peace
to the toiler who sobs for rest; peace with law,
which has leaped like the live lightning and threatened to smite; peace with mankind, whose angry
passions once we stirred; peace with conscience,
whose guilty gnawings once we felt; peace with
sin, self, Satan and hell; peace with nature and
with God.

Shod with such a Gospel of peace as this, the
Sabbatic Knight can pace the most ragged road,
tread down the direst difficulties, walk over the
most formidable enemies. He has the promise:
"Thou shalt tread upon the lion and adder; the
young lion and the adder shalt thou trample under
foot."—Psa. xci, 13. Electrified with such a promise, our Knight now exclaims: "Let me go, sandaled with such peaceful strength, and tread down
every foe." "Nay, nay; not yet; for, lo, thou art
without a shield." I return to the Divine armory
and find for him the shield, the glorious shield of

faith. Hark! he fervently exclaims: "There is none like that; give it me," and well he may so say.

In old world museums we have seen the shields of ancient time. They protected the entire body of the soldier, and defended the other segments of his armor. Carried in front by the left hand of the contestants, they could, by dexterity and strength, parry the thrusts of the foe. Full length in size, convex in form, lined inside with iron, and outside with leather; hence the Hebrew war-cry: "Arise, ye princes, and annoint the shield." Any soldier who lost his shield was disgraced. The true Sparton either carried it home, or was carried home on it. This distinguished section of armament was important, not only to the single soldier, but to the entire attacking cohorts. Commanded to scale a fortress, they formed into a solid platoon, threw their shields over their heads, formed a moving canopy, serried and mortised like the roof of a house, under which they marched to victory, over mural battlements, while stones and javelins and darts of fire flew harmlessly away.

But though these shields' were thus of much service to the ancients, it was as nothing compared with the service of the shield of faith to us. The Saviour himself, and Paul, His apostle, lift it aloft, as Samuel lifted David above the sons of Jesse. As Nehemiah was the faithful cup-bearer, so faith is the unfailing cup-bearer between here and heaven.

It makes every promise of Jehovah a fountain of power, every experience a wing of upward beating and every oppression a hand to help the true heart higher. Gabriel of the virtues, the sweet subtilty of pleasing snares it withers into weakness, and the noble graces growing in the heart, it nurtures into might. Notwithstanding all the conquests of faith she is aspersed by the slanderous as superstition.

Sceptics complain of the heavy draft Christianity makes on faith. Why not murmur at the heavier draft they themselves make upon it. The farmer is a believer in nature when he plants the seed; the scientist is a believer in nature when he calculates the occultation of a star; for he of all men makes the most of faith in nature. Darwin was a believer in nature when he wrote the "Origin of Species." He had faith in his theory, but he could not prove it, and he confessed he couldn't. Who knows that nature will act to-morrow as she does to day? Yet merchants who send their ships to sea; corporations who send their trains ahead; parents who spend their fortunes to educate their sons, all do so by faith. Take faith out of the common affairs of society and the civil commercial scientific fabric would fall to pieces; the pioneers of progress would re-call their pickets and humanity recede to barbarism. This all acknowledge. If, then, I find no fault with you for trusting nature, and carrying on the proper business of the world by faith, why find fault with us, for trusting Him who fashioned nature and is infinitely more constant and true than she—Him, of whom Nature is but the creature; Him, "with whom there is no variableness; neither shadow of turning." Once more: "The wider the connections you make the higher you rise, and the higher you rise the wider your connections." "With physical sight and mental effort I can make but very limited connections; I can make more than a flower, a tree a bird; but still I cannot think anything back to its beginning, or forward to its finish, points of interrogation and ciphers of bewilderment beset us after we go a little way back, or out, or forward into anything." It was Byron who justly said that "Science is but an exchange of ignorance for another kind of ignorance. Chemistry takes a drop of water and resolves it into two elements, and gives us two mysteries where we had but one. Science cannot bring us to the end of things, she only shifts the difficulty a step farther back." In these matters the world is little farther along today than when Sappho sang and Plato dreamed.

But right here where thought is foiled I see a conveyance ready for every hero who will venture out. It demands the highest heroism of the heart, the mightiest enterprize of the intellect, that conveyancer is the living adventurous shield of faith. Now, he who casts himself most fully into it will be carried farthest out and so farthest up. By it Columbus pushed physically farther out than any man in his time, and God and man do join to lift him highest up. Cowards refuse to venture out and the structure of this universe refuses to let them up. The shield of faith I have for you will carry you out to Calvary and then up to Creation's Capital.

This Faith breaks down every difficulty, overleaps every barrier, removes mountains, bridges, chasms, and makes all things possible to him who has it. No wonder Bailey said in his "Festus," "Faith is a higher faculty than reason;" No wonder Milton sang in his "Comus:".

> "O welcome pure-eyed Faith
> Thou hovering angel, girt with golden wings."

Faith which at first is but a shield from the fiery darts of the devil becomes the flaming chariot on which my hero rides out to meet Jeshurun's God. It becomes the glorious chain, that links him to the Infinite; it becomes the beautiful builder of the light pontoons across the gloomy gulf of death and lands the soul safely on the other shore. The faith we all need is, such as that for which William Bathurst sighed when he sang:

> "O for a faith that will not shrink
> Though pressed by every foe;
> That will not linger on the brink
> Of any earthly woe.

That will not murmur nor complain
  Beneath the chastening rod;
But in the hour of grief and pain
  Will lean upon its God.

A faith that shines more bright and clear
  When tempests rage without;
That when in danger knows no fear,
  In darkness feels no doubt.

That bears unmoved the world's dread frown;
  Nor heeds its scornful smile;
That seas of trouble cannot drown,
  Nor Satan's arts beguile.

A faith that keeps the narrow way
  Till life's last hour is sped;
And with a pure and heavenly ray
  Illumes a dying bed."

Our Sabbatic Knight exclaims: "And now I can surely go armed with faith's great glorious shield." Nay, nay, not yet; there is nothing on thy head. And if thou get no head-piece thou will have to keep parrying with thy shield to defend thy head. Let us go back to the armory and see if we can find a head-piece of defence. Here it is: περικεφαλαιάν τὸυ σωτηρίου "The Helmet of the Salvation." In foreign armories we have seen specimens of these helmets from which St. Paul takes the figure. They were made of the finest steel, inlaid with gold, surmounted with plumes and provided with brazen flaps to protect the face in action. The warrior

had little fear for the safety of his head, knowing
that the missile of the assailants, would glide harmlessly off his head-piece of defence.

But, however much the ancients gloried in their
helmets, they were worthless compared with the
helmet of salvation.   By Thess. v, 8, we learn that
this helmet is "the hope of salvation."   Highest
praises of hope have been sung :

> " Auspicious hope in thy sweet garden grow,
>   Wreathes for each toil, a charm for every woe."

So sang Campbell.

> " Hope, like the gleaming tapers light
>   Adorns and cheers our way;
> And still as darker grows the night,
>   Emits a brighter ray."

So sang Goldsmith.

> " True hope is swift and flies with swallow's wings,
> Kings it makes gods and meaner creatures kings."

So spake Shakespeare.

> "And as in sparkling majesty a star
>   Gilds the dark summit of some gloomy cloud,
> Brightening the face of heaven afar;
>   So when dark thoughts my boding spirit shroud,
> Sweet hope celestial influence shed.
> And weave Salvation's helmet round my head.' "

So warbled Keats.

"Hope springs exulting on triumphant wings."

So caroled Burns in his "Cotter's Saturday Night."

But, however adventurous flights the poets have made in eulogizing hope, yet none of them have dared to call it "the helmet of salvation." This was reserved to the inspired conceptions of the Great Apostle. It is a fitting finish to the defensive armor, the belt, breastplate, gospel of peace and glorious shield. It heartens the hero into a hope which flashes through all the faculties of his head, and circling protects them like a helmet of deliverance.

Hopelessness is the mother of despair, but hopefulness of action and energy, the hope of salvation surpasses all earthly hope; the severities of nature, the unexpected disasters of time shatter secular hopes, and poor disappointed humanity goes bereft, blinded and mangled to its grave. There are three things that have always blighted earthly hopes:

First, forgetfulness. How frequently do friends forget, though enemies seldom fail to remember. But God will never forget. He says: "Behold I have graven thee on the palms of my hands and thy walls are ever before me." Men lose hope and heart by the faithlessness of others. But this hope of salvation never can be lost because of the unfaithfulness of our God. "His counsels of old are faithfulness and he has betrothed us in faithful-

ness." Inability, too, to maintain promises shatters
secular hopes. But Jehovah is never unable to
complete His contracts—" Power belongeth unto
God." Our text indicates that it is not only the
hope of salvation, but the helmet of salvation we
are to take. This means that we may not only
have the hope of, but the crown of salvation itself.
Salvation from the two great pillars in the temple
of our modern Dagon—avarice and appetite; salvation from the subtle spell of every enticing sin;
salvation from the humiliation of defenceless exposure; salvation from Satan's victories over us
by the concentered attack of his governments,
powers, rulers of darkness, spiritual wickedness in
high places; salvation from lurking, misgiving and
gloomy fear; salvation from the clamoring crimes
and raging sins to which we may long have been
subject; salvation in love, joy, peace, gentleness,
goodness, meekness, temperance, charity and chas-
tity; salvation from every evil, and salvation to
every good; salvation so deep, broad, high, that
like God's universe, we cannot fathom its grandeur; a salvation so complete that it lifts from hell
and enthrones in heaven. Let me go now to the
fray. Nay, nay; not just yet; one more weapon.
And now we have seen, though by nature we are
terribly exposed and by Satan powerfully attacked,
yet by grace we are gloriously defended. But
man is too mighty in possibilities to rest in a mere

armature of defence. He can rise to the majesty
of attack. But as I survey the heavenly hero we
have before us, he appears with no aggressive
weapon. Let us finally re-visit the armory and
see if we can find him one. "τηv μαχαιραν του
πvευματος ö εστί ρημα θεου" "the sword of the
Spirit, which is the Word of God." As David
said to Ahimelech concerning the sword of Goliath, "There is none like that; give it me." So
saith this Sabbatic Knight. I have seen 250,000
swords framed into a flume in the Tower of London
for the Prince of Wales. A million swords have
flashed o'er the landscapes of this lovely land, and
billions of them have shimmered round the world.
But of all swords that have glittered in the sun,
there is none to be compared with "the sword of
the Spirit, which is the Word of God." It
emerged from the shroud of time, long ere Homer
tuned his lyre or Virgil his lute. More antique
than the Zendavesta, the Veda, the Sagas, the
classics, it was the first in the field. Its authentic-
ity is burned into its blade, for it bears the interior
marks of having been formed by an Almighty
Intellect, and presented by an Almighty Giver.
Its unity is complete as that of the sphere, for all
its parts work together for the production of the
greatest efficiency of the whole. Its proposition
is the sublimest that ever reached a human ear, for
it proposes to save the world from sin, and make

the bugles sound the truce of God to the whole
world forever. Its reserve force, is the most marvelous, for when men thought they had shattered
it into atoms and buried them too deep for disen-
tombment, lo! in still sublimer grandeur it rose
from its grave and commanded the amazed attention of mankind. Its adaptability is most complete, for it brings to the panting Christian mercy
or might, just as he may need, whether he be a
plebian, wearing the fustian of poverty, or a
patrician, wearing the purple of royalty. It is
quick in its movements as lightning, and loud in its
detonations as thunder. It is powerful as gravita
tion and sharper than any double-mouthed weapon.
It cuts off the soul from its sources of sorrow, and
severs it from the springs of transgression. It
cleaves a course of conquest for the immortal
spirit, and before its glittering, ponderous point,
the gates of hell close up and of glory open fly.
It deals not chiefly with outward villainy, but
with inner vice, and penetrates till it finds the
heart, and holds it up as the traitor, from which
the vices flow. It trenches upon the ideas of the
head and affections of the heart, reducing them
first to harmony and then to heaven. " For the
Word of God is quick and powerful, sharper than
any two-edge sword, piercing to the dividing of
soul and spirit, and is a discerner of the thoughts
and intents of the heart."

Such is this most illustrious weapon of attack you are authorized to take, after you have put on the armor of defense. Before that, it would be but a dangerous weapon in the hand of a defenceless child. After you are defensively armed, it becomes the most polished and powerful spear. Who can enumerate its victories? On a sword justly presented to General Grant were graven the names of the great battles he had won—Fort Donelson, Belmont, Vicksburg, Chattanooga, Wilderness, but I suppose the whole world would not contain a record of the victories this sword has won ; it will require a whole universe and a whole eternity. A great and good Being's word is that great and good Being's expression of himself. The word of Luther contained the thought, love, hate, life, power of Luther, and the word of God moves with the thought, the love, the hate, the life of God himself. This is what makes him who worthily wields it invulnerable as Deity and invincible as Divinity. All other swords shall perish ; this alone survive. All others shall be vanquished ; this alone stand forth the victor forever.

Here, then, you have the armor defensive you are to put on —belt, breastplate, boots, shield and helmet. Here, too, you have your arm of attack — "the word of God." You need no other. It is omnipotent, on the condition that you take God

with it.   In the well-known words of James Mont-
gomery:

> " Behold the Christian warrior stand,
>   In all the armor of his God;
> The Spirit's sword is in his hand,
>   His feet are with the Gospel shod.
>
> In panoply of truth complete,
>   Salvation's helmet on his head,
> With righteousness a breastplate meet,
>   And faith's broad shield before him spread.
>
> Undaunted to the field he goes,
>   Yet vain were skill and valor there,
> Unless to foil his legion foes,
>   He takes the trustiest weapon, prayer."

And so the Apostle closes this resplendent military peroration with these words: " Praying
always with all prayer and supplication in the
Spirit, and watching thereunto with all perseverence and supplication for all saints; and for me,
that utterance may be given unto me, that I may
open my mouth boldly, to make known the mystery of the Gospel."   This means, that having the
appointed armor, you are to accompany it with the
Almighty Leader; He alone makes these arms
victorious.   The absence of the right commander
means utter rout and ruin; His presence, courage
and conquest.

On the morning of the 19th of October, 1864,
the Shenandoah Valley was occupied by two hos-

tile camps. The Blue Ridge on the east, and the Allegheny mountains in the west, made it not only picturesque but fertile. Autumn had passed that way, and turned the green woods into sheeted gold. The crystal rills sang shimmering, like molten silver, to the sea. The ripe, rich grain had been stacked; birds of every wing, on their southward way, halted for the night on the trees of the lovely landscape. The Union troops slept confidently, though their General had been on business at the Capital. The darkest time of night, just before day, enabled the rebel columns to rush stealthily to the charge on the slumbering camp. The General's absence is the cause of that bold and early onslaught. When within short range, the command flies in whispers along the enemy's lines to open fire. The gloom flashed with the crash of musketry and the ground reverberated with the roar of cannon. A sleeping camp of 40,000 men had been surprised with a night attack while their commander was absent. They rose, rushed to arms; the conquering chieftain was not there to lead them, and the incoming tide of relentless and rapid battle swept like a whirlwind all before it. It was impossible to form or fight; all they could do was die or fly. Panic-stricken and flame-swept, the vast host became a mass of fugitives. The enemy, knowing the importance of such advantage, pursued in hottest haste and wildest joy.

The whole Union line was a disorganized mass of streaming stragglers. It was the greatest victory the South had won since Bull Run. Camps, cannon and men were captured, anguish wrung the hearts of the living, and torture the thoughts of the dying. But hark! There is a little dark-eyed man at Winchester, who had heard the artillery that morning, but, mistaking it for a reconnoisance of his troops, was in no special haste about leaving town; but when the thunder of battle waxed louder and louder, and nearer and nearer, the fact flashed through his mind that his army was attacked. Springing on his horse, in an instant he dashed away like an arrow. Suddenly the streams of the pursued and routed, looking along the road to Winchester, see a dust-covered speck in the distance. On it comes, horse and man. They begin to see the outline and hear the gallop. Another moment and they see a black horse, its eye blazing fire and his rider's flashing flame. With hat waving circles of command, he shouts: "Face the other way, boys; face the other way; we are going back to victory." The General's presence is electric. Instantly the fugitives turn. The whole field hears the magic word "Sheridan!" Despair gives place to determination; fear to valor. Instantly battle line is formed; every man flies to his place, and when the word is given they wheel, they form, they charge back over the ground they had lost. On, over the enemy's lines; on, like a tornado, over his entrenchments; on, over his artillery, ammunition, camp and booty, and with such cyclonic force swept the valley that Early with his troopers never entered it again, and one of the greatest victories of the war was won.

You too, my hearers, in the picturesque valley of this world, have been attacked in the night by the most pitiless marauders that ever waged a war. You have been sabered and cannonaded by the "principalities, powers, rulers of the darkness of this world, spiritual wickedness in high places." Many of you have been flying before your foes toward the mouth of hell; a few more attacks will drive you into its burning billows. But lo! coming down from heaven by way of Calvary, I see another rider mounted on a white horse. His body is cicatriced with wound prints received for you; " his head and his hairs are white like wool, as white as snow; his eyes are as flames of fire; his feet are like unto fine brass, as if they burned in a furnace; his voice is as the sound of many waters; he has in his right hand seven stars, and out of his mouth goeth a two-edged sword, and his countenance is as the sun shining his strength;" he calls to you to-night: stop, turn, form, "follow me." We stop, we wheel, we form, we follow the white-plumed Sabbatic prince. See, see, our enemies flee; He leads us on over all we had lost; on over the redoubts, and baggage

and lootings of the foe ; on over the enemies' camp;
on over all the valley of this world to heaven : nor
will he stop, till by successive victories, He has
swept this earth free from every fiendish invader
and made it a fitting brilliant for the diadem of His
Father.   [Hallelujahs and glories.]

And now, my brother knight, you need delay no
longer ; go forth in thy armor with this heavenly
Leader; and if ever you should get discouraged, look
at the long line of illustrious Sabbath Saints who
have overcome the greatest fiery trials, sheened in
this armor and under this Commander.   Clad in
this armor and under this Leader the three Hebrew
heroes emerged from the flaming fiery furnace, nor
felt the smell of flame ; Clad in this armor and under
this Leader, Daniel slept as sweetly on the Babylo-
nian lion's mane as on a pillow of down ; Clad in
this armor and under this Leader, Polycarp, when
the flames of martyrdom rose ruthlessly about his
venerable form, exclaimed : " O Father, I bless
thee that thou hast thought me worthy to ob-
ain a portion among the martyrs ; " Enfolded in
this armor and inspired by this Leader, Tele-
machus, the hermit of Syria, came from his cave
to Rome ; flew into the midst of the Colisseum ;
threw himself between the gladiators; and with his
life blood washed out the great heathen stain that
emperors could not efface, and that polluted the
church in its capital ; Enfolded in this armor and

inspired by this Leader, Ambrose, the illustrious, saved the church from the Arian Empress, forbade the blood-stained Emperor, Theodosius, to approach her altars until as he had followed David in his sin, he had also followed David in his sorrow. Girt with this armor and guided by this Saviour, John Chrysostom, the golden-mouthed, shouted from the metropolitan pulpit in Constantinople, as a reproof to the worldly Empress who had menanced him : "Again Herodius dances, again she demands the head of John in a charger," and when in exile, beneath the most flaming darts of persecution, he repeated his accustomed words : " Glory be to God for all things." Girt with this armor and guided by this Saviour, Athanasius suffered severest persecution for forty years from the Arians and the emperors, because he upheld the doctrine of the Holy Trinity ; but instead of being crushed he towered up like a giant amid the desertion of friends and the fury of foes, crying : " If no man will stand by me then Athanasius *contra mundum.*"

Armed in this armor, and saved by this Saviour; Boniface refused high church honors, penetrated the wilds of ancient Germany, cut down the great oak of Thor, built a church of the wood, baptized 100,000 souls in the name of the Trinity, and still, in his seventy-fifth year, went forth to convert other tribes, and build other churches, till he met martyrdom with a noble joy. [Hallelujahs.]

Armed in this armor, and saved by this Saviour, Elizabeth of Hungary, daughter of a king, wife of a duke, in widowhood gave all she had to the poor; dwelt among them as their servant, for the privilege of teaching them the way to, and the great love of God.

Armed in this armor, and saved by this Saviour, Rogers, the first English martyr, marched to the stake; rejected with lordly scorn an offer of pardon if he would retract, walked with a stout heart into the flames, and rejoiced in the fiery baptism through which he soared to heaven.

Armed in this armor, and saved by this Saviour, Bishop Latimer, stripped to his shroud, rose up on high, as though body and soul had both been restrung by the flames, cheering his companions by the sublime prophecy that they should that day light such a candle in England as should never go out. [Glory.]

Equipped with this armor, and led by this Lord, the Wesleys and their companions struck out from a degenerate church, charged on the streets of English cities sin, death and doom, and against the protests of prelates and the fury of mobs, laid deep, broad and secure the firm foundations of that church which has done so much for multitudes present; a church which has recalled the Protestant hosts to their first principles of progressive salvation; spread such a sentiment of brotherhood as has made Romanism ashamed longer to flaunt indulgences and flourish thumbscrews. [Praise the Lord.] Revived the Apostolic spirit of missions, and sent commissioners among the warlike tribes of the world to demand, in the name of Jesus, their swords. Given such an impetus to science, art, literature and civilization as has grouped two-thirds of the populations of the earth under Christian sway.

And what shall I more say, for the time fails me to tell of Coke, the missionary pioneer, who crossed the Atlantic eighteen times, and finished his illustrious work by giving his body to the Indian Ocean, that with liquid lips his very sepulture might kiss the shores o'er which his spirit sighed. And of Asbury, who in this armor, on horseback traveled yearly from Maine to Georgia, mid piercing cold and melting heat, and laid not only the foundations of the church, but of this Republic. And of Garretson, who kindled such lights on the banks of the Hudson as shall glow in glory after the Hudson has ceased to roll. [Hallelujahs.] And of Abbot, who spoke such words in such ways as made masses fall as if shot dead before his speech. And of Lee, who split up the hard exclusiveness of New England's life, and mellowed it beautifully with Gospel rays. And of Cartwright, who met the westward tide of empire with such sterling, manly courage as has seldom been surpassed. And of Pitman, who by his prayer amid the Jersey pines stayed the clouds till the people of the open camp have gone away thrilled by his Gospel messages. And of Simpson, another Roderic Dhu of Zion, "whose blast upon his bugle horn was worth ten thousand men." And of Janes, whose piety and statesmanship made him the Hildebrand of Methodism. And of Cookman, whose saintly life and exultant death made the church follow his white plume to track the halo of his ascent and exclaim: "My Father, the chariots of Israel and the horsemen thereof." [Glory.] And of Inskip, whose burning fervor lingers still in the memory of thousands whom he helped nearer that throne where he sits singing the song of Moses and the Lamb.

Oh, my God, let the glorious armor of these ascended fathers be fitted upon us, from head to foot, this hour, that we may carry on the wonderful war, in which they, fighting, died. For great are the battles yet to be fought; grand the triumphs yet to be won. We cannot stand an hour in the fray without this complete armor; but in it, one of us cannot, by the concentrated wrath, and skill, and power, of all the fiends, be for a moment overthrown. With it, we can measure up to the unparalleled demands of the day, and confront Satan's governments. In it, we can sweep back the floods of secularity that are settling in upon the church. [Amens.] In it, we can rouse the slumbering indifferentists from their lukewarm and perilous condition. In it, we can rally the stragglers, recall the fugitives, and form the whole church into solid line of march upon the enemy. In it, we can build the dikes and hold back the tides of Sabbath-breaking, and gambling, and Anarchism, and Nihilism, and Socialism, and violence, and rascality, and rum, till the Eternal God shall appear, and with a point of his Providence pour the whole fuming, roaring, seething, hissing, poisonous mass into the abysmal pit together. [Amens and hallelujahs.]

Come, then, my friends and take this armor and put it on. God wants to give it you. It will do no good to take it, unless you put it on; it will do no good to put it on unless you keep it on; it will do you no good to keep it on, unless you wield it. This armor is not for the camp, but for the field; for the thickest and most murderous of the battle. The more it is worn and worked, the more it glows and shines. [Praise the Lord.]

Then take it, wear it, work it, ye young men, who will be called to fill the places of these veterans of God, who in a few short years shall have gone up to rejoin their comrades above. [Amens.]

Take it, wear it, work it, ye young women, who need it to make home brilliant and beautiful.

Take it, wear it, work it, ye men and women now in the high noon of life, whose steps henceforth

8

shall be toward the valley, and before ye grow old and gray ye shall have routed hosts of the invisible enemy.

Take it, wear it, work it, ye venerable men and matrons, whose sun now sets on the eternal side of sixty, and in the wintry hours of your maturer years it will continue to be the defense and glory of your life below and your passport to the life above. [Amens.]

Take it, wear it, work it, ye unconverted, of whatever sex, age, class, and in it ye shall hew a way to liberty, life, love and heaven, through the thousands of foes who now unseen stand thick about you.

Take it, wear it, work it, ye officers and members of the churches, and it shall make you bright and shining in your business, in your homes, in your class meetings, in your prayer meetings, in your congregations, in your enterprises, until the world shall be compelled to see the splendor of your arms.

And ye brothers and Beloved Fathers in the ministry, ye captains of the troops of God, what shall I say to you; I need not say take it, ye have taken it; I need not say wear it, ye do wear it; I need not advise work it, ye do work; but I do pray you keep it untarnished. Let no speck stain your girdle, no spot dim your breastplate, no spear stab your peace, no blemish disfigure your shield, no blotch smear your helmet, no monster dull your sword, and no demon cut communications between you and your king. And now let us all unite in the most solemn determination that in the whole panoply of God we will fight until the out-mustering master, death, discharge us from the field, and that when friends ask us how we shall be buried, we shall reply like the noble Roslin Barons: " Bury us with our armor on."

Armor on, for in it we shall sweep through the black barriers of the grave; armor on, for in it we shall rush past the hosts of hell like conquering comets past fallen worlds; armor on, for in it we shall pierce swift as light the vastitudes of space, speeding past galaxies of flaming spheres to our home. [Hallelujahs] Armor on, for in it we shall fly through jasper walls, by gates of pearl, along golden streets, to take our place on that great white throne which overlooks the glassy sea. [Glories.] Armor on, for in it we shall be received with glad acclaim by angelic cherubim and seraphim, and escorted to the right hand of that Saviour who shall say : " Welcome, Sabbatic warrior, welcome from fields of strife, welcome home! lay by your battered belt and breastplate, your well-worn shoes and dented shield, your serrated helmet and your well-notched sword; all, all, lay down, the battle now is fought, the triumph now is thine. Here angel convoys take the Sabbatic knight, gather his glories round him and show him to his friends." [Amens and hallelujahs.]

The Love of the Sabbath Lord.

SUNDAY MORNING, AUGUST 9, 1891.

Mark i, 41.—"And Jesus moved with compassion."

ALL great natures have been moved by some one overmastering force. In Abraham it was faith; 'n Moses, law; in Josiah, courage; in Isaiah, prophecy; in Alexander, Cæsar, Napoleon, imbition, but in Jesus it was the new energy of love. "He moved with compassion." And this love of Him was adapted to every sufferer. Was there a distressed demoniac in the Synagogue? His love stopped the high strain of his discourse and cast out the demon; was Nain's noted widow in agony and tears bearing her only son to the dark consignment of the early grave? His love leaped to the spot and said: "Young man, arise;" did Mary of Magdala

> "Sit and weep and with her untressed hair,
>   Still wipe the feet she felt so blest to touch?
> His love wiped off the soiling of despair
>   From her sweet soul because He loved so much."

Were His disciples paralyzed with dread in a tempest? His love was heard above the hurricane

saying: "It is I, be not afraid." [Praise the Lord.]
Does the favorite daughter of Jairus lie dying? Pity
leaped to the Saviour's lips as He thrilled the little
maiden with, "talitha, cumi." Presses there an
unfortunate woman, who, in her delicate affliction,
touched His garment's hem in hope of healing? His
kindness, turned and said: "Thy faith hath made
thee whole." Lies there a lame man by Bethesda's
pool who for many years had been baffled by the
fleeter throng? His love restores him with the
words: "Rise, take up thy bed and walk." Comes
there upon Him in Sidon a frantic woman crying:
"Have mercy upon me, my daughter is grievously
vexed with a devil?" He responds: "O woman, be
it unto thee even as thou wilt." Writhes there a
deaf and dumb epileptic in Decapolis? His mercy
meets the misery with: "Ephphatha," be opened.

Begs there on the streets of Jerusalem a born-
blind outcast? His love turns into an Almighty
oculist, and gave the poor man vision. Stand there
afar off ten lepers in a community of wretchedness,
echoing that harsh, dry plaintive cry, "unclean,
unclean," to warn the wayfarer? He halts, looks,
calls, "go show yourselves to the priest," and as
they went they were released from their infecting
degradation. Meets He a woman bowed double
for eighteen years? His compassion said; "Woman,
thou art loosed from thine infirmity."

Do the sisters of Bethany weep in the paroxysms

of a hopeless sorrow, exclaiming: " Lord, if thou hadst been here our brother had not died? " He stills their despair with, " Lazarus, come forth."

Are there here this morning any who feel afflicted and cannot find a Comforter? Is there one distressed with low and evil spirits? Remember the demoniac of Capernaum and apply for freedom. Is there a widow in tears over the departed? Remember her of Nain and apply for pity. Are there tempest-tossed and storm-beaten ones? Think of the hurricane of Galilee and appeal for calm. Is there a father mourning the spiritual or physical sickness of his child? Think of Jairus and trusting plead for healing. Is there one faltering at the pool (the Church) and cannot venture in? Call to mind Bethesda and come in for blessing. Is there a mother here who mourns the affliction of a daughter? Reflect on the Syro-phenician and hear the Healer say: " Be it unto thee even as thou wilt." Is there a mute Christian here who cannot talk in meetings? Recall Decapolis and hear the " Ephphatha." Is there a man here who cannot see into the system of salvation? Recall the blind beggar of Jerusalem, and hear Jesus say: "receive thy sight." Are there here those who are so conscious of the degrading disease of sin that they stand afar off and cry : " unclean, unclean ?" Think of the ten lepers and hear Jesus say : " Go show yourselves to the priest." Is there a woman here bowed down

with trouble? Think of her who was bowed double
for eighteen years and hear the words, "thou art
loosed from thine infirmity." Whatever may be
your state, whatever your necessity, He who moves
with powerful compassion, has a blessing which
exactly fits your case.

For there was no species of human sorrow, want
or trial to which His love was unadapted then,
nor is there now. It was adapted to the poor vic-
tim suffering the tortures of dropsy; it was adapted
to blind Bartimeus and his companion in eyeless
mercy, who rushed headlong, exclaiming at each
blind bound, "Jesus, thou son of David, have mercy
on us;" it was adapted to the rich, but ostracized
and penitent Zaccheus who, with heavy heart, had
climbed up into the Egyptian fig tree to see Him
pass; it was adapted to the processions that surged
around him for it, healed their sick and pitied their
despair; it was adapted to His disciples whose feet
it washed, whose minds it enlightened, and whose
hearts it inspired with such exalted sentiments
as are found in His valedictory address and His
great high parting prayer. There is no species of
human need which His love cannot meet now.

> "For is He not the Saviour still,
>   In every age and place the same;
> Has He forgot His gracious skill,
>   Or lost the virtue of His name?"

No.

"Warm, tender, sweet e'en yet,
   A present help is He;
Since faith hath still its Olivet
   And love its Galilee."

[Hallelujahs.]

Furthermore, this love of Christ is adapted to the human race, because of its continuity. The fortunes that have been shaded, the families that have been broken, the hearts that have been crushed, the nations that have been wrecked, proclaim from all quarters the dire disasters of inconstant love. Through unrequited and unstable love the fair face has grown pale, the bright eye glassy and dim, the clear mind full of misgiving and dread, the sweet and sprightly spirit sombre and sad. The true, the good, the beautiful, have been by it deceived, and suffering from the blight of such deception, gone down to early graves. Inconstant, freakish, truant love, does its deadly work on every hand. It fills the jails with culprits, asylums with insane, saloons with patrons, and the wide world with woes. It draws the mind from lofty musing, the soul from noble trust, the heart from fond affection; mantles humanity in mourning and drenches society with tears. It haunts the very soul through all vicissitudes, burdens it with tyrannies, degrades it with oppressions, and devours it with despair.

Ah! inconstant, truant love, what shall we name

thee? Men may call thee folly; I must name thee demon. Nor is it the inconstancy of human love, flowing from sources of deception, that forces to despair; but this inconstancy is often caused by the overwhelming course of nature. The friends in whom we delight are taken from us by the inroads of dissolution; fathers, mothers, sisters, brothers, all pass away, and leave no living love behind; the choice and cherished teacher falls before our eyes; the orator, too, that lifts us from our sorrows, and plays upon our heart-chords as on an instrument, passes away, and we are left alone. We all, indeed, are passing; and amid this fluxional existence, where shall we look for certainty, whither go for stability, whither look for constancy, in love?

Rising up midway in the seething sea of human time, I see standing amid all changes the Changeless One, over whom even death had not dominion, "the same yesterday, to-day and forever," loving his own; He loves them to the end. Amid the inconstant, constant ever He. [Amens and glories.] Circumstances may change around us, laws be reversed, elements dissolve, knowledge pass down the Lethean stream, eloquence grow dumb, and all that is dear unto us wax old and wither into dust; yet, there, in the full flushed prime of everlasting youth, stands the Eternal Lover, who was the constant friend of Martha, and Mary, and Lazarus, and shall be the unflinching friend of every human soul who trusts in Him.

If you doubt, call in the witnesses. Ye brave Apostles Peter, James and John, who companied with Him, saw Him, heard Him, touched Him; what say ye? With one consenting voice they say: "He loved us to the end." Ye Apostolic Fathers—Barnabas, Clement, Ignatius, Hermas— what say ye? "Through all changes, changeless only He." Ye Church Fathers—Augustine, Athanasius, Cyprian, Cyril, Chrysostom—what say ye? "He never left us, nor forsook us." Ye martyrs of Italy. Bohemia, Scotland, England, France, rise in your red robes before us here to-day and tell us of the love of Christ. I listen for a voice from your dear, dumb wounds, and lo, each whispers: "Immutable." [Hallelujahs.] I lay my ear to the great orchestra of the Church, which voices the experiences of on-sweeping millions, and lo, with ever increasing swell comes the *vox humana* of the universal heart, laden with the one keynote, "His love is ever the same."

> " O, for this love let rocks and hills
>   Their lasting silence break.
> And all harmonious human tongues
>   The Saviour's praises speak.
>
> Angels, assist our mighty joys,
>   Strike all your harps of gold;

And when ye raise your highest notes,
His love can ne'er be told."

[Bless the Lord.]

Living as we are in these ever-changing scenes
in all seasons of life, we need this Changeless
Lover. There is, first, the season of youth,
when the ardent fires of inexperience burn ; when
young ambition over-vaults itself ; when we are
prematurely wise and think we know more than we
ever afterward do learn; when flattery and cajol-
ery spread nets for our feet ; when blinded
passion is strongest and calm-eyed reason weakest ;
when specious and fascinating temptations without
respond to plausible and impelling deceptions within ; when the bloom of the nature is rounding into
form, and its very loveliness makes it an object of
betrayal; then, in this epochal and important time,
do we need to hear that voice breaking in on us :
"I have loved thee with an everlasting love."
Again, when the springtime of our life has safely
passed and the Summer of our years comes
on ; when toilsome burdens are to be borne ;
when skillful plans are to be executed ; when the
duties of a profession, of commerce, of trade or of
domesticity, are to be discharged ; when the hard,
pitiless competition of the world is to be met with
kindness and courage ; when the pressure of multi-
plex and difficult work strains the nerves, tires the
muscle and perplexes the brain ; when the battle

for success is sore, and hot, and long; then how
consoling, cheering and strengthening it is to find
with us a constant, powerful Friend saying, "I
have loved thee with an everlasting love." [Hal-
lelujahs.]   But the Summer of human life doth not
long last.   We quickly emerge into the Autumn of
our years.   Gray hairs grow here and there upon
us; the furrows of care plough more deeply on the
features; the step may be more stately, but it is
less elastic; the fortunes of life below are pretty
clearly designated; the fruit of former years
begins to be gathered; the home is established,
the avocation prosperous, and our secular affairs
are just about as we want them; but, alas! we
ourselves have begun to change.   The fashion and
the bloom of youth are gradually giving place to
the appearance and reality of age.   Physicians,
pharmacies, food, exercise, riches, luxuries, cannot
stay the ever incoming tide of years.   At such a
time, as we look around, we discover nothing that
lasts.   All things tangible to us are temporal, and
yet, within us yearns the real self, the intangible,
the immortal self.   What can be so reassuring
under such circumstantial reveries as to look with
eyes of faith and see one standing by us who has
never ceased to love us, who will never cease to
care for us, and who, speaking out of His own
eternity, saith, "I have loved thee with an everlasting love?"   [Glories.]

And as it did not take the Autumn long to come, so it does not require long to go. The white Win ter soon approaches ; the eyes are dim and feeble now; the gleeful days of youth are gone; the insidi- ous inroads of disease (that instrument of death) are daily experienced ; the prime of life below is past : friend after friend has been called and we are left alone ; husband, wife, child and companions dear have been borne to the grave, whose very shadow now casts its gloom upon us. [Tears.] We soon, too, must go; we wait but a little longer and then the end. Ah, with what a resplendent regnancy of hope, with what gorgeous sheen of victory doth the venerable spirit clothe itself, when it looks up and out and perceives the unchanging Saviour, still standing near, awaiting the maturity of our nature through the ministry of grace and dispelling all de- jections with the words : " I am the resurrection and the life ; " " He that believeth in me shall never die." [Bless the Lord.]

Through not only the vicissitudes of this life runs this love of Christ, but also through the changes of death, and meets the disembodied Saint on the other shore ; it conducts up through the starry spaces, escorts to jasper walls, through gates of pearl, along streets of gold and up to that throne which overlooks the pavilions, encircled with light where saints in an ecstasy gaze and hang on a crucified lover. [Amens and glory.]

" Every human tie may perish,
  Friend to friend ungrateful prove;
Mothers cease their own to cherish,
  Heaven and earth at last remove,
But no changes can attend
  Our Jesus' Love."

But this love of our Saviour is not only remarkable for its perpetuity, but surpasses all else in its scope and capability. The incapacity of human love is sometimes as fatal as its inconstancy.

Two young ladies were swimming in the surf of Jersey shore, when the undertow swept them outward; their cries for help mingled with the roar of the breakers; their father and mother were watching them from the sand, and the two lovely girls were carried out to sea before their pitying parents' eyes—a specimen of the incapacity of human love in the presence of emergencies, but no emergency can arise which can thwart the power of the love of Christ.

The greater the lover the greater the efficiency of His love. This is a fundamental law. The love of a great nature is commensurate in power with the greatness of that nature. The capacity of the love is only limited by the capacity of the lover. The nature of the Christ is infinite, therefore His love is boundless. He loves with the power of omnipotence; He is omnipotent, therefore His love is all powerful.

Henry Drummond has written a clever little book on love, "The greatest thing in the world." We take a stronger stand and proclaim the love of Christ the greatest force in all worlds. Henry proclaims love the greatest thing in time; we proclaim the love of Christ the greatest energy in either time or eternity. [Hallelujahs.]

See its propulsive power. There was nothing in either eternity or time could hold back the torrent of Christ's love to man. It broke through the conventionalities of the heavenly eternities and materialized itself among the sons of men; it stayed not for public scorn, but rushed against the gathering storms of betrayal. Aristocracies trenched in the strongholds of a thousand years it faced, and policy, diplomacy, hypocrisy and shame it bore down before its overwhelming tide; nor did it turn aside for poverty, disgrace and pain. [Blessed Jesus.]

All was ready. The tempest that had for years been gathering was about to burst around Jerusalem. Our Saviour saw the impending hurricane of wrath. It was a double storm; a storm of demons and a storm of men. When the time was ripe He called His own about Him and uttered His farewell words and instituted His final rites; then plunged into the night. He passed from that upper room along the streets, through the golden gate, across the Kidron valley into the garden of

Gethsemane. A stupor of sorrow had thrown His disciples into a swoon.

But there in a secluded niche, beneath a moon-silvered olive, He is fighting the battle of the ages. Satan had fought Him for forty days and nights in the wild wilderness of Quarantania and been defeated. Now He summons all His legions to the charge. He knows everything depends on this final conflict ; He summons all His battalions and cries to His veterans : " fight neither with small nor great, save only with the King of Israel." For hours the battle seems to waver. The King of love is dashed again and again to His knees in the onset, but finally the last cohort of the enemy rushes to the attack and was swept down before the prowess of our Conqueror.

At length the bugle notes of retreat were sounded by the foe, and the Son of God, covered with blood, in great drops falling to the ground, came forth from the fray the invincible victor. Pilate afterward said, " Behold the man ! " I now say, Behold the God ! But now the human columns have been organizing. Led by Judas, I see a band of soldiers come down from the high priest's palace with weapons and torches ; they stealthily sweep through the southeastern gate, up through the Kidron valley into the garden. Judas designates him with a kiss. Such identification was needless, as He stepped forth in His robes, exuding

blood, and said : " I am He." He accompanies the
wondering soldiery to the palace; He maintains
His attitude of grandeur as the Son of God before
Annas and Caiphas; He is conducted at dawn of
day across the Tyropean bridge from the temple
platform to the prætorium of Pilate. The Roman
Governor, after inquisition and scourging, with
wondering awe brings him forth on the tesselated
pavement of the porch, and says: " I find no fault
in Him." The crowd of autocrats, hierarchs and
Pharisees, whom the noble purity and power of
his life had reproved and threatened, in a burst
that Pilate knew not how to quell, cried : " Crucify
Him ; crucify Him!" " I wash my hands of this
man's innocent blood," said the Governor. " His
blood be on us and on our children," was the clamorous response.

At length the reluctant, time-serving Governor
said: " *I miles expedi crucem* "—" Go, soldier; get
ready the cross." On Jesus, in derision, it was
laid; He bore it along the *via dolorosa* toward Calvary. The hill, shaped like a skull, at length is
reached; the cross is laid on the ground; the Christ
is flung upon it; the sacred hands are stretched
upon the transverse beam; the nails are malleted
through the tender tendons and driven fast to the
wood; the Divine feet are pinioned down on the
perpendicular section; the great spikes are driven
through the quivering ligaments and fastened to

the tree. Stalwart men now raise the cross with
its silent, suffering Lord; they carry it to the
socket in the earth prepared; they dash it down in
its appointed cavity, and there through the burning hours of a mid-day sun this Lover hung in
agony. [Weeping.] He would not even dull His
pangs by the executioner's stupefying potion. But
the agony of His body was little compared with
the torture of His soul. No cry of anguish arose
from those sacred lips on account of physical pain,
though that was excruciating beyond conception,
on account of the extreme sensitiveness of his
finely organized nature; but there was now a terrible tempest surging through His soul. He was
bearing "our sins in His own body on the tree."
The sins of all times and of all nations concentrated
there upon Him; the sins of the centuries before
the flood, the sins of the Hebraic times, the sins of
medieval days, the sins of modern years, the sins
of ages yet to come, were focusing their virus
within His sensitive Spirit; they rush upon His
holy soul with their venomous sting; He feels the
ignominious, incomprehensible torture, and yet is
still. No mind can enter into the weighty secret
of His suffering; and yet He seems impassive
and calm. But now the crisis comes, the crisis of
every other crisis—it is the withdrawal of His
Father's presence. Justice was about to strike its
final, fatal blow; a blow which would restore the

equilibrium of the moral universe; a blow which would vindicate the government of God as fully as if the whole human race had perished; a blow which at the same time would permit that human race to escape by penitence and faith. And when justice unsheathed its awful sword and enfleshed it in His quivering life, then it was the Almighty Father could not look longer upon His son; then it was He withdrew the light of His cheering face, and then it was that, treading the wine-press of the wrath of Justice alone, the first and last exclamation of anguish was wrung from those holy lips: "Eloi, Eloi, lama Sabachthani" "My God, my God, why hast thou forsaken me?" [Weeping.]

But that loving Father did not long forsake the heroic sufferer. As soon as justice was appeased, He returned and looked approvingly upon Him and His mightiest achievement, and as Jesus saw Him thus approving gaze, He knew the work was done, He knew redemption was complete; and then it was that, with a voice that rent the surrounding rocks, He cried, in all the majesty of a conqueror: "It is finished." Such, my friends, was the propulsive power of the love of Christ. But this propulsive power is, if possible, surpassed by its procuring power.

This love of Jesus makes all realms contribute to the comfort, happiness and delight of His redeemed. It enters the imprisoned chambers and treasuries of the earth and orders them to divulge their riches; and so we have the blessings hidden in the soil as well as those on the soil; it opens up the treasuries of the snow, the hail, the clouds, the seas, the laws of steam, electricity, gravity; it opens up and presents the treasuries of the skies, the sun, moon and the innumerable abysses of the golden galaxies that rule the night. What is science but the hand of the Christ helping humanity to higher and better things? This love of Christ is so great that it also marshals the blessings of all time, and treasures of antiquity, the treasures of eternity, the treasures of all the infinite past and the infinite future. It even lays claim to not only the universal riches of space and time, but it opens up all the attributes of God the Father, and converges them in coöperative action for our good. His love, His eternity, His infinity, His omnipotence, His omnipresence, His holiness, His activity—all are brought into line and beat out sweetly meted measures of favor upon every true follower. For as the inspired Apostle swept with his comprehensive mind this great theme he exclaims to the Corinthians; "All are yours, for ye are Christ's and Christ is God's. Sometimes when the mind goes out with the lamp of modern science and surveys the vastness of God's realms, the countless numbers that must hang on His providence in other grander worlds, we possibly may grow discouraged and feel that we may yet be left alone in the wild uncertainties of fate; and so we wistfully inquire:

> "Among so many can He care,
> Can special love be everywhere?
> A myriad homes, a myriad ways
> And God's eye over every place?
>
> My soul bethought of this—
> In just that very place of His
> Where He hath put and keepeth you;
> God hath no other thing to do."

[Hallelujahs.]

And still more this love of Christ is so particular
and personal and minute in the adaptations of its
power that it turns the whole troops and armies
of incidental and accidental and circumstantial sorrow into blessings. It makes us "Glory in tribulations also: knowing that tribulation worketh patience, and patience, experience: and experience,
hope: and hope maketh not ashamed, because the
love of God is shed abroad in our hearts by the
Holy Ghost given unto us.—Rom. v, 3-5. It bringeth glory out of gloom; good out of evil; joy out
of sorrow, and death out of life. [Praise the Lord.]

In this way it verifies the sublime exclamation of
St. Paul: "All things work together for good to
them that love God." We do not always see what
is best; what we most desire may be the very
worst, and hence 'tis best to leave to His sovereign

sway to choose and to command; it is best to sub-
missively and trustfully sing:

> "Not what I wish but what I want
> In mercy Lord supply;
> The good unasked in mercy grant
> The ill though asked deny."

[Amens.]
The love of Christ is so powerful that no coali-
tion of evil forces can break through it. Human
enemies may conspire for your overthrow; satanic
enemies may sally out upon you by the myriad,
but if you possess the love of Christ, the love of
Christ possesses you and will take care of you.
There is nothing in man, demon or nature
that can harm these love–enfolded souls. You
can confidently take up the gauge of defiance
and fling out the gauntlet of challenge. "Who
shall separate us from the love of Christ?
Shall tribulation or distress, or persecution, or
famine, or nakedness, or peril, or sword? Nay, in
all these things we are more than conquerers
through Him that loved us; for I am persuaded
that neither life, nor death, nor angels, nor principalities, nor powers, nor things present, nor things
to come, nor height, nor depth, nor any other creature, shall be able to separate us from the love of
God, which is in Christ Jesus our Lord."—Rom.
viii, 35-39. [Glory.] In the light of these truths

we may rest comfortably as to ourselves; but what about the rest of the world? Will the clouds never lift? Will the full flushed day never come?

The world is passing still, in parts, through the murky night and pelting storm, but on all parts of the earth the love of Christ is surely rising.

With a party of pedestrians I passed up the Tuckerman ravine, on our way to the top of Mount Washington, New Hampshire. The clouds began to gather, the storm to brew; the live thunder leaped from peak to peak, the livid lightning above illumined the way as night came on. Some lay down in despair on the cold and sleety rocks, and feared the lost path never would be found and the long night would never pass. One clear eye, now President Reeds, of Dickinson College, descried the way, and on we went to the Signal Service Hotel, clamped down by iron chains to the rocks on the highest peak of Mount Washington. Occupying eastern exposure, we watched for the coming day. Long and lone seemed that weary night, for the monstrous clouds enwrapped all in gloom. At last a narrow lane of amber hue opened up through the inky darkness toward the east; it looked as though Gabriel had dipped his wings in glory and flew that way that morn. Then a narrow yellow band marked the horizon; then a rich russet arc, and then a ruddy scarlet flame; then a gorgeous golden marge.   It looked as if the Jehovah were coming thither on His throne.   Then the glorious sun opened his great eye up out of the sea, and the battle for the day began.   The huge leviathans of cloud came rushing from the upper sky, driving into the face of the sun to prevent his rising ; the huge processions from the valley rose and ran into his disk, as if to dethrone the coming monarch ; but with the patient, silent light of his glittering rays he still shone on, till the whole canopy of sky was blue and the whole landscape clear, and the last gloomy gorgon died in dankest, darkest dell.

Like unto this, the Son of Love on Gethsemane and Calvary, rose amid a tempest full of ire and gloom.   He rose in a spray of blood that tinged the wrath clouds all around ; those clouds still continue to battle against His silent shining, but still He shines and still He rises, and every moment of His shining brings a greater force of light and love into this world.   [Hallelujahs and amens.]   In these hearts the monstrous gorgons of unbelief, of infidelity, of idolatry, are daggered by his spears of truth, and the hour is coming when all the nations shall walk in the sunflood of His love.   [Amens.]   The watchman's report in response to the traveler's question is being realized :

" Watchman, tell us of the night,
    How doth olden promise run?
  Traveler, o'er yon mountain height
    See that glory-beaming *Sun!*
  Watchman, does its beauteous ray
    Aught of hope or joy foretell?
  Traveler, yes; it brings the day,
    Promised day of Israel.

" Watchman, tell us of the night;
    Higher yet that *Sun* ascends.
  Traveler, blessedness and light,
    Peace and truth, its course portends !
  Watchman, will its beams alone
    Gild the spot that gave them birth?
  Traveler, ages are its own,
    See, it bursts o'er all the earth !

" Watchman, tell us of the night,
    For the morning seems to dawn.
  Traveler, darkness takes its flight;
    Doubt and terror are withdrawn.
  Watchman, let thy wandering cease;
    Hie thee to thy quiet home !
  Traveler, lo ! the Prince of Peace,
    Lo ! the Son of God is come !"

Meantime, let us keep marching steadily, firmly
on. Standing one sunny morning on the Hima-
layan mountains, I saw an officer operating a heliograph. Going up, I found he was signaling the
British soldiers, twenty miles away. I asked the
import of his signal. "In obedience to the com-
  9

mander," he replied, " I am signaling them forward
to take the passes of Thibet, which have been blockaded by marauders." To-day, as I stand in this
church, I hold a heliograph within my hand; it is
the word of God. I watch for the signal from my
Commander; it comes; it is " Forward, and take
the blockaded passes between here and heaven.
Forward, and open the passes closed by worldliness
and dissipation. Forward, and open the passes
closed by unbelief and Sabbath desecration. Forward and open the passes closed by strong drink
and licentiousness. Forward, and open the pass
closed by pride and profanity. Forward, and open
the passes closed by every sin, that my redeemed
may come home." I listen, and lo, again I hear
other cries coming, like a swelling sea, from the
lofty heights, and it is the myriad voices of
saints ascended sounding:

> " Forward ! be your watchword,
>   Steps and voices joined;
> Seek the things before you,
>   Not a look behind:
> Burns the fiery pillar
>   At our army's head;
> Who shall dream of shrinking,
>   By our Captain led ?
> Forward through the desert,
>   Through the toil and fight:
> Jordan flows before you,
>   Zion beams with light !

Forward ! flock of Jesus,
  Salt of all the earth,
Till each yearning purpose
  Springs to glorious birth:
Sick, they ask for healing;
  Blind, they grope for day;
Pour upon the nations
  Wisdom's loving ray.
Forward, out of error,
  Leave behind the night;
Forward through the darkness,
  Forward into light !"

The Supremacy of Law in the Sabbath Sphere.

SUNDAY EVENING, AUGUST 9, 1891.

Deut. xxxii, 46, 47.—"Observe to do all the words of this law. For it is not a vain thing for you; because it is your life."

> "That very law which moulds a tear
> And bids it trickle from its source.
> That law preserves the earth a sphere,
> And guides the planets in their course."

THIS stanza our schoolmasters taught us when boys, to illustrate the universality of the law of gravitation. This law of gravity is the grip of God upon creation, and we cannot take time now to explain it. When we rise up higher than materialities and seek to pursue any one branch of law in its differentiating ramifications, we find illustration necessary to trace the object of pursuit in its multiform out-branchings and operations. After leaving the domain of general laws and coming into the realm of special, we discover that every particular class of creature has its own special laws, so nicely meted and adjusted that any violation of them is detrimental to that creature's welfare.

The laws of horticulture must be observed, else flowers droop and die; the laws of agriculture must be maintained, else cereals wane and perish; the laws of stock raising must be practised, else the herds diminish and degenerate; the laws of humanity as given by Divinity must be executed, otherwise the race must suffer proportionately with the violation of the laws. The Author of law deemed this so important that He has not only written His laws within human beings, but has furthermore, given them a direct written document concerning what they should do and not do; wherefore "Observe to do all the words of this law. For it is not a vain thing for you; because it is your life."

One of these life and death laws relates to a septenary of our time. It never has been annulled and never shall be abrogated in time. It is rooted in the very nature of all beings and things, and cannot be uprooted without tearing the social, civil and evangelistic fabric to pieces. God alone is competent to be the Fountain-head of Law. Even Plato was able to see that "No mortal can frame law to purpose;" Demosthenes was sagacious enough to discern that "Law is the invention and gift of God;" Sir Matthew Hale affirmed that "Almighty God by an ample foresight foresaw all events and could therefore fit laws proportionate to the things He made," and Thomas Carlyle declared "The laws are there; thou shalt not disobey them, it were better for thee not, for penalties, terrible penalties there are for disobeying."

This is true of all God's laws, and is therefore true of His Sabbath law. In general law is a system of beneficent limitations; in this Blackstone, Hooker, Montesquieu, Johnson and Burke all accord. A child can see the reason for these limitations by law in the natural sphere, and the natural is only a projected image of the moral. Without legal restriction, trees might grow to the stars, whales might grow too large for the ocean, elephants for the landscape; worlds would throw off their orderly procession and rush upon each other in wild collision. And what is true in the physical orders of being in this matter is equally true in the moral. Excesses must be curtailed, indulgence must be limited, exuberance must be restricted; hence, "Thus far shalt thou go, and no farther," must bind every man in his dealings with his fellows and his God. The responsible Governor of the natural, the juristic, the moral realms, with all their inter-dependence and inter-play, alone is competent to declare what His creatures ought to do, and not do. His right to rule lies not in His will, but in His complete possession. What we make we have a right to guide. What God creates He has a right to control, especially when we know that such sovereign control is the har-

mony of the world, and the Divine way by which
we climb to affluence and rest. Obedience to the
law of God is the exit from conflict and care; disobedience the door to impingement at a multitude
of points, and to embarrassment in a myriad of
ways. History, observation, experience, like a
Divine trinity, demonstrate this. The very severity
of the law is, therefore, an expression of infinite
loving kindness, whilst its beatitudes lead on to the
land of eternal youth. It stands forth before the
eye of every competent investigator as "Holy,
just and good," and shall so forever stand. Wherefore, "Observe to do all the words of this law, for
it is not a vain thing for you, because it is your
life."

Having glanced at the origin and mission of law
in general, I now come to deal with that part of
the law that relates to this septenary of time in particular. This sacred septenary is as old as the finish
of creation. We read, "For in six days (eras) the
Lord made heaven and earth, the sea, and all that
in them is, and rested the seventh day; therefore
the Lord blessed the Sabbath day and hallowed it."
—Ex. xx, 11. As this seventh day (era) is to be
used as a resting period for the Creator, so the
seventh of this seventh period, through all its ages
is to be used as a resting and refreshing time by
the creature. Strange to say, all creation, except the
sinner, seems in sympathy with this announcement.

Clip off a piece of steel from the block, watch it a moment through the microscope, and you will see that the particles have been disturbed: watch another moment, and you discover that they begin to readjust themselves as soon as you give them rest. This is necessary to restore integration and cohesive equilibrium. The same is true of the whole material fabric of the earth, and of all things in it and on it. The soil, as every agriculturist knows, needs rest to continue productive, and every seven years is a boundary, over which few farmers wisely go before they return it to fallowness. The Children of Israel were ordered to let the whole land lie fallow at the end of the square of seven—that is, at the end of every forty-ninth year—the fiftieth year was to be a year of utter land rest; and so long as they observed this, they had a year of jubilee. This sacred number seven runs like a line of gold through many historic dealings of God with His people, as recorded in the Bible, and comes forth most conspicuously in the Apocalypse with which the Great Book ends. "The seven stars in His (Christ's) right hand, which are the seven churches; the seven seals opened by the slain Lamb; the seven thunders detonating; the seven angels sounding their trumpets and pouring out their seven vials upon the earth." Symbolic, doubtless, of some great mysterious methods of adjustment which the Father gives us but hintings of here and there, but which are yet to be unfolded when man becomes so sagacious by law-keeping as to read the archives of the Divine jurisprudence. [Amens.]

And we are not without demonstration by experiment of the high utility of the observance of this septenary law upon even the animal creation. During Sir Robert Peel's time, an hundred horses were worked in England for ten months annually, without regard to Sabbath rest, and then allowed to rest two months consecutively. Another hundred horses, at the same time this test was made, were wrought six days in the week, at the same kind of work, so as to make the test equitable, and then rested on the seventh. And what was the result? That result was two-fold; first, the horses that wrought six days a week and rested on the seventh, were in much finer condition to go on working, and second, they did one-ninth more work than the others. The same Sabbatic law has been tested by cattle drivers from the far west, and the testers have in every instance found that the droves that rested on the seventh day arrived sooner and in better condition at their destination than the droves that paid no regard to the Sabbath. Thus it is seen that the septenary law of rest is interwoven with the whole fabric of materialistic and animal life.

We now approach its application to and influence upon the human being, for whom all other creatures were made. Is he an exception? Can he rise above this law, and pay no heed to its dictates, with impunity? The human creature is no exception, and this has been demonstrated so often and so satisfactorily, that if it were not for the army of impingements and impingers that rise up around us, it would not be necessary to re-demonstrate it.

The English Parliament in 1832 (the same year the great political enfranchisement took place), formed a committee, of which Sir Robert Peel was chairman, to determine by actual experiment whether men who labor six days in the week are really better off than men who work seven. The test was made on two thousand men, for a number of years, who worked seven days in the week, each man receiving double pay on Sunday. What followed? Physical deterioration and spiritual demoralization.

That all ought to work six days in the week every industrial economist will admit. That all ought to rest one day in the week every philanthrophic economist cannot deny. The human being is constructed on principles as mathematical and as minute as any machine ever invented. He is made to run six days in seven, then rest; and all experience proves that when he runs more than that, at either manual or mental labor, he violates, injures and frequently destroys himself.

Several years ago, in one of my pastorates, on a Sunday morning, I observed a large black-eyed, well-dressed, thoughtful-looking, but haggard-featured man, a few pews from the pulpit. I observed him specially for his imposing personal appearance and profound attention. He came that evening, and for several Sundays following. Aware he was not one of my own people, I began to think by this time of a personal interview. Accordingly, at the close of the service I stepped down, and was very graciously received. The result, as follows: "I am a New York merchant, and have for years been employed on Sunday. My nerves began to give way, and my health, too, so I resolved to stop before I committed suicide. I found it impossible, however, from long habit, to keep my business from haunting me, even at home on Sunday. My wife said if I came down and heard you, you would give me something else to think about. I came, found her advice salutary; and so have kept coming, and I am happy to say I am now out of the doctor's hands, and quite myself again, and so here we are, the whole seven of us (pointing to his family), delighted to know we have found out how to spend Sunday."

That man lost his overworked, pensive, despairful appearance, and became one of the finest looking and one of the kindest-hearted men I ever saw in any part of this planet, and his business, his family and his soul prospered marvelously by the change. It would be easy to add many more instances of the advantages of obeying this septenary law that have in my brief and limited life come under personal notice. But I will let others speak. Here is Sir Matthew Hale, who affirmed he prospered during the week day in proportion as he kept Sunday; here is William Wilberforce, the philanthrophic emancipator of shackled millions, who said his mental vigor and persistence were ascribable to Sabbath rest.

On the other hand there come to us from all quarters the sad results of disregard of the Sabbath by earnest and otherwise admirable workers. There is Sir Humphrey Davy who, through brain weariness, sleeplessness, palsy, apoplexy and death, was obliged to forego his splendid career because he would work on Sunday. Here is Hugh Miller, the giant of the rocks, who was so devoted to his geologic science, that he thought he could not spare Sunday, and the results were madness and suicide. Nor need I detain you to describe Castlereagh, England's greatest Minister, and Cavour, Italy's grandest statesman, both of whom were cut off, the former by suicide, the latter by overwork, because they insanely insisted that they could not spare the seventh of time for restful worship.

The Germanic Government itself has been looking into this question, "The effect of Sunday toil upon the people?" The investigation occupies 1,000 pages. Four hundred industrial representatives were brought to the dock to testify with thousands who had worked on Sunday, and the result of it all is, that from their evidence the Holy Day had degenerated into a holiday, and then into a secular day, and then into a toiling day, and finally into a damning day, through whose ministries of destruction the people are falling into drunkenness, debauchery, infidelity and atheism.

American citizens, how great reason you have for gratitude that this sacred septenary, that is evidently a part of the web and woof of things, has never been so perversely prostituted by our best and loftier statesmen and soldiers.

Washington, the father of our country, issued the following order to his army, 1776: " That the troops may have an opportunity of attending public worship as well as to take rest after the fatigue they have gone through, the general in future excuses them from fatigue duty on Sundays. * * * We can have little hope of the blessings of heaven upon our arms if we insult it by our impiety and folly."

Abraham Lincoln, who, with the boldness of his strategic pen, clove asunder the whole system of Southern slavery and wiped away one of the greatest, foulest, political stains that deformed this commonwealth, in 1862 issued this order: "The President, Commander-in-Chief of the army and navy, desires and enjoins the orderly observance of the Sabbath by the officers and men in the military and naval services. The importance for man and beast of the prescribed weekly rest, the sacred right of Christian soldiers and sailors of becoming deference to the best sentiment of a Christian people and a due regard for the Divine Will, demand that Sunday labor in the army and navy be reduced to the measure of strict necessity. The discipline and character of the national forces should not suffer, nor the cause they defend, imperilled by the profanation of the day or the name of the Most High."

These are but samples of a host of stately quotations that might be made to prove that ours is by its laws, its usages, its history, not a Sabbath-violating, but a Sabbath-keeping nation. The Legislature of every State in the Union, with one exception, has recognized that the Sabbath day is an American as well as Christian institution. That exception is the State of California, and if I were a statesman in Washington I would move to put her under martial law, until she recognized the laws of the Almighty. The New England puritans, the Maryland Catholics, the Pennsylvanian Quakers and even the New Jersey Dutch, all regarded the Sabbath of the Lord as a sacred day, and kept it as such. It was this made them powerful in war and successful in peace ; it was this formulated the foundation thoughts of our immortal Constitution ; it was this worked its humane way up and out among the masses, making us the man-building nation of the earth.

And now that all this has been done, shall we here in Newark lower the Holy Day into a half holiday, or a whole holiday, or a secular day, or a toiling day, or a day of dissipation, debauchery and death? By the help of heaven, it shall not be, and by the help of the State and municipal laws it must not be. [A shower of amens.]

This brings us to the great present practical questions before us :

(1) Have we city laws that can protect our Sabbath?

(2) If so, does wisdom dictate that they should be enforced?

(3) And if so, who is responsible for their execution?

First, then, have we city laws that are capable in this city of protecting the Sabbath? The answer to this is found in our city ordinance, page 304, and following sections :

"*Section 647.* No person or persons shall, on the first day of the week, commonly called Sunday, sell, dispose of or deliver for money, or any thing of value, or on credit, or shall cause or permit to be sold or delivered, any spirituous, malt, vinous, fermented or intoxicating liquors, or any lager beer, or sour wines, in any saloon, restaurant, or other place, within the limits of the city of Newark. And no person or persons shall, on the first day of the week, commonly called Sunday, cause or permit the store, shop, saloon, cellar or place of business, or other place by him, her or them occupied, to be open for the sale of any spirituous, malt, vinous, fermented or intoxicating liquors, or any lager beer or sour wines. And no person or persons shall, on the first day of the week, commonly called Sunday, cause, suffer or permit any persons to assemble in his, her or their store, shop, saloon, cellar or other place of business, by him, her or them occupied, for the purpose of there drinking of any such liquors as aforesaid. And any person who shall violate any of the provisions of this section, shall, for every such offense, forfeit and pay the sum of ten dollars, or be imprisoned for the term of four days.

"*Section 648.* No persons shall, on the first day of the week, commonly called Sunday, assemble or meet in any street, vacant lot, or other place within the city of Newark, for the purpose of there engaging in any games, plays, quarrels or disorderly conduct, and all persons are hereby prohibited from assembling on the said day, in any of the said places, and there engaging in any games, plays, quarrels or disorderly conduct; and each and every person who shall violate any of the provisions of this section, shall, for every such violation, forfeit and pay a sum, not less than three dollars, nor more than twenty-five dollars, or be imprisoned for a term not exceeding ten days.

"*Section 649.* No person or persons shall, on the first day of the week, commonly called Sunday, sell, dispose of or offer or expose for sale, or cause or permit to be sold, disposed of, or offered or exposed for sale, any segars, oysters or confectionery, under the penaly of ten dollars for each offense."

It is evident that here are five distinct departments of offense in these three sections against which the Sunday law of our city is directly aimed:

I.—Selling intoxicating drinks on Sunday.

II.—Open stores and places of business.

III.—Congregation of people assembled for drinking purposes.

IV.—Games, plays, quarrels and disorderly conduct.

V.—Sale of cigars, oysters or confectionery.

These statutes, written and proclaimed by our City Fathers, are clear, definite and comprehensive enough to insure the protection of the Sabbath.

That they were on the 5th of July, 1891, all flagrantly violated, every citizen knows. That they are every Sabbath defied, set at naught, and trampled under heedless, desecrating feet, no observer can deny. The trouble is to get away from the sound of their violation. The streets that on week days are quiet and uninvaded by the shocking yells of news hucksters, are on the sacred Sabbath vociferous with the competitive cries of news venders. The loud, long-piercing yells about New York *World*, *Herald*, *Sun* and Newark *Sunday Call*, invade with distracting vociferations the Sabbath morning devotions of an hundred and fifty thousand professedly Christian people in Newark every Holy Day throughout the year. And this in a city whose statutes proclaim " No person or persons shall on Sunday sell, dispose of, or offer for sale " so quiet and innocent things as " oysters and confectionery." The best and most loyal citizens are waylaid and distracted on their way to church, and even in church are disturbed by this outrageous, omnipresent newspaper bellowing. The whole city, instead of being a Sabbatic Beulah of rest, and Bethesda of blessing, is turned into a pandemonium of hell, because these newspaper pests want, by loud clamor and crying, to earn a few cents, even though it be at the expense of the Holy Day of God, and of the spiritual welfare of multitudes.   This also helps to keep our dissipated newspaper Na-bobs in Europe spending in brothels the blood-money of souls.   Scores of thousands of the best citizens feel outraged and indignant, and yet this sore evil goes on without an Aldermanic protest, or even a finger lifted by the Mayoralty. [Cries of shame.]   Fellow citizens of Newark, the " right of petition " belongs to you, and you should roll up such a scroll of petition as would girdle this city, and sweep this crying Sunday nuisance from every block and street.   .

And now, as to the places of business that are kept open either part of the sacred Sabbath or the whole of the Holy Day.   " Their name is legion, for they are many."   To accommodate whom?   Certainly not to accommodate the average citizen, much less the best citizen.   They are open for the accommodation of all that godless crew, who drink so much on Saturday night, that in their maudlin condition they fail to provide for themselves beforehand on Sunday. Thus vice, crime, immorality, are being fostered before our very eyes; the people perish, and no man says much, and few do anything. Oh, for seven years of Mayor Perry, to sweep these abominations into the Passaic.

And as to the saloons, it is a well-known fact that there are hundreds of them in this city that make thousands of people drunk every Sabbath Day by selling, in defiance of the promulgated law, to all comers.

It is no part of the plan of my present discourse to set forth the hellish evils of Sunday intoxication. It is enough to say here that this great red dragon is devouring the vitals of our dissipated fellow citizens every week, and yet no man seems to love his fellows enough to raise a cry for their rescue. Oh, my God, help us here to create such an interest in the deliverance of our fallen fellow men, that all this city shall be stirred, from the river to the hill, and rush to the rescue of the lost. [Amens.]

And now my next question is, seeing we have the laws which are capable of preventing all or most of this sin, shame and destruction that are going on, accumulatively, on the Day of the Lord, in our midst, should these laws be executed? Or, should they lie dormant in the statute book, and let the people perish? You might as reasonably ask, Shall the other laws of our ordinance be executed? Shall the laws concerning streets, sewers,

obstructions, encumbrances, markets, Fire Department, Health Department, weights, measures,
assessments, public grounds and contagious diseases be executed? Every citizen of common
sense says, Certainly! And, as a rule, these laws
are executed by the proper executives. Shall the
laws concerning stealing, arson, burglary, assault
and murder be executed? You all say, Surely,
otherwise there would be no security for person or
property. And I rise here in my place, and proclaim that just as surely as the laws touching these
outrages should be executed, so surely should the
laws against the prostitution of the Sabbath by the
open stores, by the side-door saloonists, by the
avaricious swarms of news venders, and the more
secret cliques of gamblers, be also executed. [Ap-
plause, and amens like a flood.]

The law of this city gives us a civil Sabbath, and
I stand here in the name of the welfare of this city
and demand that it be executed. [Amens.] The
Sabbath law ought to shine as conspicuously in the
policeman's toggery and the detective's badge as
any other civil law in our code. Then would we
have a quiet, decent, Divine day. [True.] Then
would the Sabbath no longer be scouted as a puri-
tanic and fanatical nuisance; then would its holy
hours be no longer employed in dragging our
people down to deeper disgrace, poverty and distress, but in educating, refining, elevating and evangelizing them. [Many voices, " That's so."]

In the next place, it is proper here to inquire who is responsible for the execution of these Sabbatic laws which I find in our city ordinances? On whom does the weight of responsibility rest? Who holds the secret spring of execution? You may say the Common Council. Not exactly, for that is more of a legislative body than executive; still, they have certain responsibilities. You may say the police. True, the police are an executive body; but the city ordinance places a man of vast responsibility and power between the legislative Council on the one hand and the executive police force on the other, and this man is the Mayor.

Page 14, section 16, of our City Ordinances, distinctly legislates: "The Mayor shall supervise the *conduct and the acts of all city officers*, and in case of violation or neglect of duty, or other misconduct of any officer he shall transmit information thereof to the Common Council, with such facts and particulars as he may deem it important to communicate, and for the performance of *his duty* in this respect and otherwise he shall at all times have full power to examine all books and papers in possession of such officers, and to examine any deputy clerk or other subordinate."

Page 178, and section 399, are still more emphatic in placing the weight of the proper execution of the city ordinances by the police on the Mayor. They emphatically state that he shall see that the

several officers enforce the laws and ordinances of
the city :

"*Section 399.* The Mayor shall be the head of the police department, and shall superintend and direct the police generally; *he
shall see that the several officers and members of the department are
prompt and faithful in the discharge of their duties, and from time
to time take such measures as he may deem necessary for the preserva-
tion of the peace and good order, and the enforcement of the laws and
ordinances of the city.*"

By page 184 we learn:

"*Section 410.* The Mayor and the Committee on Police are
hereby authorized and required, from time to time, to make and
establish such rules and regulations not inconsistent with the laws
of this State, or the ordinances of the city, for the government
and control of the members of the police department as may be
deemed expedient and proper to carry out the objects of this
ordinance, and with a view to making the police department and
all the officers and agents appointed under it, efficient, vigilant,
prompt, and useful to the city. Such rules and regulations shall
be duly reported to the Common Council, and when concurred in
by them, shall be in full force, and shall be styled ' The Police
Rules of the Police Department.' "

Thus it is evident that the city ordinance places
the Mayor at the head of the executive department
and even authorizes him, with concurrence of the
Police Committee, to make regulations, if the old
are insufficient for the proper government of the
city. The main wheel is the Mayor, the next the
Police Committee, the next the Common Council,
and these being inter-active, convey their commands to the police for execution.

It is plain now where the responsibility for the violation lies. It lies namely on the Mayor; nor can that undemocratic and iniquitous measure, recently passed by our State Legislature, which wrests the civic power from you, the people, and places it in the hands of an autocratic oligarchy, exculpate the Mayor from discharging his prescribed duties. It lies partly on the Police Committee; it lies partially on the Common Council and police. But the Mayor is the mainspring. The subordinates will not likely act where they have a feeling that he and the Common Council do not wish them to act. There is such a thing as being too active as an officer—policy comes in here. The tip of political strategy is easily given and received. The unwritten law and caution and prudence for our own sake comes into play, and the Sabbath is allowed to be looted and polluted because certain cautious, knowing ones want to stay in office. [That's it.]

Mayor Haynes is a paternal old gentleman with a certain shew interblending of the pedagogue and demagogue that is not altogether despicable. He also, I believe, in monetary matters, is honest, and in application to business, industrious and patient.

These are good qualities for any Mayor, but he needs holy electricity in his backbone, and if he will now walk up and give us a civil Sabbath, according to the demands of the city ordinance which, according to his oath of office he is bound to do, we will thank him very much, and we will do more, something which he very much appreciates, we will consider his re-election to office. But if he will not wake up and protect our Sabbath according to the laws laid down for him in the statute books, then I call upon every Christian voter, be he Democrat or Republican, to come forward and elect a man who will execute the laws he is sworn to execute, according to the demands of the book which has been accepted by the people as their municipal guide, and not according to prudent and private whims of his own, salted down with a strong layer of political craft and selfishness. Wake up the Mayor to his duty, or give us a man that will make duty his watchword ; duty and not finesse, duty and not duplicity. [Showers of Amens.]

Then we shall have a Sabbath which shall by its ministries bless the whole people; then we shall have a Sabbath expurgated from open stores and back door saloons, drinking carousals and the pestiferous, ubiquitous army of newspaper criers. We shall, indeed, have a day of devotion, of religious recuperation and rapture; a day which puts its precious hours with its priceless teaching and inspirations around the wearied bodies, tired minds and wounded hearts of the thousands upon thousands of our factory workers and shop-keepers and poorly paid clerks, and lifts them up to greet the

Sabbath as the day of their delight. Then will we all with the eloquent Morley Punshon sing:

" Sweet is the sunlight after rain,
And sweet the sleep which follows pain,
And sweetly steals the Sabbath rest
Upon the world's work-wearied breast.

" Of heaven the sign—of earth the calm !
The poor man's birthright and his balm !
God's witness of celestial things !
A sun 'with healing in its wings.'

" New rising in this Gospel time,
And in its sevenfold light sublime;
Blest day of God ! we hail the dawn,
To gratitude and worship drawn.

" Through the hot world from week to week,
'Twere vain the soul's repose to seek;
But on the Sabbath restful air
Is nature's voiceless call to prayer."

———

" O ! naught of gloom and naught of pride,
Should with the sacred hours abide;
At work for God in loved employ,
We lose the duty in the joy."

Wherefore " Observe to do all the words of this law. For it is not a vain thing for you, because it is your life." [Amens.]

The Tides of Music's Sabbath Sea.

SUNDAY MORNING, AUGUST 16, 1891.

Eph. v, 19.—"Speaking to yourselves (one to another), in psalms and hymns and spiritual songs, singing and making melody in your heart to the Lord."

Rev. v, 9, 10.—"And they sung a new song, saying, Thou art worthy to take the book, and to open the seals thereof; for thou wast slain, and hast redeemed us to God by thy blood out of every kindred, and tongue, and people, and nation; and hast made us unto our God kings and priests; and we shall reign on the earth."

THIS earth is more than a splendid sepulchre rolling round the sun. Harmonic Life may hide herself, but she can be caught. She shall be caught when we learn how to sing the bridal of the earth and sky; when we become suffused with the light of that morn that cannot sleep and never dies. The bards of brightest minstrelsy have shown us the receding skirts of this coyest queen. While in pursuit of her, each wrinkle in our forehead becomes the furrow of a star. Let us, therefore, take a Sabbath morning walk among the hills of God, and see if we cannot descry a life that will lift us into song, and a song that will lift us into love.

The soul of man is the fountain of emotion, but objective beings or things only can rouse this emotion to its highest grandeur, or depress it to its deepest degradation, or swell it to its widest range ; and, that man's soul may sink, soar and fly, nature is full, not only of depth, height and expanse, but filled with many-phased and multiform forces, that keep beating in upon the senses and rousing the soul.

(1) There is form, for instance, which assumes all sorts of shapes and positions—round, square, rough, smooth, small, great, symmetric, irregular, low and lofty. The sculptor tries to imitate these varied forms, which so entertain the eye, and delight the mind, and relieve the dull monotony, by vivacious variety. You may pass through any part of earth you please, you may go on any tour through nature you wish, and you will find nothing exactly alike in all respects. Even the little things—the tiny insects, the useless reptiles, the fish of the lakelet, the beasts of the jungle, the fowls of the air— are all various. This vast variety carries itself up into all ranges of life—into the stately horse, the patient ox, the form and features of the man. And when you trace the lakes, rivers, seas, valleys, mountains of the world ; when you trace the immense oceans and mighty continents, you find in

all a brotherhood, a similarity, but also a difference in aspect and in form. And when we leave the terrestrial, and soar up through the spaces of the sky, with star-revealing eye, the layers of air, frescoes of cloud, rain of stars in their immeasurable deeps, are all various. And this vast variety of all things, from the smallest animalculæ to the mightiest orbs, keeps offering to the mind of man fresh phases of being, which stir his emotions with something new and strange. Surely in love and wisdom thus "hath God wrought."

(2) But again, there exist on the surface of nature not only these vast varieties in form, but also great variety in color. All the colors of the prism are used, to lend an ever varying expression to grass, herb, flower, fruit, bird, fish, beast and man. This variegation of color is represented by the painter rather than the sculptor. But what a poor effort is the greatest ever flung on canvas, by the most cunning hand of deftest delineator, compared with the wealth of shade and color in the magnificence of nature herself. And these colors, whether sober gray, or living green, or imperial purple, or ensanguined scarlet, or chaste violet, or the skillful interblending of each and all in the billowy arches of nature; all are full of forces, which, often unconsciously to ourselves, soften and sweeten our emotions and gratify our love of change. But these forms and colors, in all their variations, appeal to the eye.

(3) This brings us to another class of variations which appeal, not to the eye at all, but to the ear. These ear variations are not visible; they are not made for us; they are not on the surface of nature; they do not grow in the valley; they do not spring up spontaneously in the forest, nor appear anywhere on the surface of nature. They are hidden in nature's breast; they dwell in the recessional of man's own soul; they love the inner chambers of nature's palace. And it is when man opens with the golden key of melody, these hidden forces of harmonic sounds, that we have the highest style of emotion. We have in nature many things which have been called song that have not been evoked by man. These are but mere tokens of what can be done by nature's Master and by nature's King. We hear of the lovely song of the lark, of the dulcet warblings of the nightingale, and of the delightsome music of the thrush; but if any human debutant were to appear in opera, yielding such sounds, he would be hissed from the footlights: if in church, he would be invited from the choir gallery. We hear of the melodic song of the waves, and the soughing rhythm of the winds, and the dignified music of the storm; but any human melodist · appearing before men and producing such sounds, in such monotonous measures, would be deemed unfitted for any choral society.

No, the harmonics of nature are only metaphors

of what can be done; only prophetic notes of that mighty musical pageantry, coming steadily upon human time, through human depths, from Divine deeps. The prophetess of song has long been in the world. She has piped through the throat of the bird; she has crooned and strummed through the voices of the wind; she has screamed through the yells of the savage; but she has been but a prophetess still. There could be nothing but scrunching and scranching sounds, till the great Harmonist of human hearts appeared, reconciling the faculties of men, and setting them to the symphonies of heaven, by opening the mystic volume of eternity.

There were some efforts at song among the heathen of the olden time. The Egyptians, the Persians, the Greeks, the Romans, and the barbaric hordes of the far Orient, tried to sing, but all lamentably failed. They could not rise higher than the minor key; they never felt the conquering swell of the sealed Book opened by the slain Lamb, because they themselves were filled with a barbarous dissonance which would not let them truly see, and therefore, they could not sweetly sing. Even David himself, the poet prince, and the minstrels of the prophetic schools, and of the holy temple, could not reach the highest notes nor sublimest strains of human melody. And it was only when that mighty Harmonist of the human heart appeared amid Judean hills, in peasant garb and godlike grandeur, bringing life and immortality to light by the Gospel, that men began to "sing with the spirit and the understanding also." And even then, amid the general clash of Christian creeds with pagan systems, the real goddess of song only occasionally appeared; and although epistles, and gospels, and sermons, and speeches, were recorded and handed down through the ages, yet, singular to say, except the Magnificat, there is not a single original stanza of song in all the New Testament, and few hymns in all the voluminous writings of the Church Fathers.

Those were times when men and women had more cause to contend than sing. Those were days when men and women had to encounter in hand-to-hand fight the assailing enemies of the truth, and so, whilst snatches here and there of sacred symphony appear in early ages and medieval times, there was but little of the real spirit and expression of triumphant song.

But when at length the most violent and bloody battles had been fought ; when at length four hundred years ago the placid light of redeeming truth touched Bohemian hills and commenced to sweep through the forests of Germany, then the goddess of an exalted symphony began to touch with heavenly fingers the happy human heart—the real harp of song.

From the days of Huss, Luther, Calvin and Knox, the spirit and power of music has assumed a real importance among the children of men. From then till now it has kept growing and gaining steadily an exalted sway. It bids fair to become the greatest art known to the human race. Raphael, Phidias and Michael Angelo, the mighty masters of sculpture and painting, wane before the incoming presence of Beethoven, Haydn and Mendelssohn, the human seraphs that swam in the skies of symphonic thought beneath the wand of sacred melody. " Then the waves of music's purest sea began to flow for the good to be." And now let us see a little farther into the philosophy of this.

(1) Music is the language of the felicitous emotions. Discord and dumbness form the language of the conflicting emotions. Examine yourselves and you find this illustrated abundantly. Diagnose yourselves and you will discover you are structures of sensitiveness, on which sounds make much impression. A foe speaks harshly to you and some of you fly into a towering passion ; a friend speaks soothingly to you, or a foe seeks, by due reparation, reconciliation, and you fly into a state of composure and calm. A horrible set of savage yells and scranching sounds breaks suddenly upon you, and you spring up disconcerted as though you had suddenly been stabbed. But a most melodious voice projects soft, mellifluous sounds gently over you

and you are the willing captive of a soothing charm.

When you are harassed by harshness, your emotions sink; when you are sweetened by harmony, your emotions rise, and the more complete the velocity, intensity, variety and form of these har monies, if adapted to your condition, the more complete will be your sense of exalted feeling. Human nature itself is the ground form of music. Therefore another quality must be taken into this delineation, and that is what I have already hinted at, namely, the harmony of human nature. If in your body, the brain and nerves and thews and muscles and arteries are all out of order, there is no use of you trying to be musical; there is no use of anybody trying to make you so. But if your whole being is in perfect pose, symmetrically strung, so that all factors accord, you rush out into the morning air like a lamb into a grassy pasture on a June morning and you can scarcely keep from singing.

If in your family there are savage discords and barbarous dissonances, caused by clashing interests and cruel naggings, you are disturbed almost as much as you would be by physical ailment, and even the skillful harp of David does not drive away your soul-like sorrow. If in your business the leading lines are at variance and your leading interests collide and destroy each other, and your accounts are in an inextricable tangle, unless you are exceedingly dishonest and careless and phlegmatic, no minstrel can make you feel, for any length of time, musical. But if there be perfect health in your mind, in your soul, in your body, perfect felicity in your home, and a fair share of prosperity in your business; if the past of your life to you is satis-factory and the future is blossoming with hope, almost any melodist can make you merry. But then this merriment may be but for a time. There is something more which we must take in before we can be perfectly melodious all round the circle of every possibility and probability. When you add to this physical and family and business happi-ness, another and a still more important happiness; when you add to security for this world security also for the world to come; when you add to it the prospect of a happy death, the glory of a harmless judgment, the lustre of a heavenly home, the grand-eur of the best society, the best place, the best Father and the best of all things under His benignant smile; when, I say, you add these high spiritual states of heart melody to all the forces of natural harmony, with all the powers of governmental goodness, then you are in a truly melodic state, as well as condition and are prepared if God has given you a voice, to rise to the highest emotions and moods of the very sublimest song.

But you must not here misunderstand my mean-ing. I do not mean to say that experiences of trouble and winnowing tribulation, prevent the

purest musical moods and highest musical ecstasies.
Indeed, the contrary of this is true. It is the soul
that has passed through the most fiery afflictions,
that has meekly endured the deepest ploughshare
of sorrow, that comes forth with the most sensitive
chords all tensely strung to some sweet soothing
strain. It is such a soul that can enter into real
sympathy with human anguish, and if possessed of
a voice can project all that magnetic tenderness
that soothes, and softens the listeners, through a
voice that comes from a soul which has suffered
sorest sorrows.

It was for this reason that a great teacher was
accustomed to ask his intending pupils whether
they had seen sorrow, and if not, rejected them as
unable to rise to the finest strains of sympathy in
song ; it was this that gave such touching grandeur
to the Apocalyptic Song—those who sang it had
" come up, through great tribulation ; " and He,
through whom they came, had seen more sorrow
than any of the sons of men, and had been " more
marred than any man."

No! sorrow makes song all the sweeter if it be
sorrow which has swept us up out of grossness and
sin into faith and refinement before God. Wherefore, ye suffering ones before me to-day, do not
despair. Every affliction nobly borne, every trial
prayerfully endured, every heart-spasm and recoil
that comes to you through dire adversity, if they

but draw or drive you nearer to your God, will give a fresh richness to your soul, and new tone to your heart, another flood of feeling to your spirit, by which you shall sympathetically sing out your victories to others in such sonnets as

> " In the midst of affliction my table is spread
>   With blessings unnumbered my cup runneth o'er;
>   With perfume and oil thou anointest my head,
>   O what shall I ask of thy providence more."

It is harmony with God under all circumstances for which I plead, and when this is realized, even straits, difficulties, embarrassments, toils, poverty and distresses, become mellow and mighty to urge us with more rapid feet up that rugged, narrow path to purest harmonies. [Amens.]

But there is another important point which I wish to impress on you. Music is so versatile, so accommodating, that she casts a glamour over all things worthy or unworthy which she sings. In this respect, like all art, she is not at all fastidious. I have heard her chant with delight "Brennen on the Moor" and "Bonnie Annie Laurie," and "The Lone Barren Isle " and "Lord Ulin's Daughter." Brennen was a savage outlaw and "Bonnie Annie" was not so delightsome as many I see before me, and "The Lone Barren Isle" was certainly weird and desolate, and "Lord Ulin's Daughter " was a disobedient girl who ran off with the Duke of Ulva, broke her father's heart and lost her life by it. But yet, when these worthless themes are set to lovely music and sung by a sweet sympathetic voice, they will start tears of emotion to our eyes. But the power is not in these subjects of the songs but in the music which celebrates them. "The Last Rose of Summer" is but a worthless thing, but sung by some persons it will make your heart melt, sentimentalize and weep. Music can take the "rustic minstrel boy" and make a conquering hero of him. It can take such a rude, rustic combatant as Brien Boru and make him appear as the heart and soul of honor; it can take the "Banks of Doon" and make them shimmer like the banks of the River of Eden; it can take the homely Scotch face of "Peggy," by Burns, and make it shine in a soft sweetness which would be sufficient to charm a king. Music can take even corrupt, ignoble and cruel persons and practices and make them appear in all the resplendence of noble and exalted character.

And this is why music is at once delightful and dangerous. Delightful, if it sing a worthy and ennobling theme; dangerous, if it polishes pollution or attracts by its melodious sounds, unwary youth from the ways of virtue and religion to the ways of vice and vagrancy. This power of music is why she is used in all the haunts of evil. The lowest resorts of shameless vice and buffoonery must have their orchestra. Sometimes, even in our own city, they are so bold as to place them in the casino and saloon to attract the innocents and draw the unwary. The great dramatists, tragedians and stage managers all appreciate and use music as a part of their attractions, and indeed, sometimes, she is the queen of the whole entertainment, as in the high opera. These facts simply prove her power, and although she is the daughter of heaven, yet she is by the inventive genius of men used, alas! too often, to lead the way to and through the gates of hell.

I will pass by the milkmaid as she sings on her homeward way with the milk-pail on her head; I will pass by the swain who drives away his disappointment by the strains of the violin of Stradivarius; I will pass the civic virgin who soothes her sorrows and banishes her blues by the deftly fingered melodies upon the piano-forte of Christofali; I will pass by the Carilons pæan-pipes, organs, harps, clarions, clarionets, flutes, etc., of the orchestras of the world. They are all trying to get happy or to make others happy, or to make money by making melody; but the truth remains that they are all preparing the thought and feeling of the world for better things; although we do not see it they are all preparing the world for that better melody which is as high above all mere earthly music as the sky is above the earth, and that is the music which comes from a heart which has come into harmony with itself, with nature and with God, through Jesus Christ, the only Heart Harmonist, so that all circumstances are but the hands that strike the well-strung lyre, and make it give forth a melody which is preparing for that great song the redeemed sing in endless rapture around the throne of God in glory.

The music of Italy shall lose its voluptuous languor; the music of France its gay frivolity; the music of Germany its intense realism; the screeching of the savage coming forth from discordant hearts shall lose its harshness; the degrading music of the ballet, and of the worthless and of the vile, shall all lose their defiling innuendoes, and men everywhere shall feel the thrill of that new song which will be forever young.

Hence it is that the years as they pass pour out their pearls of hymns from a host of hymnists, and hence it is that never since the world began were there so many musicians who sing of Jesus and His love. And as the heart of the Italian dilates and loses its stageyness when Garibaldi's hymn is sung; and the soul of Frenchmen becomes serene and pathetic when the Marsellaise is played; and the German turns from his beer and stupor when " Die Wacht am Rhein " is chanted; and the English, Russians and Americans are alert and dignified when their national anthems are encored, so the time is coming when the vast masses of humanity will sway with delight and sing with an imperial joy, when the songs of God the Father, and of God the Son, and of God the Holy Ghost, and of truth, and of holiness and victory, and home are sung by the multiplying pilgrims of the cross.

That time will come just as soon as men and women learn how good, and near, and great, and lovable, God Almighty is; that time will come just as soon as men will learn how weak and worthless comparatively are the things of this present life; that time will come just as soon as men know how attractive is duty, and how delightful is religion, and how important is salvation, through our Lord and Saviour Jesus Christ. [Amens.]

Therefore, what is the business of the hour for every Christian?—I had almost said honest Christian, but you cannot be a Christian without being honest; I had almost said true Christian, but you cannot be a Christian without being true. As an artis*an* follows art, so a Christi*an* follows Christ, and He is the life and soul of honesty and truth. Hence, I will only ask, What is the business of every Christian in regard to music? The text yields the answer: "Speaking to yourselves (one to another) in psalms and hymns and spiritual songs, singing and making melody in your heart to the Lord." This is the delightful method you have of enjoying yourselves. I know one man in this church who has fifteen different hymn books in his house; I know that no good hymn by any American publisher escapes his eye; he cuts it out and pastes it in a book of his own, and when the time comes he has his musical supplies ready, and you all know how useful that man is in this city and church. Nor is he alone. There are others of you, who, perhaps, in a less extensive way, practice the same method. I am happy to notice this is not confined to the class-leaders and the men, but that very many of you Christian women delight yourselves, your families, your friends and your church in the same way. We have a heaven here in Franklin street every time we have a meeting, and it is in no small measure due to the fact that you are now cultivating the grand old Apostolic and Methodistic custom of "speaking to one another in psalms and hymns and spiritual songs, singing and making melody in your hearts to the Lord." I I want to encourage this; I want your singing to become so powerful and persuasive that it will lay hold of the ear of this city, with still greater strength, and woo and win many a wanderer from scenes of profanity and death. [Amens.] We have a thousand song cards printed, and we want a thousand singers, that will sing more powerfully and sweetly at the shrine of God, than did the Sængerfestites lately at the shrine of art. Observe I do not despise art.

The science of music is important. Indeed, you
cannot have good time and true symphony without
it, and therefore I encourage those of you who can
use notes to use them, and those of you who cannot, to be led by the leaders who know the notes,
and not by quavers and semi-quavers of your own.
Moreover, we do not want any such ridiculous
repetitions as a choir once exemplified, which
undertook to sing—

> " I love to steal awhile away
>   From every cumbering care,"

Commenced and continued with—

> " I love to steal—
>   I love to steal—
>   I love to steal."

A stranger who was in the audience, rose up and
announced : " If you love to steal so much as that,
this is no place for me." We want no such vain
repetitions in our singing. We want the best
hymns in the world, set to the best music, and we
believe we have them. And now it remains for us
all to set out with two things in our minds :

First, That music is fast becoming the great
melodious tide that is going to carry this world
forward on its way to God ; that although it began
with the sharp, shrill notes of the savage, it,
through the modulating feelings and tones of the

church, has become so deep, rich and strong, that it lifts and soothes the souls of men as it never did before. That all these advances in the science of music by great composers are to be brought in and used by the church: that art, science and Satan must not be permitted to use all the gay, glorious and stirring tunes; that whenever and wherever we find a lofty and beautiful melody, no matter what it is attached to, it is a child of the Church, for had it not been for the Church it never would have been born, and that it must be lifted up and brought out of its secular and salacious setting and made a conveyancer of heavenly love and calm to the aching hearts of the multitudes. I regret exceedingly the stupidity with which our hymnists and musical publishers suppress in this matter. There are scores of the most delightful melodies, that have been allowed to float, like orphans, through the air, and flow only from the lips of profanity, which, if caught and set to some sacred sonnets, would swell millions of souls with joy. [Amens.] But the Church is moving, and it is moving in this direction.

The other fact that I mention for your encouragement is that no instrument, however much is paid for it, however deft the operator, however grand the thunder tubes, and soft and sweet the minor strains; no instrument can ever equal the human voice that flows forth from a Divine and redeemed soul. [Hallelujahs.] An instrument, however grand, is but a wind machine; that's all. It has no feeling; it has no thought; it has no soul, but that which flows through the fingers of the operators, and that, I fear, in many cases, in these times, does not amount to much. But the human voice has thought, and sentiment, and feeling, and sympathy, and hate, and love, and joy, and sorrow, and glory, and God, all in it, and hence it is that your singing lifts me up; hence it is that I feel like a man floating in glory, swimming in bliss, when you sing well; hence it is that I feel so free in speaking, because your very songs move me with the Holy Ghost. I would rather have those Christian people up there in that choir, who pay such regard to God's Word and Day, who come down here to the Lord's table with us on Sunday, who sing not so much for pay or position, but because they love to sing out the holy joy of their happy hearts; I announce to you that I would infinitely rather have them than all the artistic, godless, irreverent, giggling choirs that ecclesiastical caterers are able to pay for. [Amens.]

Now mark, I am not despising the art, it is the godlessness of the art. Sanctify Art, and she is Divine; desecrate her, and she is all the more devilish because so artistic. Let us have artistic singers, let us have scientific voices, let us have highest types of intelligence and refinement in music, but before they can pass the threshold of my judgment into my church and choir, I want to know whether they have been sent by God or the devil. If by the latter, then I say, Go away, and sing his songs, and don't come in here to pretend to sing God's songs, when you are living a sinful life. [Amens.] My friends, I find I have enough to do to keep the devil out of the church, without inviting him in to receive pay, for doing the praising that the people ought to do for themselves.

No! Out upon this villainous custom all over the land, and let the Church be vital enough to raise up a race of holy men singers and women singers, who will be as scrupulous in their lives, because they occupy so responsible positions as that of leaders of sacred praise, as the minister in the pulpit is required to be, who is the leader of the people's prayers, and thoughts, and emotions. Then we will have spiritual services, then we will have full churches, then will we have many conversions, then will we advance upon the world, instead of the world advancing upon us, then will God be glorified and sinners saved on every hand, and "the kingdoms of this world will become the kingdoms of our Lord and his Christ."

There is the old creation, that is the material; there is the new creation, that is the spiritual; there are the old songs, they are the secular; there is the " new song," that is, " Thou art worthy to

take the book and to open the seals thereof." Seal
after seal of mysteries flies open as the Son of God
becomes immanent; problem after problem of life's
dark enigma is solved with satisfactory solution by
the approach of the Mediator between God and man.
" For thou wast slain and hast redeemed us to God
by thy blood out of every kindred, and tongue,
and people, and nation, and hast made us unto our
God kings and priests, and we shall reign on the
earth." This is the keynote of that new song; the
note all men need to hear and heed; the note that
lifts the heart, the mind, the life, the family, the
State, the Church, the world, up into that harmonic
realm where they "cannot keep from singing."
Thousands of hymns and tunes flow from this
heavenly, this prolific note, all over this emerging
world, and as more and more benighted and belated men and women, are made to hear these
hallowed strains, the farther will this earth, with all
its nations, emerge from intellectual, moral and
spiritual gloom, until, rising up, all shall see the
strange consistency of the death of Death by
the death of The Deathless; the slaughter of sin
by the Sinless; the dissipation of suffering by
the suffering of The Sufferer; the destruction
of discord by The Harmonist, who hath been
slain that every tangled chord in human nature
should be renewed, reset, retuned, and that every
perturbation of law in all man's moral universe

should be stilled and made harmonic with human
welfare forever. [Hallelujahs.]

Meantime, let us keep on singing; singing in the
sunshine; singing mid the shadows, for the sake of
the hearts that are dying in decay; singing in your
heart; singing in your home, singing by the death-
bed of the sick and the poor; singing in your
school; singing in your meetings; singing in your
shops, streets and stores; singing with the sinners;
singing with the saints; singing for souls that are
sick, sore and sad. And in the great congregation,
when the masses meet to hear God's holy word,
then, and I say it strongly, let every soul break out
in hallowed song; song so rich, so deep, so sweet;
song so melodious and mighty in its meaning and
its swell; song so tender, touching and triumphant; song so full of faith, love, hope and joy; song
so full of rapture and the sympathy of tears, that
the poor wanderers afar from our Father's Word,
Day and Love, shall catch the strain and feel the
power, and falling in with its mighty tide, be swept
in penitence to their knees and then on promises to
their God. [Amens.] Oh, comrades, sing on, till
your own hearts glow and luke-warm ones grow
warm, and back-sliders be healed, and the whole
army of the Church launch out upon the tides of
Music's Gospel Sea, bearing all nearer to that
great melodic throng who are singing still that
new song to Him who is worthy because He was

slain. Sing on, then, ye pilgrims of Franklin street,
with Flora Best, such strains as—

" There are songs of joy, that I lov'd to sing,
When my heart was as blythe as a bird in Spring;
But the song I have learned is so full of cheer
That the dawn shines out in the darkness drear.

[CHORUS.]

" O, the new, new song; O, the new, new song;
I can sing it now with the ransom'd throng:
Power and dominion to Him that shall reign,
Glory and praise to the Lamb that was slain.

" There are strains of home, that are dear as life,
And I list to them oft' mid the din of strife;
But I know of a home that is wondrous fair,
And I sing the psalm they are singing there.

" Can my lips be mute, or my heart be sad,
When my gracious Master hath made me glad?
When He points where the many mansions be,
And sweetly says there is one for thee.

" I shall catch the gleam of its jasper wall
When I come to the gloom of the Even-fall,
For I know that the shadows dreary and dim,
Have a path of Light that will lead to Him."

I look forward to the time when every church
choir shall be an orchestra of heaven; when every
old twanging bell shall be taken from every steeple
and replaced with melodic chimes; when all the
best voices, trained in highest art, shall feel hon-

ored in singing our Saviour's praise; when floating out in broad, deep volume from the universal human soul, shall flow such a tide of song as shall set and keep going heavenward, the vast multitudes who, inspired by this "new song," "speak to each other in psalms and hymns and spiritual songs, singing and making melody in their hearts to the Lord." [Amens.]

11

This Sabbath Land and Its Mission to the Nations.

SUNDAY EVENING, AUGUST 16, 1891.

Isaiah lxii, 4.—"Thou shalt be called Hephzibah and thy land
. Beulah."
Mal. iii, 12.—" And all nations shall call you blessed, for ye shall
be a delightsome land, saith the Lord of hosts."

SCIENCE shows us all beings are evolved through
the instrumentality of internal and external
factors. Man himself is no exception. Inward forces
originally given operated on by outward powers
conditionally conferred, produce all the physical,
intellectual, social and spiritual phenomena known
to us in the history of man. The present stage
we have reached implies a vast number of progressions by successive metamorphoses, every one
of which is evidently intended to take us farther
on in the great evolutive march toward that destiny
mapped out for us in this and other worlds. Such
progressions imply an organic system, a distribu-

ting, a regulating and a sustaining system. These systems have been in operation in nature, in man's body, mind and soul, and naturally give rise to certain social, intellectual and spiritual types in man's sociological sphere.

Nature is not a mere husk of the spiritual; it is a material pattern of the spiritual. The natural realm is pervaded by the spiritual presence; the spiritual presence is environed with the natural realm; the continuity and supremacy of law, in both spheres are the agencies with which the Supreme Being works, and while it may be that natural law overlaps and to some extent pervades the spiritual sphere, yet it never can monopolize nor dethrone it. These laws are not necessarily heterogeneous. Indeed, the frequency with which our Saviour illustrated spiritual truths by natural phenomena, indicates they are homogeneous; so homogeneous that the natural laws are but differentiations of the spiritual. The spiritual, therefore, is Supreme; the natural, subservient. This was demonstrated in the career of the Christ; it is demonstrated in the evolutions of the Christians. The spiritual being naturally Supreme, has its purpose and its plan. That plan and purpose, when we think back, lead us to a person. That person points us to His laws, by which we rise till the mind touches His intelligence and the heart—His love. Then we involuntary exclaim: *This is He;* He must control all natural essences and moral systems. That He has planned beings to evolve under his own supervision and according to His own model, there is every reason to believe. The story of human life proves an intelligent progression. Progression, from the unit to the family, from the family to the clan, from the clan to the tribe, from the tribe to the nation, and from the nation to the race.

Herbert Spencer's main postulate in his development of sociology is that everything advances from homogeneity to heterogeneity. This he demonstrates by so many examples that no fair mind, after thorough examination, is disposed to doubt the truth of this part of his theory.

In a preceding discourse, not of this series, however, I have demonstrated that the Spencerian theory of evolution serves a high and important function to advanced thinkers and readers, and will continue to do so to all men in the proximate future, who make the domain of truth and love among men the main objects of research. On that occasion, you will remember, I presented four leading parallelisms between Mr. Spencer's sociology and the doctrines revealed by the Bible. These parallelisms do not appear at first reading, but only begin to body themselves forth after his books, have been beaten again and again by the flail of patient and persistent thought. I do not believe that these fundamental parallel-

isms have ever appeared to Mr. Spencer himself. But God has made him (unconsciously
to himself) the great collaborator of such facts
from all races and times as when placed together and thoroughly analyzed, demonstrate that
the underlying doctrines of human nature and of
the Holy Bible are the same. I say the same; I
do not say similar.

But I go farther than Herbert Spencer in this
and announce that after full development, under
differentiating laws and environments, that naturally lead to heterogeneous products, then the
spiritual wave comes in and makes the heterogeneous homogeneous. The world is not far enough
advanced in its development to afford as many
multiplied demonstrations as Mr. Spencer finds in
his hemisphere of truth. I say hemisphere and not
sphere, because Mr. Spencer, like almost all other
sheer scientists, ranges only through half the sphere
of truth, and leaves the other half uninvestigated.
This is why science (so called) is often atheistic.
The other hemisphere of truth which Mr. Spencer
and company have not entered is that which I now
propose to explore, and whilst time will only permit a bald outline, yet it will give us a general idea
of the Divine drift, flowing through the Divine plan,
producing products worthy of a God. That plan
has behind it a purpose; that purpose is human
interior homogeneity from human exterior heter-

ogeneity, which is yet to retain its exterior heterogeneity. That plan at first proceeded through one human being operating upon other proximate human beings. Now that plan, according to the phases of the times is proceeding to work on a more extensive scale, by making one nation operate upon many nations, not to produce human uniformity but to effect interior human homogeneity, and yet retain exterior heterogeneity. The natural laws produce divergencies; the spiritual laws produce convergencies; the former prepared for the latter, the latter completes the work of the former. This brings me to my theme, "This Sabbath Land and its Mission to the Nations."

As men were chosen to operate upon men in the beginning of the spiritual development, so now nations are chosen to operate on nations. Where shall we look for the nation that bears the marks, that carries the credentials of apostolicity to the other nations in any preëminent sense? We look over China, the most populous nation, but her stagnant millions have evidently no high commission to the rest of the world, from the high source of things, except it be the mission of conservatism. We investigate India, the next in population, and discover no signs of commanding progress in the " Dreamy Hindoo." The other nations of Asia are out of the question, and as for Africaand Australasia there are few signs of cosmopolite advancement in either continent. We come to continental Europe and we find her various nations straining under great standing armies, and balancing diplomacies which absorb their strength and materialize their motives.

Entering England, we discover the heraldess of the great work, on the very eve of whose accomplishment we stand. Coming to America and looking southward, we see no leader of the hot heart of the world that pants for freedom. Looking northward we descry an expansive territory, which is a mere dependency of Britain. Where, then, shall we look for that great administratrix, whose mission of humanity, civility, evangelicity and consequent interior human homogeneity is to all other nations of the earth? There is but one answer, and that is, the Commonwealth of America. It looks, at first sight, selfish, and perhaps, to some who have not thought this through, silly, to make such a statement as this to an intelligent and mighty audience like you; but, have patience, and I will present such proofs as have set my own mind and heart in this direction. And I do not do this, I trust, through either vain vaunting on the one hand, or excessive patriotism on the other. If I were living in Patagonia, with the same knowledge and impressions I now possess, I would express the same important inter-evangelistic doctrine, for the following weighty reasons:

(1) This land long lay embosomed in the ocean, hidden from the eye of the rest of the world. None but a few aborigines, who probably came in some stray skiff that floated from some proximate point of Asia, were in the land. Here, through the long, lone ages, it waited in silence, maturing its forests, its prairies, its metals and minerals, for its destined populations. God could have conveyed Noah here in his ark, or Abraham with his faith, or Nimrod with his bow, or Moses with his law. He could have put it into the mind of Pythagoras, or Archimedes, or Alexander, or Cæsar, to seek these shores. He could have inspired the Syrians or Phœnicians to sail hither; but the fact that they never set out is presumptive evidence the Divine Supervisor of human events did not want them to come. The world was not ready; the Church was not ripe; the people were not prepared for the great social, political and religious emancipation which are the necessary factors in a nation that could be fitly chosen to bless all the other nations of the earth with civil, social, material, educational and evangelistic emancipation.

You will now notice a strange coincidence, showing that when America was to be unveiled to the old world, that old world was to be prepared to populate it with a new life. Just as a great gaunt heroic Florentine was crying, " O, Florence, the

Church must be renewed, the Bible is the true guide, the Christ is the true pope, love to God and love to neighbor must be the rule of life; to this cause there can be no other outcome than victory; but to me it will be death; mine shall be the red hat of martyrdom." Just as the glorious Savonarola was with such words shaking the infamous pope, Alexander VI, and all the Italian papacy simultaneously, another great Italian was rushing from court to court of Europe, seeking exploring outfit to sail westward across the Atlantic, in the hope of finding a westward course to India, but really to discover America. And, finally, as the grand Savonarola towered in San Marco as the great expositor of the prophets and of Revelations as if he himself were a prophet, Columbus had by his pleading secured an outfit for his illustrious expedition, and was actually on his way to this long-shrouded land.

Dull must be the mind that cannot see in this the Divinity marshaling the co-related events to suit His own benignant designs for the welfare of the human race. The God who inspired Savonarola to initiate a new reformation, also inspired Columbus to discover a new world, to care for and develop the rich results of that reformation. Columbus, therefore, is a name of which every American should be proud. Columbus is a name that should have been stamped on this land forever, as an acknowledgment of how he had by fortitude lifted it up out of the floods before the eyes of men determined to be free.   Columbus, a brave soul, that dared to sail with his convictions against a world of scoffers and a storm of scandal.   Columbus, who by his eighteen years of persistent thought, explanation and pleading, won a queen to his side, and through that queen's supplies, this land was discovered.   Hear that, O ye who would refuse womanhood enfranchisement equal to that of man. Ye who would not permit her to vote for civil purity and for ecclesiastical law, hear it, and learn that woman at the civil polls and woman in the General Conference would, by her intuitive sagacity and her superior benevolence, prove herself the best human friend of both State and Church. Material America undiscovered but for Isabella! Spiritual and moral argosies undiscovered, if we further refuse womanhood its place in the legislative and administrative diplomacies of both Church and State.   Heed it, ye who would keep her back, and break the prejudicial bonds of ages, and set her fully free.   Thus, then, Columbus, who, white-haired with thought at thirty, battled not only against the wild, lonely, unkeeled, unexplored, ever-expanding deep, but against his one hundred seamen, who again and again during those seventy strange days would have mutinied and turned back but for the imperial grandeur of that one hopeful soul. Columbus, who on his return, was at first feted like a lion and then spurned, calumniated and imprisoned like a traitor, till finally, death disimprisoned his victorious spirit, and coming generations, by the perfidious inconstancy of man, were left to garland his name with immortality. One year after next October 12th, the world ought to celebrate the quadri-centennial of this, the greatest discovery made by man. And the name of Columbus will tower high, afar above that of Amerigo Vespucci, who by his own craft and the stupidity of the times, was able to displace that of the real discoverer and engrave his own name on this continent; far above that of Fernando Cortez, who, through cupidity, conquered the Montezumas; aye, far above Magellan, Narvaez, De Soto, Melendez, Cartier, La Roche, Champlain, Cabot, Frobisher, Drake, Gilbert and Raleigh, and all other adventurers who came hither, backed by avaricious companies, to hunt for gold. Above them all, that solitary soul shall stand, in the esteem of an admiring and benefited world. Hence, learn one lesson, learn it well; that you are persistently to follow your conscience, though all the world is in arms against you; since God is with you, all is well, and all shall be better by and by.

It is well for you also to remember how as discovery after discovery continued to be made here of new territories, by the various explorers, so simultaneously, in the Old World the reformers Luther, Melancthon, Calvin, Knox, Ridley, Latimer and a host of others were discovering new inlets of truth, new valleys of blessing, and new mountains of vision in the Holy Scriptures, and were displaying their loveliness, to the multitudes whose sons in later days would populate this land.

Nor is it less strange that at the very time the patriot fathers were, through the stubbornness of King George III, and the political mal-administrations of his minister, Lord North, seriously contemplating a revolt from the exacting and imperious domination of Great Britain, there rose up a multitude of lay evangelists under the rousing preaching of Whitefield, and the still more efficient administration of the Wesleys. The doctrines of the Lutheran Reformation which had, to a great extent, only reached the heads of Protestants, were now vitalized with a fresh vitality and visited their hearts. Thus, contemporaneously, did the two great works proceed, doubtless under a divine providence—the emergence of the magnitude and fertility of this land on the one side of the Atlantic; the emergence of a divine doctrine, producing new specimens of redeemed human lives on the other. I call this the harmonics of history. But behind the harmonics was the Harmonist. [Hallelujahs.]

(2) The next important point worth considering is the location of this Sabbatic land. How it dif-

fered from that of ancient Canaan! Canaan, a little
strip of ragged, rugged, rocky country, graced with
a few fertile valleys, the chief of which cut it in
two, and known as Easdraelon; the other, the
Shephela, which skirted the sea. A land bounded
by the red rocks of Edom on the south; the desert
of Arabia on the east; the white-hooded mountains
of Lebanon on the north, and the Mediterranean on
the west. Beset by Ammonites, Perizzites, Hittites
Moabites, Philistines on the one hand, and by ban-
ditti of the desert on the other; a land with less
cultivable area than that of New Jersey alone.

Contrast this with the expansiveness, the fertility,
the variety, the serenity of this new Canaan. Cut
off by thousands of miles of ocean on either side
from the flames of Old World war; capped at either
end with the crystals that crown the poles; situated
serenely from all foreign domination, and utterly
independent of all balances of power; left to pursue
her own clean, clear God-given way without a
trammel and without a foe; widest in its temperate zone; narrowest in its torrid; navigable by
great rivers; gemmed with expansive lakes; graced
with a thousand blessings to other lands unknown,
there is nothing left for us but gratitude to the
Giver, and admiring utilization of the gift. Truly
we may call it Hephzibah (my delight is in her) and
Beulah—(married). But it is ours to see to it
that she is not married to old-world customs, de-

caying with the wrecks of crime; not married to old-time prejudices and dominations that grind the very faces and hearts of the poor; but married to that God who, like an Infinite Husband, casts around her the embracing fortresses of the seas and kisses her with the crystal lips of the waves.

Finally, the time came for the first important deportation of the prepared Pilgrims to set out for this prepared land. Political and ecclesiastical establishments in the old world were both against God's chosen. They were slaughtered like sheep; they were burned like felons, and those that remained of them were exiled in various parts of the earth. "Oh, Lord, how long?" rose from many a heart in remote dales, glens and deserts.

Finally, a colony of English refugees, who were in Holland for conscience sake, resolved on putting the ocean between them and their proscriptionists and persecutors. After innumerable difficulties they succeeded in embarking in the Mayflower, from Plymouth, and one hundred and two souls said adieu to tyranny. Pilgrims had been their name at Leyden, Holland; Puritans they have been called by the historians of America. There was Standish, and there was Bradford, leaders of the most resolute band of men and women that ever settled in any country; resolute because they were religious. They would have freedom to worship God in spirit and in truth. They would brook no interference with their sense of duty. The Bible was their one book; the Sabbath was their sheet anchor. They studied and obeyed the one; they sanctified the other. Through unutterable inconvenience, deprivation, disease and danger, after landing at New Plymouth, they pursued the strange tenor of their way. The Winter and shelterless wilderness bore many of them rapidly to unknown graves; but that very wilderness they turned into a cathedral to worship God. They soon were joined by others of kindred spirit. As time passed on they multiplied; as they multiplied they kept close to God through Sabbath ministries. And so that serene Sabbath devotion instructed their minds with truth, inspired their hearts with love, and spread a sacred halo round their lives, that began to glow far and near.

O, blessed year 1620, and blessed month December, and glorious day Monday eleventh, when, after a Sabbath of devotions, the Pilgrim Fathers landed on Plymouth Rock. Here was the nucleus of the young nation's life. Hollanders might settle in and around New York; Episcopalian English might colonize Virginia; Roman Catholics might populate Maryland, and Quakers Pennsylvania; but, Massachusetts, it was thou that furnished heart and brains for all of them in the time of trouble; it was thou protested against George the Third's intolerant domination; it was

thou threw Lord North's diplomatic tea into thy
harbor; it was thou roused the crunching lion from
his lair and " fired the shot heard round the world."
Because thy Sabbath-guarding God was with thee ;
because thou wast true to Him, He could not be
false to thee.   And so, through all the succeeding
vicissitudes of this nation's life, the might of Massachusetts has been felt through every State, by
every change, and God delay the time when, before
the persiflage of an iniquitous Sunday press, and
an intolerant invasion of foreign criminals, thy
statutes, thy example, thy purity and thy prowess
shall be forgotten.   Nay, rather let the sacred principles that were in thee and made thee great, continue, and spread, and ramify, and differentiate in
various forms, till all these forty-two States shall
be restrung with thy Sabbath-keeping customs and
thy man-building actions. [Amens.]

Thus, then, we see God chose the right kind
of human stock to found the new nation here.   If
He had selected the Irish, then the curses of Romanism would have been rampant ; if He had chosen
the French, then infidelity would have prevented
integration ; if he had chosen the German, then
rationalism and Sabbath prostitution would have
ruined us ; if He had chosen the royalists of
Britain, then we should still have been a mere
tributary offering, the ignoble perfume of flunkey-
ism, to that royal baccaratist, the Prince of

Wales. But God chose His own people, and hence His own are determined to defend His cause at risk of all things, and to spread the glory and honor of His name through all the earth. [Hallelujah.] O, land of God! Sabbath land! Jehovah calls thy faithful Hephzibah and thee He nameth Beulah. [Hallelujahs.]

Thus three facts are plain:

1. God permitted this new world to be discovered at the best time.

2. In it He has given us the best located and the most richly endowed segment of the earth's surface.

3. In it He planted the best human stock on the planet.

And from these three facts, judging by the analogies of both nature and history, as well as by the suggestions of intuition, I am disposed to think that the great Administrator of human affairs, proposes to emancipate all the other nations of the earth by this land, and that, according to the text, these nations shall call this land blessed.

Again, it is presumable Jehovah has the blessing of the nations of the world in view through America, because of the cosmopolite population that He directs to these shores. We are unique in this regard. No nation under heaven has so great variety of people as this republic. There is scarce a nation on the globe but has sent its deputies here.   But is not this an evil?   Would it not have been better to have limited immigration, and closed our ports to all but a selected few who can prove by culture and wealth that they are worthy?   Yes, if you want to ruin this Republic and bring upon us the scathing scath of an eternal malediction, exclude the pauper and the poor.   Ninety-nine out of every hundred people have come hither because they were poor.   The rich did not need to come, and so they stayed at home.   And if I were to make an analysis and trace back to the original emigrant trunk, the various millionaires and influential citizens of this land, I would find that those trunks were in most cases ragged, stormbeaten and gnarled by the sore trials and storms of the old world—trials which became so tense that they drove them to poverty and emigration.   Thus hath God chosen in this sense "the weak men of the world to confound the mighty, and the men that were not to bring to naught the men that were, that no flesh may glory in His presence."

But it may be said, what will be the result of so much intermingling of racial stock.   Do not so many intermixtures weaken race?   Just the opposite, if those intermixtures are under the generalizing wisdom of the Lord.   Amid such intermingling there is the better chance for the procession of that basal law of life, the "survival of the fittest."

Then, too, there is presumptive evidence that God intends this Beulah to bless the nations from the reflex influence of the lives of those that came from other lands. I make no extravagant statement when I say there is not a nation on the globe to-day but is in one way or another being molded, instructed, inspired, developed, physically, intellectually, industrially, commercially, mechanically, civilly, morally, philanthropically and religiously, by the influence of the successes of those who come here.

If I had time to take up each nation one by one nothing would be easier demonstrated than this. But I must keep to my subject and proceed furthermore to state that it is evident God intends to bless the other nations through this commonwealth on account of the unprecedented powers He has given us.

If God give a man superior knowledge, virtue or tact it is for the purpose of blessing some one who lacks what he has. It is a law of nature that the strong shall help the weak ; it is a law of barbarity that the strong shall devour the weak. If God give a community a surplusage of wealth, genius and influence it is not only for the purpose of helping that particular community, but that through that community others may be aided. And so, if God give a nation a surplusage of gifts and blessings He no doubt intends to bless therewith that particular nation, but He furthermore intends that that nation shall bless other nations. That God has blessed you in a most marked manner no investigator can for a moment doubt. He has blessed your farmers, your miners, your merchants, your mechanics, your traders, your teachers and professors and preachers as they never have been blessed in any other land, so that there is more wealth now in the United States, made by the people of these States, than was in the whole world when Columbus discovered the country nearly four hundred years ago. And this wealth is increasing rapidly, and is to continue to increase.

The Baltimore *Manufacturers' Record* states—

" The business men of this country are too apt to forget the soundness of America's vast progress. The United States is to-day almost the only great country in the world whose future is brighter than its past. Great Britain has in many respects reached the limit of its greatness. It can no longer be the manufacturing centre of the world, for we have taken the foremost position in that line. Its vast iron and steel business is yearly increasing in cost of production, while ours is decreasing. It cannot meet the world's ever growing demand for iron and steel, because it cannot increase its prodnction to any great extent in competition with this country. It produced no more pig iron in 1890, notwithstanding the high prices prevailing, than in 1882, while we more than doubled our output. Much of its ore it imports from far distant regions. Its cotton is all imported, It spends about $750,000,000 a year for foreign food stuffs. On the continent every nation is burdened with debt, and none can ever hope to pay off its obligations. Measured by their natural resources and their possibilities, they are bankrupt. In all of them the cost of production and of living is steadily increasing. In the United States we have scarcely laid the foundation of our future greatness. In natural resources we are richer than all of Europe combined; we are paying our debts faster than they are due; we have barely scratched the ground in the development of our mineral wealth; we are rich enough to stand a decrease last year of 900-000,000 bushels of grain as compared with 1889, on account of bad weather; we are rich enough in addition to this to send $70,000,000 in gold to Europe within a few months without creating any financial trouble, and that, too, after Europe had unloaded on us millions of dollars of our stocks, because our securities were the only ones in the world that found a cash market when the Barings and others were trying to save themselves. In ten years, from 1880 to 1890, we have added $2,000,000,000 to our capital invested in manufactures, an increase of nearly seventy-five per cent. In the same time the value of our manufactured products has risen from $5,300,0000,000 to $8,600,000,000, a gain of $3,300,000,000; or, in other words, we are producing manufactured goods at the rate of $3,300,000,000 a year more than we were ten years ago. The increase in capital invested in manufactures in ten years, from 1880 to 1890, was greater than the entire amount of capital invested in 1870, or only twenty years ago. In these ten years the growth of our manufacturing interests was greater than the growth from the settlement of America up to 1870. In these ten years we have built 75,000 miles of railroad, almost as much as our total mileage in 1880.

Now, the question arises, What are we going to do with these enormous augmentations to our wealth? I answer, We are either going to ruin ourselves, or we are going to save ourselves and the world. Which shall it be? The answer lies in whether we shall use our Sabbaths to teach the masses of money-making people how to benefit themselves and others by their wealth ; or, whether, untaught and uninspired, they shall prostitute their Sabbaths in finding means to spend their money in ruining themselves, and consequently the nation.

Thus, at a glance, it is seen that everything hinges on sanctifying the Sabbath. The greatest opportunity ever enjoyed by any nation of blessing the world is open to us. But the greatest opportunity of ruining ourselves through that very same opportunity is also open to us. Which shall it be? O heaven, which shall it be? That is the question. The Sabbath, again I say, is the pivotal axle that shall roll us one way or the other, up or down, forward or backward, according as we use it. The destiny of all the other days of the week depends on how we use the Sabbath. The destiny of the units, the families, the towns, the cities, the people of this country depends on how we use the Sabbath. If they use it to dissipate, and drink, and carouse, and learn the black arts, and to practice the devil's doctrines, then the Sabbath shall damn us. But if we use it to rest, recuperate, to instruct, to educate, to inspire, to elevate, and to learn the bright arts, and to practice beautiful graces, then the Sabbath shall enthrone us; and the people of this Republic shall, through their various successes in art, in science, in literature, in mechanics, in finance, in industry, in humanity, in education, in evangelism, and all that variegated web of national, civil, domestic and ecclesiastical blessings implied under these genetic heads, rise so high and spread so wide their elevating influence, that they shall take the whole world in their arms of love and liberty, and lift it up from its bondage and tears, to shine as the most resplendent jewel in Jehovah's crown. [Amens and glories.]

The Necessity of Sabbath Conservation in Our Great Cities.

Psl. cxxvii, 1.—" Except the Lord keep the city, the watchman waketh but in vain."

"WHAT a fermenting vat (says Carlyle) lies simmering and hid in the great city." The record of great cities is the record of the race. They have taken the most prominent part in politics, science, art, literature, evangelism, de-vangelism and destiny of both men and nations. Extinguish the history of Babylon and Nineveh, and you blot out the history of Persia. Abolish the history of Athens, and you abolish the history of Greece. Annihilate the archives of Rome, and you ruin the records of ancient Italy. What the cities of Egypt were, the valley of the Nile was. Palestine rose and fell with Jerusalem, for great cities are the commercial aggregations of the resources, characters and lives of nations. Paris,

Berlin, St. Petersburg, London, focus and represent the features of France, Prussia, Russia and England, respectively. These great capitals are the creations of their respective countries, and by reflex influence re-create the countries of which they are the products. Countries nurture the cities into strength, but after they have become strong, they mould and control the countries.

Our own large cities are approaching maturity. New York, Brooklyn, Newark, Philadelphia, Chicago, Cincinnati, St. Louis, San Francisco, New Orleans, and the other four hundred and thirty-two at the past and present rate of increase, will control this Commonwealth ten years from now. The gravitation toward these centers is relatively immense in this country. The ratio in fifty years has advanced from four and a half per cent. to twenty-two and a half per cent. From 1790 to 1880 the population of this country increased thirteen times. In the same period the population of our cities increased eighty-six times. In 1800 there were only six cities with a population over 8,000. In 1880 we had two hundred and eighty-six cities with a population over 8,000. In 1890 we have four hundred and forty-three cities with a population over 8,000. The influence of these four hundred and forty-three cities on the Republic is almost resistless even

12

now. That influence will be all controlling a quarter of a century from to-day.

Whilst it is with pride we point to the power, population, wealth, learning, present and prospective prosperity of these cities, yet it is with apprehension and dismay we look upon their morals. It is with a feeling akin to agony and despair we contemplate their Sabbath-breaking, dishonesties, saloons, theatres, libertines and houses of death. These I dread more than socialism, anarchism, rationalism, and the hounds of war. These corrode, corrupt, eat up honor and virtue, and prepare for the desolating revenges of history which overtook Babylon, Jerusalem and Palmyra. The Erinnys of an outraged justice are in pursuit, and like Byron, in his Childe Harold, succeeding poets, alas, again may sing:

> " The Niobé of Nations, there she stands,
>   Childless and crownless in her voiceless woe."

It is not to be regretted that the old world is pouring in upon us her surplus populations, but it is to be lamented that she pours in their shameless depravities — depravities which could not be brooked at home, and cannot with safety be tolerated abroad.

As in the time of Tacitus Rome had become the *colluvies gentium*—"the sink of nations"—so in our time, our large cities are becoming cesspools of the putrid streams that flow from the old world—effete through the drunkenness of crime. Scarcely one-third of the country's population is foreign by birth or parentage, but yet, such is the strength of the disposition, of foreigners to settle in our cities that sixty-two per cent. of the population of Cincinnati are foreign, sixty-three per cent. of Boston, eighty-three of Cleveland, eighty-eight of New York, and ninety-one of Chicago, with an equal average per cent. in Newark. These are surprising facts, but the reason for alarm is not in the figures, but in the social ideas, the political affinities, the hate of religion, the love of license, the ignorance of liberty, the power of infidelity, the prevalence of anarchy, the domination of drunkenness, and, above all, the abandonment of God. These are the forces that sweep out salvation, peace and happiness, and bring in restlessness, despair and destruction. Think of another truth. There are 200,000 saloons in the country. This, estimating the population at 60,000,000, gives one saloon to every 300 people. Bad enough, indeed; but when we come to Brooklyn we find one to every 250 of the population; to Chicago, one for every 179; to Jersey City, one to every 150; to New York, one to every 125; to Cincinnati, one to every 124; Newark, one to every 130. Thus, you see, there are about double the number of drinking places in the large cities in proportion to the population that there are in the rural districts. This is a pretty sure sign, that there is double the general corruption of tastes and manners.

Now, let us see what is the relation of the Church of God to this immense growth of city population and wickedness. Is the Church keeping pace with this incoming population? Sorry am I to have to say, that the Church is far behind *relatively*, and appears to be losing actual hold of the masses. There are a million of people in and around New York, over whom the Church, has as little saving power as if they lived in the centre of Africa

I have examined statistics and conversed with ministers, statesmen and laymen of the various denominations on this question, and find that, *relatively speaking*, the Presbyterian, Congregational, Reformed Dutch, Baptist and Methodist Churches, are ten-fold less in influence and membership than they were thirty years ago in the city of Brooklyn, and what is true of Brooklyn is also true of New York. Sunday newspapers, Sabbath dissipations, saloons, theatres, places of vile resort, gambling dens, prison population, suicides and insanities have *relatively* outstripped the increase of population; but the Protestant churches have *relatively* fallen far behind. This condition of affairs is preparing the way for such scenes of violence, rapine, and murder as will throw into the shade, the terrors of the French Revolution. What are the causes of this dreadful outlook?

I dare not locate them altogether in rationalism, agnosticism, materialism and immigrated infidelity. I must look deeper and nearer home, and when I look I find them in facts which you will bear me witness I have been preaching against. I find one of these facts in the false attitude that the vast body of professing Christians assume toward the people. That attitude is one of *general indifference* about the personal salvation, of the foreigners and strangers who come into our cities. The feeling of the great majority of professing Christians, appears to be, now we are in the church we are converted; we are all right if we are faithful; we shall receive the crown of life; hallelujah, we are saved, and we are going home to God.

Aye, what are you saved to? Saved to sublime selfishness; saved to self-conceit and abominable exclusivism; saved to an un-evangelic morality and an un-Christly churchism, that are as barbaric and heathenish in the sight of God, and angels as was the phariseeism of Judea, or as is the idolatry of Brahma or Buddha.

Verily I say unto you, if you are merely trying selfishly to save your own soul, you have not learned nor experienced the first principles of the Christian religion; you cannot save your soul and be selfish, for the very first and all-pervading principle of Christianity is loving, living, undying, laborious activity for the lost; a loving, earnest, sincere anxiety and action which will speak to others, pray for others, implore, beseech, obtest and cry for others; aye, which will lay down life itself for the salvation of the ruined.

Now, where in the churches do we find this kind of Christianity? Once in a while we meet such a soul; but where is the church whose members in the mass, measure up to this unselfishness of Christ and of Paul. Let the churches of these cities get at the throne of grace, such an unselfish, burning, soul-saving spirit, as Christ had when he laid down His life for redemption, and as Paul had when he could have wished himself "accursed for the sake of his kinsmen according to the flesh," and let them move out upon advancing hosts of Germans, Jews, Italians, saloonists, Sabbath-breakers, and haters of churches, and you will see such a revolution as will imparadise in the arms of salvation, this million of our fellow citizens in and around New York who now scout the Sabbath and scorn the Church.

Another fact that accounts for the fearful inundation of infidelity in our midst, is the misapplication of what little unselfish zeal we have as churches. We have been reading, thinking and praying about India and China, Africa and the Western frontier, and we have been giving to send out missionaries to these regions beyond, and we have been forgetting to stretch out the hand of help to the heathen at home. God forbid that I should advise less help to the heathen abroad; I don't think we do half enough for them; but God help us to see that the barbarians at our very doors, have a Christian claim to all we can say, pray, give or do to help them to see and seek the world's Redeemer.

What else are we in this world for, my hearers? Is it to join a church, give to its support, offer up a few general prayers, observe moral lives, live in fashionable homes, conduct respectable business, make money, save the most of it, to spoil our relatives, and die and have the church sing us to heaven, when God Almighty shall appear and say to us from His judgment throne: " Depart from me ye cursed into everlasting fire prepared for the devil and his angels. For I was an hungered, and ye gave me no meat; I was thirsty, and ye gave me no drink: I was a stranger and ye took me not in: naked, and ye clothed me not : sick and in prison and ye visited me not. Then shall they also answer him saying, Lord, when saw we thee an hungered, or athirst, or a stranger, or naked, or sick or in prison, and did not minister unto thee? Then shall he answer them saying, verily, I say unto you, *inasmuch as ye did it not to one of the least of these, ye did it not to me.* And these shall go away into everlasting punishment."—Matthew xxv.

Another fact that accounts for this deluge of infidelities in our large cities, is the misdirection we give to our Sunday-school zeal. Now I am treading on delicate ground, and may say some things unpalatable. But let the truth be spoken, though the heavens fall, and let the temple of Dagon be uptorn, if Samson perish in the ruins. I hold, from my experience and observation, that some Sabbath-school teachers and officers appear more anxious to teach the lesson, keep up the number of their classes and their school, than to get the pupils converted to Christ and united to the church. I am now speaking on general, and not on particular terms—of schools generally, and not of our own particularly. To teach the lesson intelligently and thoroughly is good; to keep up the number of the classes and prestige of the school is excellent; but if you succeed eminently in doing both, and fail to lead the scholars to give themselves, body and soul to Christ and His Church, the whole of your successes are deplorable and remediless failures. And now with these three facts in mind:

(1) The false attitude of the great mass of church members toward the world.

(2) The misapplication of much of our zeal in neglecting the heathen at our doors.

(3) The want of direct work for powerful, personal salvation that unites the rising youth to Christ and the Church.

Let us see how we can so affect ourselves as to avoid these dangers, and do our full share toward staying the invading tides of worldliness and wickedness with which our great cities are already blighted. And first, remember the example of Jesus in regard to cities. He made them the centers, the strategic points of his preaching. Saint Matthew says: "And it came to pass, when Jesus had made an end of commanding His disciples, He departed thence to teach and to preach in their cities." Luke represents Him as saying: "I must preach the Kingdom of God to other cities also, for therefore am I sent." When on great field days He preached in rural districts, it was to the cities that emptied themselves to hear Him; hence we read, "The whole city came out to meet Jesus." So important did He deem the salvation of the Jewish capital that He wept over it, crying: "Oh, that thou hadst known, even thou, in this thy day the things that belong unto thy peace," and went through it sobbing, "Oh, Jerusalem, Jerusalem, * * * how often would I have gathered thy children together, even as a hen gathereth her chickens under her wings, and ye would not." The cities of Capernaum, Chorazin, Bethsaida, Jericho, Jerusalem, were the head-centers of His entire ministry, and whilst He often retired to the country to commune with His Father, yet, with the exception of His sermon on the mount, which was intended for His disciples, He delivered most of His great discourses in the cities. He also instructed His disciples to follow His example. "Into whatsoever city or town ye enter," etc. "When they persecute you in one city, flee unto another." And among His last words were, "Beginning at Jerusalem."

This was His policy, and it was both sensible and successful. He knew that the word thoroughly preached in the cities would "sound out in all the region round about." He and His Apostles made the cities great speaking trumpets, which branched out their voices through all the land. It was a masterly diplomacy, a politic stroke of strategy, because these were the attractive hives of human beings, to whom the world lent its ears. Paul (though of the Apostolic band, abortive born), recognized this masterly strategy, and commenced and continued his marvelous ministry amid the densest masses of human beings he could find. Damascus, Jerusalem, Antioch, Paphos, Derbe, Lystra, Phillipi, Thessalonica, Berea, Athens, Corinth, Ephesus, Rome, were the great cities of the world in his time, and there he preached nearly all his great discourses and wrote all his epistles. This accounts for his unprecedented success.

But alas, there has been a great mistake in America made by the Protestant churches in these last three decades. We have been opposing and counteracting to a great extent the plan so prudently presented by Christ and so faithfully executed by Paul. We have to a deplorable extent, as a national ministry and membership, been founding and fostering feeble churches, in sparsely settled rural regions, and neglecting to focus the bright, burning rays of the glorious Gospel on the masses in our great cities. We of course have some fine churches, and powerful preachers in the cities, but "what are they among so many?" There is more spiritual destitution in New York and Brooklyn than exists in any other part of the country, and yet these are the two cities which should, on account of their commercial relations with the world, be kept beating highest, cleanest and mightiest under the banner of Immanuel. Nevertheless, below Fourteenth street in New York is a population of 550,coo, with but 60,000 sittings of Protestant churches, sittings which are constantly decreasing, and the outlying wards of Brooklyn are known to be in a worse condition. Now you will say, why do you speak about New York and Brooklyn? Because the same state of affairs has begun to appear in our own city, and by the appalling pictures, on the other side the river, I desire to rouse you to take the field in the name of the Lord God of Hosts, and stem the tide of worldliness and unchurchliness that is sweeping up against our breasts at this very hour.

What are we going to do about it? I hear some

rationalistic philosopher exclaim: " Let us do something new.   Let us cast around for some new plan and pursue it with manly intelligence and vigor."

> " New occasions teach new duties;
> Time makes ancient good uncouth;
> They must upward still and forward
> Who would keep abreast of truth."

The first two lines of this stanza may be made to contain a great and grave blunder, however poetic, however scientific.   Such novel experimentation suits very well in agriculture or manufacturing, in mechanical contrivances and practical sciences, and even in physical pharmaceutics.   But the spiritual sphere does not change; like gravity it is still the same. Its laws, its forces, its methods of operation, so far as fundamentals are concerned, are fixed.

The old truth and the old plan may be capable of many adaptations and ramifications, but the moment we diverge by subtle modifications, and plausible differentiations, from the fountain-head, that moment the conductors of power become clogged, and befogged and we are left in our apostacy to suffer ignominious failure.

The fundamental facts, forces and plans promulgated by the Word of God must be as strictly obeyed, as must the laws of electricity by the electrician. As in the natural sphere there are inerrant laws, forces and methods of operation that must not be relegated to obscurity, and cannot be impinged with impunity, so also, in the moral and spiritual realm are mighty, majestic principles that underlie and pervade all successes. One of these principles is promulgated in our text, "Except the Lord keep the city, the watchman waketh but in vain." What this city needs most of all, therefore, is more of the Divine guardianship of the Almighty. We may sing and soothe ourselves with—

> " Right forever on the scaffold,
>   Wrong forever on the throne;
>   But that scaffold sways the future,
>   And within the dim unknown
>   Sitteth God amid the shadows
>   Keeping guard above His own."

And this is excellent, but what about the great sweltering, swaggering, seething, drunken, dissipating masses that have taken themselves from neath that guardian care, and are by their numbers and their sins making us a second Nineveh or Babylon? How can we save them? "That is the question."

The primordial principles of God's word show us very plainly, and we have no other standard we dare trust. One foremost practical principle teaches, get thoroughly saved yourselves. The pentecostal fires had to come and cleanse, illumine, inspire and thrill, even the personal disciples of

Jesus, before they were fit to move a hand toward saving the world. The same practical principle is as true now as then, and always shall be true. What, then, we first of all need for the renovation of Newark, and the salvation of the various slaves of Satan in this city, is such a power of the Holy One within us, and upon us that it shall be not we that speak, but "the Holy Ghost within us." This is the old-time power. But it is also the new-time power [Amens], because there is no other in heaven or earth that can edify saints and save sinners. All Christians in all times who have had their hearts, minds, words and manner filled with this Holy Ghost, sent from the Father by the Son as His ubiquitous representative, have ably fulfilled their mission and left behind them halos of glory and gardens of the Lord full of the "trees of right-eousness." And all professing Christians who have permitted themselves to be decoyed aside to some one, or some thing else, have left behind them a heritage of desolation. Now then with this his-toric and scriptural evidence before us, it is clear what we are first to do to emancipate Newark.

We are to seek by personal prayer and faith, for the fulness of the spirit. Such a fulness as will fill all our feelings, thoughts, words and acts with the convicting and converting power of Almighty God. [Amens.]

Such a fulness of blessing as shall make us overflow, as the abundance of water makes the spring. [Amens.]

Such a fulness as lifts us up above sin, and fear, and diffidence, and makes us easy and able in speaking to, and pleading with sinners to come and be saved. [Amens.]

Such a fulness as makes us happy, glad, rapturous, and leads us to take chief delight in making others so. When we secure and retain and live in such a blessed state as this, we shall not live for naught. Even David understood this when he prayed; " Restore unto me the *joy of thy salvation, then* shall I teach transgressors thy ways and sinners shall be converted unto thee."

After securing such exalted, joyful power for ourselves by prayer, faith and fidelity, next comes the duty of strengthening "the brethren" and sisters of the churches. Bring them all in. Lead, gently lead, and lift, lovingly lift them all up, to the same mount of blessing. I say all. [Amens.]

This can be easily accomplished by the inspiring songs you sing ; by the fervent prayers you utter ; by the glorious example you show ; by the elevated, bright, beautiful life you lead. [Hallelujahs.] I have found nothing easier and more delightsome in my ministry, than the blessed work of encouraging the discouraged, of strengthening the weak, of comforting them that mourn in Zion, of fusing into flaming heralds the lukewarm ones, and placing arms of pity, of sympathy and of love around the backslidden, turning them round and cheering them on up to the heights of joy, through the hope which is in Christ. [Hallelujahs.]

Then having been filled with the glory of the Holy Ghost ourselves, and having led the whole church all along the line, men, women and children, rich and poor, learned and illiterate, up to the same celestial rapture, what is our next step? That next step is to go after and bring home the sinner. Here comes the tug of war. The sinners in these times, and in this place have become intrenched in the saloons, in the clubs, in the pleasures of the world and in the deceitfulness of riches. Moreover, multitudes of them are said to be prejudiced against the churches and the Christians. What is the cause of this? Who is to blame for it? What has been working this alienation? What has been digging this impassable gulf between the unsaved people and the church, their best friend? The answer is at hand; ponder it well. The cause of this alienation of many from the churches lies in Sabbath desecration. That is the scooping scoundrel that has through these twenty-five years in our large cities, been digging the chasm between the people and the Church of God.

By Sabbath violation they are kept away from the churches; they become prepossessed with adverse principles, purposes and pursuits. They become enamored of pleasure, and license, and revelry. They go on bringing their children up, after their Sabbath spoliation ways. They are shut out from the softening, sweetening hymn; the pathetic, uplifting prayer; the instructive and inspiring truth; the tender and genial brotherhood and sisterhood of Christ; and so they and theirs become morally hard, and corrugated, and gnarled, and spiritually deaf, blind and dead, till finally, alas, they and theirs fall into the great gloomy chasm of despair and destruction which their own Sabbath breaking has dug for them.

Oh, my God! Is there no help? Is there no remedy? Must these aberrant masses, for whom Thy Son has died, be engulfed forever? Is there no help? Yes, there is help. Help only in manly, united, sustained Christian effort. Help only in the Christian people of Newark laying aside their sectarian differences and their political prejudices, and coming together as one man and demanding from the officers of this city that Sunday desecration shall now and here forever cease. [Amens.]

That Christianity and the Sabbath and the thousands of poor dupes who enter into its defilement with zest, have been trampled on long enough, all for the purpose of catering to, and pleasing a foreign element, in hope of securing their political support.

That the officials of this city shall either execute the city ordinances, in regard to the Sabbath laws with the same fidelity that they execute other laws, or they must give place to those who will execute them. This is a political and civic duty that every Christian should take a part in by his vote and voice. The city officers, as I have shown on a former occasion, are bound by the laws of this State and this city to give us a civil Sabbath. They themselves know, and everybody knows, that they give us an outrageous Sabbath. Wagons flying through the streets on business, stores open in all quarters, saloons filling the unfortunate with drunkenness, news hucksters and traffickers (those blatant curses of the modern city Sabbath), crying all over their secular wares, making a human pandemonium here in Newark. How, in the name of heaven, can the Lord, (one of whose fundamental commands is " Remember the Sabbath day to keep it holy,") keep in loving guard such a city as this? What else can happen but what we see does happen—that men and women shall be blasted and blighted, that families shall be disrupted, that society shall degenerate, that corruption shall ensue, till the curse of God shall strike us and turn us into another Sodom. [Cries of God have mercy!]

O Newark! Newark! thou art destroying thyself. But in God is thy help; now is the time for

Christian men, for all lovers of this city and all lovers of their fellow-men, to rise in mass and demand the rectification of these shameless, glaring Sabbath evils. Then shall the poor, toil-worn and unfortunate thousands, who are going to destruction through desecration of God's day, stop, think, turn and begin to emerge up out of their Sabbath follies, and commence to move toward reconstruction through the consecration of the Lord's day to sacred, instructing and inspiring purposes.

Before any great religious movement takes place in this city, this work must first be done. No church, no minister, no member, can reach the masses of Sabbath-breakers till this city lifts up its civic hand and says, according to the specifications of our statutes, " Remember the Sabbath day to keep it holy."

You might as well suppose that the day-school teachers of the public schools, could make scholars of the pupils if the pupils were all playing truant, as to suppose that we can Christianize and educate the masses of this city on Sunday, when so large a portion of them are making it a play day. [Cries, That's so.]

O! our God, our hearts bleed for these fallen, deceived ones. Do Thou interpose, O Thou most mighty, and make such a revelation by Thy Spirit of the horrors of Sunday prostitution, to the municipal authorities of this city, that they shall say, We have erred; we have gone too far; we will go back to the statute book, and we will give the City of Newark a civil Sunday.

I believe this will happen. When it does, O ye blood-washed, spirit-inspired pilgrims, be ready! Be ready to be good Samaritans; be ready to pour in the oil and wine; be ready to bandage up the bleeding wounds; be ready to set the wounded victims on your own beasts; be ready to bear them to the hotel (church) of healing and of joy; be ready to say, take care of this poor wounded traveler and I will discharge the bills. [Amens and hallelujahs.] Then gathering up and bringing in, all these maimed and wounded ones, and seeing them restored once more to manhood and womanhood, we will lock arms with them and each other, and march through this New-Ark of probationship to that New-Ark of glory. "Then the Lord will keep the city and the watchman will not wake in vain." [Amens and glories.]

Garland of Gratitude. —No. i.

For the Prosperity of This Land Under Sabbath Ministries.

Psa. lx, 4—"Thou hast given a banner to them that fear Thee
that it may be displayed because of the truth."

Psa. cxv, 1—"Not unto us, O Lord, not unto us, but unto thy
name give glory for thy mercy and for thy truth's sake."

THE Hebrew נֵס here translated banner,
means a glittering standard around which
warriors gather. I shall use this standard
as the variegated banner, of multiform prosperity in these United States through Sabbatic
ministries. Without the vitality which flows
through such sacred ministrations, the tree of the
Republic should have been a weakling of gnarled
and stunted growth. But with this vitality per-
vading roots, trunk, branches, leaves, flowers and
fruit, that tree has become so ample and umbrage-
ous, that emancipated millions sing beneath its shade;
and Jehovah, from whom all blessings flow, has
given them this multiform "banner to be displayed,

because of the truth." Turning to the first fold of this standard, I find—

He has given us the banner of prosperity in initial settlement. When the old world was groaning under the hard heel of tyranny; when the masses sighed and wept under the remorseless and defiant sway of a fierce feudality; when the people wore themselves out under abject servility, to their exacting lords, and slavery was the unjust and cruel lot of man, this virgin land in all her early charms, rose up out of the floods before their wondering gaze. It had shone like a strange asylum, before adventurous Icelandic and Norwegian sea kings as early as the tenth century.

It had shimmered like a new Canaan before Spanish explorers in the fifteenth century, and it sparkled like a Divine El Dorado, before the avaricious eyes of Europe in the seventeenth century, so that French, Spanish, Dutch and English vied for its possession.

Britain (that prophetic chieftainess of modern history) procured the lion's share and resolved to colonize and defend it. But it was on the 11th of December, 1620, when the Pilgrim Fathers, glowing with the love of God and freedom, landed on Plymouth Rock, that the real genetic seeds of unity, fraternity, equality and liberty were sown.

From that day this land of the setting sun, became the land of the rising sun to all who determined to be free. Vessels were chartered, thousands upon thousands sailed, under the golden marge of closing day and reached in safety these shores of the morning.

Great Britain, by boldness in battle and diplomacy at court, secured uninterrupted Northeastern sway.

The French lost their last foothold there when the heights of Abraham were captured, by the gallant, but expiring Wolfe from the great Montcalm.

And now Britain levied taxes, discouraged development, clasped her strong restraints upon this youthful Hercules who, feeling himself cribbed, caged, confined, expostulated at first, and finally expressed a resolution to be free. This only exasperated the victorious lion on the other side the flood, who, mid much indignation, sent over 30,000 warriors to subdue the refractory and ungrateful child.

The first sounds of their castigations were heard at Lexington, Concord and Boston. It was there Britains, misjudging the metal of their foe, hoped to quell and crush colonial aspiration. But it was there also "The embattled farmers stood and fired the shot heard round the world." This shot was the slogan that summoned the colonists throughout the land, and marshalled them in serried echelons for action and for arms.

Appeals to that greatest of Protestant Kings (George III) at first were made, declarations of colonial rights drawn up, exhortations to unity expressed. Hancock exclaimed, amid all conflictions, in the Colonial Congress, "Let us hang together." And Franklin replied facetiously, "Yes, let us hang together; for if we do not we must hang separately."

Vacillation seemed for a time the genius of the deliberating members. But there was one young man blazing with patriotism, and the love of liberty who rose amid distracted delegates, and swept by his eloquence the wavering into line, as he cried, "Tarquin and Cæsar had each his Brutus, Charles the First his Cromwell, and George the Third may profit by their example." The royalists shouted treason, but Patrick Henry, flaming with the prophetic message that burned within him, fearlessly towered up like a messenger from the Almighty and replied, "If this be treason make the most of it," and went on bearing the main body of the Congress with him, as he protrayed their wrongs, and capped the climax of his seraphic speech with, "My countrymen, you may do as you please in this matter, but as for me, gentlemen, give me liberty or give me death."

Not from the eloquence of Pym, Hampden, Wentworth and Falkland; not from the impassioned style and dramatic manner of Lord Chatham, Fox, Sheridan and Grattan; not from the easy, brilliant oratory of the younger Pitt, the charming Canning, the epigrammatic Sheil, and the practical vigor of Castlereagh, have ever flowed more powerful and pregnant utterances.

The halting Congress thereafter verged toward efficient and enthusiastic action. The people waited in breathless expectancy the result of its deliberations. When, at length, on the Fourth of July, 1776 (a day to be forever memorable), Richard Henry Lee, of Virginia, rose in his place with the Declaration of Independence on fire in his heart, the House was hushed to solemn stillness as, with flaming tongue, he moved, " Resolved, that these united colonies are and ought to be free and independent States, and that all political connection between them and Great Britain is and ought to be totally dissolved." The crisis had come. The resolution was unanimously adopted. The news found the ready and expectant bellman, and that old bell, which seems pro- phetically to have had graven round its rim, " Proclaim liberty throughout the land to all the inhabitants thereof," tolled out the tidings of political joy. The news flew up the Delaware, across New Jersey, over New York, through New England, like a sacred emancipation. The voice of trumpets, and clangor of bugles were in the air. The ubiquitous energy of the popular will was swift as lightning and loud as thunder. The clerk left his page unwritten on the desk, the youth

13

elt himself a man, the veteran forgot his years, the mother gave up her darling boy, the pure and noble wife, relinquished the husband she adored, and the patriots (against the persuasions and the plots of royalists) rushed to the battle, as to a feast. This is the political crisis which was brought about by Sabbath-keeping heroes—a crisis which neither Phœbus of Rome, nor Demos of Athens, nor reformers in Venice, nor Cromwell nor Hampden of England, had dared inaugurate. A crisis for which the multiplied, wailing, down-trodden millions waited and watched with eyes of tears, through the gloom of unpitying ages; a crisis for which philosophers had sighed, and philanthropists prayed, and poets wept, and states-men planned, and soldiers fought, and yet, on account of the tyranny of man, it was long in coming.   But now it had come.   Come to bridge the gulf between the rich man's castle and the poor man's hovel; come to hew down the assumptions of the rich, imperious and proud; come to lay in the very dust the scepters of cruelty, the swords of barbarity, and the crowns of an unlimit-ed and monarchic wrath; come to go down beside the beggars in their want, the culprits in their chains, the poor in their sorrow, the weak in their desolation, and whisper in the ear of each: "Arise and stand upon thy feet, for thou also art a man."   [Hallelujahs.]

At this time, however, the governmental Swells of England, had but sneers and bayonets for such degenerate rebels, as in these western wilds desired to be free. No man of commanding and acknowledged ability, had as yet been permitted to rise to supreme prominence in the New World. And so long as the colonists were content to dance attendance upon the flute of British lords, and submit to every measure which would enrich them and impoverish themselves, all was calm. But when the colonial patriots arose and protested ; when George Washington, Benjamin Franklin, the two Adamses, Alexander Hamilton and Thomas Jefferson rose up to assert natural and Divine rights, then all was storm. But when the smoke of battle had cleared away from Bunker Hill, Trenton, Charleston, Saratoga, and the lofty Lord Cornwallis, with his seven thousand beleaguered troops, marched out of Yorktown to stack arms and surrender to Mr. George Washington (as Lord Howe, refusing him his military title, scornfully had called him); then the sneers of royalty were changed to a most deplorable and irremediable chagrin, and the ridicule of aristocrats to a ridiculous respect, and the prophetic utterance, " My lords, whatever else you can do, you cannot conquer America," of the great Lord Chatham was realized. The energy of a Sabbath educated people triumphed, filled the world with wonder and England with defeat. And well might the world wonder. Look at the conditions of the two opposing powers. Then only a thin line of insignificant towns stretched from Maine to Georgia; then, save when crossed by the war-whoop of the Indian, unbroken silence reigned from ocean to ocean; the inhabitants of New York were confined to the bay and shores of the Hudson; the fertile fields of the Genesee valley were held by the savages.

Schenectady was a frontier hamlet and Albany and Kingston villages exposed to Indian incursions. Pittsburgh was a mere military post, surrounded with woods, swamps and mountains. The fine regions of Kentucky, Tennessee, Ohio, Illinois, Indiana, and all the other westward territories were one vast wilderness, untrod by the white man's foot, unseen by the white man's eye. Those immense realms beyond the Mississippi were tablelands of dread, where hordes of savages were believed to roam over interminable plains. A disconcerting sense of mystery haunted all territories west of the Alleghanies.

Scarce three millions of people, were sparsely scattered over a long strip of land, bounded by the ocean on the one side, by the wilderness on the other. Eight hundred thousand of these were New Englanders; eight hundred thousand more belonged to the Middle States, and the residue to the Southern.

Virginia surpassed all others in wealth and splendor. New York and Massachusetts had not as yet thought of shining like such aristocracy. The roads in all regions were bad, and modern appliances of travel, agriculture and manufacture impossible.

Around these nature-besieged colonists raged malarial fevers, wild beasts and wilder men. Before them lay the dark and trackless woods, behind them the raging seas, on every hand the foe.

Chicago, soon to be the seat of the World's Fair, was unborn. St. Louis unstaked out. New York town extended only from Castle Garden to City Hall. Broadway penetrated no farther than Chambers street. Philadelphia was an insignificant hamlet clinging to the bank of the Delaware. Baltimore and Boston were small towns, and Newark had not 1,000 inhabitants. Passage from one town to another was tedious, difficult and dangerous. Such was the material setting of this infant Republic, when so fiercely attacked by British arms.

Scan the foe as he approaches, radiant with the terrific plumes of a thousand victories, venerable in prowess, fierce in diplomacy, warlike in strategy, uncompromising and unfaltering in the fray. What nation dare stand before him? The braves of Ireland, the heroes of Scotland, the warriors of Denmark, had all been reduced to submission by his ancient valor.   The victorious legions of Spain, France and Holland, all had crouched at the feet of this imperious and warlike conqueror.   Since then this great military power, exceeding ancient Assyria, Greece or Rome in the efficiency of his legions and the vastness of his conquests, has cut to pieces on the famous field of Waterloo the troops of Napoleon the Great—troops that all but overrun the world; conquered by the sword two hundred millions of warlike people in the Orient— people of the genuine Aryan stock—and so has gone on and strung upon his spear nation after nation, till now in every quarter of the globe his war drums salute the ascending sun.

What a tremendously dangerous foe was this (with his leaders here in possession of the field) for an infant Republic, just emerging from its cradle, without the sinews and experience of war, to dare to repulse.   But your patriot fathers did attack in his new made lair, this world-conquering lion.   Cut off his mane, plucked out his teeth, clipped his claws, stifled his roar, bayoneted his sides, swept him with a simoon of buckshot front, flank and rear, and sent him back bleeding, wondering, wounded and dismembered, across the sea, to hide within his Angle Isle and lick his gory wounds. [Applause.]   There never was such a defensive victory.

It was Horatius keeping the bridge—it was

more; it was Gideon, with his three hundred lappers, routing the Midianites—it was more; it was Leonidas, with his three hundred Spartans, guarding the pass of Thermopylæ against the whole Persian army—it was more; it was the victorious battle strokes of Sabbath-keeping Christians, who cried through a trail of tears and blood, "Give us liberty or give us death." [Glories.] Aye, it was more; it was the triumphal march of Jehovah in His people through the land, crying, "Men of England, give place to my people, that 'they may dwell here' in a land which is not 'too strait for them.' You have persecuted them in a strait land; now I give them a large land. You have proscribed them in your own country, and now do I sweep this new country clear of you, and give them incalculably better than ye have yourselves." [Hallelujahs.]

Thus we see God has given us the glittering banner of prosperity, so far as obtaining possession is concerned. And so we display this fold of our flag to the world, as we adoring cry, "Not unto us, O Lord, not unto us, but unto Thy name give glory." But again, by opening another fold, I perceive He has given us the banner of physiographic superiority. Three million five hundred thousand square miles of territory, ten thousand miles of ocean frontage, twenty-four thousand miles of river navigation, nine thousand

miles of island shore line, prairies that for expanse
and fertility are unequalled on the earth, lakes that
for size and beauty excel all others on the globe,
mountains that with granite fingers wring out
the clouds over the plains, valleys so rich and
fertile that the surplusage of their productivity
is being exported to the extent of six millions
of bushels of wheat in the one week ending August
22, 1891, oil wells that produce one hundred and
thirty thousand barrels a day, forests that turn
out lumber which I found docked on the Para-
matta river in Australia nine thousand miles away;
black shale regions containing enough of oil to
cover Pennsylvania and New York States, with an
ocean of illuminating liquid fifteen feet deep;
floral belts that (as in Texas) lift up their golden,
scarlet, violet hues laughing to the sun; fruits of
every species, vegetable of every genus, cereals of
every shade, flocks of every variety and herds
almost numberless, climate of every temperature—
thus, laden with a richness of blessing, with an
affluence of capacity, that could feed and clothe
the population of the whole earth, does the land
lie before us, pillowing its cool and quiet head
amid the crystal palaces of the north, and stretching through thirty degrees of latitude, bathing its
emerald feet in the balmy waters of the south.
Truly God has given us, the banner of physiographic grandeur, and therefore we gratefully

weave it into our garland of praise and cry, " Not unto us, O Lord, not unto us, but unto Thy name give glory."

I open another fold of this great standard of prosperity, "to be displayed because of the truth," and I find furthermore He has given us the banner of agricultural prosperity. Every nation on the earth in this regard is now left far behind us. To such an extent has agriculture grown that as early as 1870, the value of the farm implements alone was $337,000,000, and the value of the live stock was $1,500,000,000, and the cash value of farms, implements and stock was over $11,000,000,000, and the annual production was in value $2,448,000,000. The number of farms was 2,600,000, the number of farmers and helpers 6,000,000, and so large and lavish were some of these farms that 2,000 of them produced $50,000,000 worth in one year. And such was the increase that during the decade between 1870 and 1880 the number of farms increased to 4,000,000, the number of farmers and helpers to 7,670,000, and the worth of farms only, to $10,000,000,000.

But in no decade, either in this or any other country under the sun, has there ever been such materialistic progress as in this land from 1880 to 1890. It is utterly unparalleled in all history. I have received and am receiving through the courtesy of Gen. Robert P. Porter, Superintendent of

United States Census, every bulletin that comes out, before finally forming the national volumes which will be published, of the state of the country, and from these I gather that such has been the marvelous growth during the ten years ending with 1890, that the absolute wealth of this country now has risen to the almost unthinkable sum of $62,610,000,000, or about $1,000 for every man, woman and child in the land.

And this enormous wealth, all in one way or another, has come forth from the soil. Most from the surface, but much from the bosom.

Since 1770, when the wondering hunter picked up a swarthy diamond, and carried it to his hut amid the mountains of Mauch Chunk, there have been over $13,000,000,000 worth of merchantable coal, quarried from these beds of anthracite. And the bituminous coal beds are even more extensive than the anthracitic. The great Appalachain ranges contain inexhaustible supplies. The State of Mich igan contains 6,700 square miles of it, and Illinois 47,000 square miles more. The iron, too, packs the mountains. The gold, the silver, the copper, the lead, rib the hills.

Our barren and rocky wilds seem set on founda tions of wealth, and our fertile valleys cover illim itable beds of jewels. Such is the wealth in the soil and on the soil that if the whole earth were to form a conspiracy to boycott America you could, with the utmost indifference, play " Yankee Doodle Dandy," and go grandly marching on. [Applause.]

This, through Sabbath-keeping coöperation, God has done for us. Therefore, this also I reverently weave into his chaplet of praise, and coming forth I devoutly lay it at His feet saying, " Not unto us, O Lord ; not unto us, but unto Thy name give glory." But I open another fold of this great, glittering standard He "has given us to be displayed because of the truth," and discover the banner of financial prosperity. For in this, too, we lead the world, not, however, without a great, protracted struggle.

The common currency of the early colonists consisted of beads made of clam shells, known as wampum. These they used in dealing with the Indians. This was abolished as a nuisance in 1650. Ten years after the Revolution the first bank was proposed in Massachusetts. The country swam through the British war on $140,000,000 bills of credit. There was then no national mintage. January 15, 1782, Robert Morris, the noble financier of the Revolution, proposed a coinage, and the much appreciated dollar was adopted as a basis.

This worked well up till 1843, when the paper money complaint broke out in Ohio, Illinois and Indiana. This bank script was called by various rude names, as white-dog, blue-pup, according to the purposes for which it was devoted. But the

" rag-baby," as it since has been called, has been of great service, especially during the Civil War.

When the South seceded in 1860 our debt was about $90,000,000, and had it not been for this same baby secession could hardly have been prevented. At the beginning of the war, sufficient gold and silver not being procurable, $10,000,000 treasury notes were authorized. February 8, 1861, $10,-000,000 more, and as necessities arose by the terrible and unexpected drainage of the war, government bonds, bank notes and legal tenders were issued till, in January, 1875, you were $2,242,-301,082.43 in debt, and during July, 1864, so much was the nation's credit strained that it required $2.85 to procure a $1.00 in gold.

But this over two billions and a quarter, I am happy to say, is being paid off as soon as it comes due. Over one billion has been paid during the last decade. We are now considerably below a billion in debt. The foreign nations are twenty-five billions in debt, and two billions of this have been contracted during the last ten years. Thus it is evident that while Sabbath-desecrating nations are falling into embarrassment, we, a Sabbath-keeping nation, are emerging from embarrassments.

The French Cession was secured in 1803 from Napoleon for the small sum of fifteen millions. It is now worth more than that number of billions. The Texan annexation was ratified in 1845, which gave us territory large enough for a new empire. Alaska was purchased April 10, 1867, and since then the eleventh census states that seal-skins to the value of $33,000,000, and other furs to the value of $16,000,000, have been sold in the London market. Owing to these successes, there is no part of the civil world where at this moment an American dollar, whether in paper or metal, will not bring its full value in gold; for you have taught the nations, the detestable character of repudiation, by your unflinching honor in assuming and paying, the very last dime of your obligation. Your financial basis is as solid now as the gold-packed mountains which look out on your Golden Gate, and it is known all over this earth that, as sure as thirty-six inches make a yard, so one hundred cents make an American dollar. As a travel-er, I have been charmed with the recognition of this fact in many parts of the earth. There is nothing of a secular sort, does a man more good when abroad, than to feel that he is trusted for the sake of his country. This, too, hath God wrought through the agency of a Sabbath-keeping people; therefore I weave this golden strand into the gar-land of gratitude we owe, and with you, casting it at His feet, adoringly exclaim, "Not unto us, O Lord, not unto us, but unto Thy name give glory." But I open another fold of the great standard "to be displayed, because of the truth," and I discover, furthermore, He has given unto us the banner of scientific prosperity in the practical and mechanical arts. There is no nation that ever has begun to compare with the American nation in inventive and applied genius, in the mechanical arts and sciences. Other nations, from old Egypt up, have been making things to stay—pyramids to sit and moulder, statues to lean on pediments, pictures to hang on walls. But the genius of Americans is applied to making things to go. To my mind, in this vast distinction, there are a promise and a prophecy. The mandate of the Master was "Go." Scientifically, we have been obeying, and in this obedience there is a preparation for something soon to follow. The best place to study the mechanical "go" of our people, however, is in the Patent Office in our National capital.

There you can see the 250,000 inventions which have been flowing from American minds. Machines for almost everything under the sun. Machines for ploughing, and drilling, and grubbing, and sowing, and reaping, and winnowing, and grinding. Machines for cultivating wheat, corn, rye, oats, barley, hops, cotton, cocoons, hay, sugar, molasses, potatoes, beans, peas and honey. Machines for the management of horses, oxen, pigs, sheep, goats, boys, girls, men, women and mosquitoes. Machines for manufacturing cloth, flax, hemp, jute, boots, brick tile, clothes, hosiery, rubber, iron steel, nails, tacks, prints, salt, tar and turpentine. Machines for diving into the deep and scanning the submarine regions of mystery, and the subterranean realms of dread. Machines for penetrating the azure depths of the celestial worlds and descrying their order, number, distance, size and speed. Machines for sweeping through the continent with "wheels of thunder and banners of flame," in a capital stock of ten billion, and on a mileage that is creeping up toward 200,000 at the rate of 6,000 miles a year. Machines for capturing and controlling one of the greatest invisible forces of nature, discovered by our own Benjamin Franklin, and trained to do message service by our own Samuel B. F. Morse, and set by the energy of American genius, to silently carrying annually 50,000,-000 messages over 300,000 miles of line, and weaving the world into one great brotherhood of commerce. Telephonic machines breaking down both space and time, and uniting by their net-work our great cities into one grand bourse of business. Electric light machines, brought to the birth by the splendor, of the inimitable genius, of our own Wizard of Menlo Park—blazing with a light before whose brilliancy and beauty, the golden stars themselves grow dim. So numerous and so mighty are these industrial machines, that with them we can accomplish more work, in this land than could all the world two hundred years ago. This, too, "hath God wrought," through a Sabbath-sanctifying people, and as I take these ever-active, ever-advancing, mechanical labor-saving powers, and work them into that garland of gratitude we all owe the Almighty, and as we adoringly lay it at the foot of His throne; let us together exclaim, "Not unto us, O Lord, not unto us, but unto Thy name give glory." [Amens.]

Garland of Gratitude.—No. 2.

For the Prosperity of this Land Under Sabbath Ministries.

Psa. lx, 4.—"Thou hast given a banner to them that fear Thee, that it may be displayed because of the truth."

Psa. cxv, 1.—"Not unto us, O Lord, not unto us, but unto Thy name give glory, for thy mercy, and for thy truth's sake."

IN our first study of our banner of national prosperity we discovered physiographic, agricultural, financial and scientific supremacies. In looking at it again I discover unequalled educational, humanitarian, heraldic and religious prosperities. 'Tis flags within The Flag. So, then, in opening another fold of the great, glittering standard God has given us, I find the banner of educational supremacy.

The time was, even in this land, when universal education was looked upon by many with leerful scorn. Thank God those times are forever past, for universal education is not only the grand fostering parent, of our advancement in the mechani-

cal arts and sciences, but is also the palladium of
our civil, social and religious liberties.

It was Numa in Plutarch said, "the fair fabric of
freedom passed away because it was not founded
on education;" it was Zaleucus, Pythagoras, Plato
and Aristotle who vainly tried to teach this blinded
world, that education was the only custodian of
civil liberty; it was the filibustering feudalities
who, in their imperious pride, denounced the general education of the people; it was the dignitaries
of Rome, who seconded them in their diabolical
denunciations. The poor world groped and
groaned on in darkness, beneath the lash of its
pitiless tyrants, without knowing the source of its
weakness, poverty and sorrow. But when Washington the great, and Jefferson the good, and
Adams the brave, rose up in the initial stages of
the integration of this Republic, and declared with
earnestness that an ignorant people could not be
free; when in later days Jedediah Peck, Adam
Comstock and DeWitt Clinton reiterated and re-
emphasized the educational principles of the patriot
fathers; when these never-to-be-forgotten gentlemen took hold with manly hand of the public
schools, and lifted them up out of their obscurity
and obloquy, and placed them in the very front
rank of our institutions and practically said, Now
let education become free as the light of heaven;
let her go forth untrammeled into every county

and State of this Union ; let her soften, soothe and
sharpen the rising race of this Republic from
ocean to ocean; let her re-cast the savage youth
who would grow up into desperadoes and outlaws,
and remold them into pleasing and profitable factors of society.   Then our statesmen generally
began to see that what they would have come out
in the state, they must first put into the schools.
And so all the States have come· into line, old
Massachusetts, who never yet failed in a vital
measure, leading the way.   Such has been the
progress, that far-off Illinois, according to the
eleventh census, is now abreast of Massachusetts.
And such has been the rectification of public senti-
timent, that the public schools are no longer looked
upon as only fit for pauper pupils and charity
scholars.   They are looked upon now as the bul-
warks of the State, of which every intelligent
patriot is proud.   There are, however, objectors
still.   But when you meet them say, Hands off the
poor man's child !   He is our child because he was
born in our country and could not help being so
born, and we mean that he shall have as fair an
opportunity, to equip himself for, citizenship as it
is possible for the state to give him.   Say hands
off to every aristocratic and exclusive scuttler, who
would selfishly keep the children of the poor and
unfortunate, in ignorance and obloquy that they
may govern them.   Educate the poor, inspire the

unfortunate, and they will govern equitably themselves. Experience proves the equity of this principle. As the schools increase, crimes diminish ;
as the schools flourish, pauperism hides its head in
shame. Three-fourths of the paupers and prisoners
of this Republic, are of those who have not been
brought up in our public schools. And as I look
over the entire field, at the 68,000,000 acres of land
granted, at the $82,500,000 of regular income, at
the 225,000 schools, at the 236,000 teachers, at the
$96,000,000 annually expended, at $211,000,000
worth of school property—figures which have
been greatly increased during the past decade, but
whose increase I cannot furnish because the bulletins are not all published—as I survey these educational expenditures, I say that in no department of
either State or National government, did this
country ever invest capital, which has brought and
will bring so immense returns, as that invested in
our public school system. We have yet almost
five million of people over ten years of age who
cannot read, and over six millions who cannot
write. This should not so be under a paternal
government like ours. Go on, then, great Instruct-
ress of the people, go. Woe be to the man who
would bind thy wings; woe waits the man who
would embarrass thy march, through poorer doles
dealt out to faithful teachers. Shall the officers of
the navy roll in luxury, and our hard-toiling

teachers groan in grinding poverty? Perish the thought! Away with the dull eyes, sunken cheek, anxious, haggard, care-worn looks, of these under-paid pioneers of learning. Let them be better fed, better clad, better supplied with books and apparatuses of experiment, and the reflex influence on the schools, and on the land will repay in plenty this added liberality.

There are sections, as Wyoming and Dakota, into which populations are pouring at a ratio of 200—300 per cent. increase each decade, and there the educational banner is floating high. But there comes a flood of immigrants, who settle in the large cities along these Eastern shores; and I, for one, say, let them come. Let them come, from the Isle that hangs bleeding and crying at the belt of Britain; let them come, from the historic, priest-belabored land of Italy; let them come, from the easy-going, beer-bibbing land of Germany. Aye, let the almond-eyed Oriental come. Let all come. But let all be taught, when they come, the majesty of American law, the sacredness of American institu-tions, and let their children be most thoroughly transformed into Americans, through the public school system. Thus will the body politic assimi-late to itself what the public schools put into the national hopper, and men will no longer feel that they can come here and de-Americanize this nation. The movement, in the minds of many of our statesmen, to curtail emigration, is neither wise diplomacy nor good humanity. It has reacted, and will react bitterly upon us. The suppression of Chinese emigration, to please a few demagogues like Dennis Kearny, has done more to alienate the Chinese nation from us than any measure that has ever passed Congress. We can afford to take care of the world's poor. It is by taking care of the world's poor that we have become richer than the world. Singular, statesmen cannot see this. Surely we have proved the imperishable truth of the words of the Lord Jesus, " Give and it shall be given you, good measure, pressed down, shaken together and running over, shall men give into your bosoms." Thus, then, let the Old World's poor come. The fact of their coming demonstrates they mean to do better. But let every one of their children (for we cannot do much with the old folks, and a few years will end them) be brought up to understand, and to obey the constitutional genius of this commonwealth, through the agency of our public schools. O! school commissioners, in this and every city, hear these words and heed this counsel. There is only one feature of our American school life, that I survey with serious alarm, and that is the stand that the administrators of the Roman Catholic Church, have taken in regard to the education of their youth. They refuse to receive our public school education on the plea that it is a Godless education and, paradoxical though it seem, these were the men who clamored for the expulsion, from the schools of the only Book that presents, an authoritative revelation of God to mankind. And so the blessed Bible, upon which this Republic is built, was in many instances expelled to please the adherents, of an ecclesiastical system, which history proves to be the subverter of nations. Well, even that would not work. They insisted on having the education of their own children, and disclaimed all paternity the State assumed, in regard to their educational welfare. They now are building parochial schools all over this land, and propose sectarian education only for their children. I look upon the coming results of this with anxiety. It cuts off one-tenth of the youth of this country from the other nine-tenths, and educates them as aliens, in sympathy with a foreign system, which assumes absolute authority over men, body and soul. There can no good come out of this scholastic schism. I apprehend much evil. Nevertheless, our duty is plain. God has given us the educational banner of the world. Our duty is to hold it high, and make it float over every palace and hamlet, and hut, in this realm till all the people are cultivated, and having done our best, still humbly say in our hearts, "Not unto us, O Lord, not unto us, but unto Thy name give glory."

By opening another fold in our great, growing,
national standard, I discern, furthermore, that God
has given us the banner of supremacy in humanitarianism, "to be displayed because of the truth."
Inhumanity has been one of the haggard and
horrid features of human history. The cruelty of
man to man; the rancour of clan against clan;
the rapacity of tribe to tribe; the hostility of
nation against nation; the slogan call to arms;
the trumpets summoning to war; the enlisting of
powerful armies; the drilling them for the field;
the leading them to the fray; the fierce onset of
mighty battalions on the battle plain; the crash
and gash and gore of encrimsoned butchery;
the groans of the dying; the shouts of the captains; the cries of the vanquished; the yells
of the victors; the rush of retreat; the storm of
pursuit; the enslavement of captives; the looting
and occupation of the territory — these, alas!
are the leading features of secular history. Chief
against chief; king against king; wars and
rumors of wars, have, up to a recent date,
monopolized the time, talent and resources of
mankind, the object of the whole being that
the one might subdue and tyrannize over the
other. But these shocking barbarities and this
fiendish ambition, have never had for any great
length of time the ascendancy in this Republic. The Revolutionary war was undertaken to

defend ourselves against just such barbarous impositions on the land; the War of 1812 was waged to defend ourselves against the impressment of our sailors on the sea; the Mexican war was undertaken to defend ourselves against incursions of the Mexicans on our southwestern border; the civil war was undertaken to prevent the westward spread of slavery. Thus it will be seen that there was a legitimate cause for every war we have yet waged, and every one of them has proved eminently successful. But still, humanitarianism had not gone very far when this nation was founded. For years after the Declaration of Independence, culprits were treated with much inhumanity. Prisons had no reformatory tendency; in many cases they created greater vagabonds. The innocent were thrown in with the guilty; youthful offenders with hoary scoundrels; women, too, with men. Disease, crime and demonry were the products. Ten crimes were punishable with death, even in glorious Massachusetts. In Kentucky, twenty-seven offences were followed with death or maiming. In those days, perjury, obtaining money under false pretences, horse stealing, writ stealing, breaking a jail, stabbing, etc., were punished unhesitatingly as capital crimes, probably because all such crimes were similarly visited in the Old World. But in 1822, Edward Livingston, the American Howard, rose and cried down and out

14

such inhuman barbarities; so that, now, only murder in the first degree is punishable with the loss of life. Prisoners, too, are classified; criminal children sent to the house of refuge or school-ship; chaplains appointed to instruct and reform the erring. The prisons are becoming reformatories instead of deformatories, places of sympathy and prayer instead of slaughter-houses, and the last report of the prison of Massachusetts demonstrates that 85 per cent. of criminals who come under this new and humane treatment slough off the old rags of rascality and put on the new garments of manhood. Similar reports come from New York.

The national census bulletins for 1890 say the total number of prisoners in county jails throughout the land June 1, 1890, were 19,538. The number reported in 1880 was 12,691, an increase in ten years of 6,847, or at the rate of almost 54 per cent. The increase in population was not quite 25 per cent. In 1880 the ratio of prisoners in county jails to the population was 253 in each million; in 1890 it was 312. The increase, therefore, has been 59 to the million. The largest increase has been in the North Atlantic division, where it was 95 to the million.

These figures prove that crime is on the increase only where Sabbath breaking is on the increase. Other statistics prove that crime is on the decrease where Sabbath keeping is on the increase, demonstrating the humanizing influence of Sabbath keeping and the demoralizing power of Sabbath breaking. In Sabbathless lands prisoners are treated with the most shocking barbarity. I have seen in Canton, China, a prisoner tied up by the thumbs and great toes, so that the weight of his whole body came on these four small members. I have seen another, before the eyes of the Mandarin, flagellated till the blood flowed in streams and the poor creature could scarce crawl away, and this was only his "first dish," as they call it. I found torture inflicted upon criminals and witnesses. Here are some of the modes: Striking the lips with sticks till they are jellied; nailing criminals to boards by malleting spikes through the palms; thrusting their head through the Cangue; throwing them on beds of spiked iron; using boiling water and red hot spikes, and cutting the tendon Achilles; compelling them to kneel on pounded glass, sand and salt mixed together, till the knees grow excoriated; ending up with an hundred blows with the bamboo. The quivering lips, the pallid face, the shuddering frame, all proclaim the agonies of these poor creatures.

Such is the inhumanity of the greatest Sabbathless land on earth. How different the humane treatment in this Sabbatic land. No torture permitted on prisoners except that of confinement.

Books, papers, chaplains, church, admission of friends and advisers, and every other element that can reform and renew the culprit and send him forth a new man. These, of course, are privileges of recent prison life, but they have come to stay and grow, until our prisons, shall assume rather the function of renovators than inquisitorial and murderous Bastiles.

Anæsthesia, too, has been born in this land. Before her birth the sufferer had to endure, the lacerations of surgery and tortures of dentistry with no alleviation. But since the demonstration in Boston, in 1846, of the harmlessness of inhaled ether, millions have been relieved of their sufferings and the sources thereof, without passing through the old time pangs. The thanks of the world are due such men as Horace Wells, of Hartford, and Morton, of Boston, who by their experiments have shown humanity how to shun the abnormities of disease and enormities of pain.

Nor has the spirit of humanity forgotten the jeopardized seamen on our coasts. All along the Atlantic and other dangerous shores life-saving centers have been established. Fitting men and apparatuses, such as the car and breeches buoy, are appointed to deliver seamen in distress, and so successful have these surfmen been in rescuing imperiled lives, that out of 1,989 endangered seamen 1,980 were saved in a single year.

I need not mention the 6,000,000 slaves recently
emancipated, nor stop to portray our homes for
the friendless, foster homes, asylums, reformatories,
houses of refuge, relief bureaus. Nor need I wait
to paint the munificent responsiveness, of our people in the presence of any great calamity, such as
the Chicago fire or the Johnstown flood. The memories of these are fresh in our minds. I have traveled and investigated patiently in twenty-three of
the leading nations of the earth, and I have no hesi-
tation in announcing that for sympathy in sorrow,
for helpfulness in distress, for a humanity that is
prompt, practical and abundant, America easily
leads the world; and furthermore, I have no hesi-
tation in declaring that this fairest of all the humanities has flowed from the love of Him who
went about healing the deaf, dumb, blind, halt,
withered, palsied, leprous and demonic, and finally
suffered His loving hands and feet to be nailed to
the bitter tree for our advantage. [Praises be to
God.]

Thus, then, hath God given us the banner of
humanitarianism "to be displayed because of the
truth," and as we gather up all these expanding
charities in our hearts, we bring them adoringly
to the foot of His throne and humbly exclaim:
"Not unto us, O Lord, not unto us, but unto Thy
name give glory." [Hallelujahs and amens.]

Again, by looking for another flag folded in

this great standard, I discover our heraldic emblem which God has given us "with a star for every State and a State for every star," "to be displayed because of the truth." All nations have their symbolic standards—China her couchant dragon, Japan its rising sun, England her rampant lion, Russia her volant eagle, Turkey her crescent, etc. But of all the national ensigns, for significance of symbology, we prefer the flag of the United States. Those red stripes symbolize sacrifice, a law which is as universal as space and time; those white stripes symbolize purity, an excellence which is primal in every noble character; that ground of blue symbolizes liberty, an exhilarating, exalted possession, which flows from sacrifice and purity; those stars symbolize light, an essential essence emanating from the introduction of the other three in human character. But our flag is not only intrinsically significant; but it is extrinsically powerful.

Joel R. Poinsett was United States Minister to Mexico. The election of Pedraza as President was distasteful to many Mexican people. The mob rushed to arms, took possession of the Accordata, and thence rushed out upon the government troops that were posted in steeples, convents and churches. Building after building was demolished, massacre after massacre committed, when, at length, the excited murderers came to the house of our Minister, who had in his humanity admitted refugees. A shot was at once fired through his cloak, and the wild insurgents cried, "Fire into the windows; burn the building; bring up the cannon." In the height of this furious infatuation, Mr. Poinsett marched out on his balcony, wrapped in our flag, defiantly shouting to the sea of savages, "Fire on that if you dare!!" Instantly every musket was unleveled, every threatening voice hushed, and the assassins slunk away as if they had suddenly been confronted with an exploding Vesuvius. And if the united savagery of the world were to besiege these shores, crying, Disrupt the Union, abolish the commonwealth; a proper exhibition of the same grand flag, with all it represents, would blaze out with the splendor of Jehovistic victory. I believe God is as much with our national banner now as he was with the Ark of Israel, the talismanic ensign of His chosen people; and from observation in many realms, I am convinced there is no pennon that floats from masthead, no standard that streams from flagstaff, that commands the reverence and awe which the flag of our country inspires. It represents a genuis for man-building as well as for man-ruling. This genius enabled the second son of Ebenezer Webster, a small New Hampshire farmer, to rise gracefully from poverty and obscurity to be the first orator, the foremost jurist, and the leading statesman of his day. This genius led

forth from the solitudes of the woods, the young
Kentucky rail-splitter, and taught him first to be a
soldier, then a grocer, then a surveyor, then a
lawyer, then a legislator, then President of this
Republic, liberator of Cis-Atlantic Africa, conser-
vator of this Union and martyr for his country.
This genius led by the hand the child of impecunious Jesse Grant, the Georgetown tanner, up from
the swill of the tan vats, to and through West
Point, through the Mexican war, the civil war,
whence he came forth Commander-in-Chief of one
of earth's mightiest armies, the conqueror of a formidable Rebellion, the rebuilder of this Commonwealth, the President twice of this Confederation of
nations he had saved, the silent sufferer and the
military ideal of an admiring and benefited world.
This genius which this banner of our country
represents, not only overawes insurgents without
and integrates giants within, but creates admiration
around, extending possibly to the other life. If we
could summon from the shades, Washington the
great and the good, what entrancing pictures that
have grown up under this Sabbatic flag might we
present before his appreciative gaze? I seem to
see his venerable form slowly rise from its long
repose on the lovely slopes of the Potomac. A
certain complaisant sweetness casts a radiant glow
over his firmly fashioned features, as he contrasts
the condition of this country now with what it was

when he left it on that cold December morning of
1799. As he ascends some mount of all-embracing
vision and looks out upon our fruitful farms; as he
descends into the underground treasuries and be-
holds our well-worked mines; as he emerges to
our trade department and investigates our world-
commanding system of commerce and finance; as
he looks into our immense works of practical arts
and applied sciences, lifting the land to unheard-of
splendor; as he critically surveys our educational
system, making education free as the light of
heaven, from ocean to ccean, and elevating the
young to intelligent citizenship; as he pauses
before our humanitarian institutions, studding with
stars of love the whole body of the land for relief
of the belated and benighted. And then, as he casts
his military eye over our history; as he spies
Andrew Jackson's troops drive back, once and forever, his old-time enemy (the rattling, rollicking,
appropriating, attitudinizing Johnny Bull, who
never misses a chance of being under the branches
when the tree of nations is shaken, to pick up
his swell share of the fruit) from behind the cotton bales in New Orleans; as he reviews the
grandeur of our troops in the subsequent Mexican war, on the heights of Alto, on the plains of
Palma, amid the smoke of Vista, and coming off
more than conquerors through the rush and roar
of Contreras and Monterey; and, as coming down

to later times, he scans with his fine sense of
martial frenzy the forty-five battles of the civil
war, till freedom for the slave and solidarity to the
Union were forged with a skill, courage and persistence that never have been surpassed ; and then,
finally, as he turns and surveys the resumption of
unparalleled peace and prosperity at home, and the
unequalled credit and eclat abroad, would not our
venerable founder forget his accustomed calmness,
and rushing rapt in a flame of patriotic admiration,
grasp that flag as the symbol of our powerful
privileges, and in the fine poetic strain of Francis
Scott Key, exclaim :

> " 'Tis the star-spangled banner ! Oh long may it wave,
>   O'er the land of the free. and the home of the brave."

And would not these over sixty-two millions of
ever-increasing Americans respond, with a reson-
ance that might shake the world :

> " Forever float that standard sheet,
>   *As valiant sons rise up before us,*
>   With freedom's soil beneath our feet,
>   And freedom's banner streaming o'er us."

And then, together addressing that Supreme
Being before whom Washington himself often
prayed, and who delivered him out of all his sore

distresses, we would together say, "Thou hast given this banner of great secular prosperity to them that fear Thee, to be displayed because of the truth." We will display it, therefore, nevertheless, "Not unto us, O Lord, not unto us, but unto thy name give glory for Thy mercy and truth's sake." [Amens and hallelujahs.] But I unfold again this great substantial standard of our nation, because I finally discover another banner within its pattern—the banner of religious prosperity. This is the most important of all. Indeed, to it all the others owe their unexampled development. The prosperity of this nation, under the sway of the Lord of the Sabbath is a fulfillment of many prophecies. Take but one—in Deut. xxviii, 1–13, of which this new Israel is a literal fulfillment in every respect:

"And it shall come to pass, if thou shalt hearken diligently unto the voice of the Lord thy God, to observe *and* to do all His commandments which I command thee this day : that the Lord thy God will set thee on high above the nations of the earth :

"And all these blessings shall come on thee, and overtake thee, if thou shalt hearken unto the voice of the Lord thy God.

"Blessed *shall* thou *be* in the city, and blessed *shall* thou *be* in the field.

"Blessed *shall be* the fruit of thy body, and the fruit of thy ground, and the fruit of thy cattle, the increase of thy kine, and the flocks of thy sheep.

"Blessed *shall be* thy basket and thy store.

"Blessed *shalt* thou *be* when thou comest in, and blessed *shalt* thou *be* when thou goest out.

" The Lord shall cause thine enemies that rise up against thee to be smitten before thy face : they shall come out against thee one way, and flee before thee seven ways.

" The Lord shall command the blessing upon thee in thy store-houses, and in all that thou settest thine hand unto: and He shall bless thee in the land which the Lord thy God giveth thee.

" The Lord shall establish thee an holy people unto Himself, as He hath sworn unto thee, if thou shalt keep the commandments of the Lord thy God, and walk in His ways.

" And all people of the earth shall see that thou art called by the name of the Lord ; and they shall be afraid of thee.

" And the Lord shall make thee plenteous in goods, in the fruit of thy body, and in the fruit of thy cattle, and in the fruit of thy ground, in the land which the Lord sware unto thy fathers to give thee.

" The Lord shall open unto thee His good treasure, the heaven to give the rain unto thy land in His season, and to bless all the work of thine hand : and thou shalt lend unto many nations, and thou shalt not borrow.

" And the Lord shall make thee the head, and not the tail : and thou shalt be above only, and thou shalt not be beneath ; if that thou hearken unto the commandments of the Lord thy God, which I command thee this day, to observe and to do *them*."

These are blessings that have come to us through obedience. Those interested in seeing the terrible curses awaiting disobedience can do so by reading the rest of the chapter, as I am not on that side of the subject to-night. These blessings were just so far given to old Israel as it obeyed the Lord.

These blessings have been conferred upon, and shall be continued to us, in exact ratio as we are sub-missive to the Giver. The lapse of time has not altered the Divine method of moral government one millionth part of an hair's breadth. The great men and nations of the past, and of the present are but the volitional chariot, on which Jehovah rides, and all who will not be obedient to the Divine procession upwards are swept, and must forever be swept, into utter desolation downward. They become the flying drift from the wheels of Jehovah's train, flung out of the way to make it easier and safer for the next procession that comes on God is in this world and those of you who are making your reckoning, without reference to Him are making it without reference, to the only Being on whom you are utterly dependent. This would not be good business policy. How can it be good religious diplomacy? For the most part our people early caught hold of this great idea of utter dependence on God. They seem to have said practically, " We will do our best, O Lord, now do Thou thy best with what we do." Hence there has been a marvelous progression, in the very nature of religion itself in this land.

Before the Declaration of Independence religious toleration was unknown among even the colonists. They had an idea that to be intolerant was to be religious. Hence Congregationalists persecuted Episcopalians, Episcopalians persecuted Puritans, Roman Catholics persecuted Quakers, and Quakers proscribed Roman Catholics, whilst Stuyvesant sent religious cranks in chains to Holland. Before

the Revolutionary war these five sections—New
England, New York, Virginia, Maryland and Pennsylvania—were bitterly intolerant of each other in
religious matters, and dissenters from either by
each were deemed worthy of death. If our roy-
stering "Robert" had ranted in those days as in
these, he would have been hung from the first limb
of the nearest tree. But now men more tolerantly
say, if any man be such an avaricious lunatic
as to close his eyes, and go forth crying up
and down the world to scoffers for fifty cents a
head, that there is no sun; we simply continue our
way in the full splendor of his blessed beams, balancing in our minds, which exhibited the greatest
folly, the speaker, or the pitiable creatures who lost
their time, money and hope by listening to him.

This spirit of toleration began with this Republic. It was unknown in any part of Europe till
after it had spread from hence. Religious rancour
ran riot through every land. Many of the people
who joined the churches seemed "tenfold more the
children of the devil" than before. But after the
Declaration of Independence New England, as
usual in every advance, set the example and became willing to give other people a right to think.
All the other sections followed suit and abolished
religious oligarchy and adopted religious equality,
at least in theory. But it was hard to break up
the petrified incinerations of ages, and it was not

really till the Methodist itinerant appeared, hovering over every frontier, distributing chapters of charity from his saddle-bags and volumes of love from his sermons, that the whole Republic was smelted into one great sisterhood of amicable States, where a man was only valued for what his life weighed, and his opinions were only regarded in proportion as they produced good fruit. And so it has come to pass that no man is considered any the less valuable, on account of his religious shibboleths, provided his life is a well rounded reproduction of our Lord's.

This great growth is bringing the pilgrims together. Congregationalists, Baptists, Presbyterians, Episcopalians, and even Roman Catholics, have all found out that in order to be good Christians they must be good Meth-od-ists in reality if not in name, for all good beings go by method. The bad alone are methodless. In this way all the denominations fall in love with the name Methodist, and the only trouble with the Methodist is that he can jump, out and into another fold as easily, as a young colt can clear a fence on a June morning, because he fancies there is better pasture or more privilege on the other side. They are generally glad enough to jump back, however. There are some things that need mending with us. We need to stop our flight from down town churches, by which a monumental beauty as St.

Paul's, New York, is sold and the fortress that should have detonated with living truth, till this world's end, to crowded congregations, is given up.

We need to reform our inequitable methods of administration, by which a church, because it is strong and rich, secures its choice of pastor, whilst a church which is weak and poor is refused its preference. If it is right for the former to have its choice, it is right for the latter, and there ought to be no respect of churches in this matter. I think I am inside the bounds of truth, when I say that scores, if not hundreds, of churches and ministers are hurt every year by such partial, inequitable and diabolical administration.

These and kindred defects, it is to be hoped, will be remedied to good degree next General Conference, unless we send up old-time ring-masters, who have their own preferment, more at stake than the welfare of God's militant host. God forbid that such should be the case, for the stone taken "out of the wall" of a church like St. Paul's " cries out," and "the beam out of the timber" in many a church like Fulton street, Elizabeth, "answers it."

Notwithstanding these and kindred defects, such is our vitality, that the reflex results of Methodism on other denominations, in quickening them are acknowledged to be greater, than the direct results in making and keeping Methodists themselves. And such is the vitality of Methodism that she can

give a crop of malcontents, to other churches every
year, and go grandly on multiplying without them.
My own opinion of the mission of Methodism is
commensurate, with my opinion of the mission of
Americanism. My conviction is that as God intends America to emancipate, and civilize the
world politically, so He intends Methodism to elevate, and regenerate the world spiritually. The
work of the one is simultaneous and commensurate
with that of the other.

John Richard Green, in his admirable history of
England, in speaking of what Methodism has done
for other churches says: "The least results of
Methodism are the Methodists themselves." I say
the same of Americanism; "The least results of
Americanism are the Americans themselves."
Such a statement may seem startling and unsup-
portable, but when you have read history backward, forward, across, and have confirmed the
same by personal inspection, you will come to the
same conclusion. These views of mine will explain
why I flame and storm when any villainous hand is
thrust out against Americanism, on the one side, or
Methodism on the other. I believe they are the
Jachin and Boaz of Jehovah's civilizing, emanci-
pating and evangelizing temple in this era.

The history of Methodism is closely interlaced
with that of this Republic. The history of this
Republic is closely related to the history of Metho-

dism. The one could not have existed in such world-moving form without the other. The one cannot advance, in its intended mission to the nations of the earth without the other.

There are many other organizations in this land. They have fine churches and many members, and I pray God to bless these more and more, but when I take into consideration that more of this world has come under the scepter of The Christ since Methodism was born in John Wesley's heart under Peter Böhler, February 7, 1738 (inside the space of 153 years), than had come under its sway during all the 1,738 years that preceded, I cannot but think that Methodism is to be the great spiritual power of the future, unless she, too, ripens into corruption, by falling into lust of secular power instead of spiritual blessing. If ever the preachers come to have a keener relish for a rich official than for a lost soul; a fleeter foot toward the house of the luxurious sinner, than toward the hut of the impecunious saint; an "itching palm," a winking eye, a caoutchouc conscience, a man-pleasing, time-serving, place-seeking and preferment-adoring spirit. In a word, if ever the time come when, as a body, Methodist preachers make the church dependent upon rich sinners, then we shall wither up by the roots.

What we need is not more contracted churches, but bigger and better preachers ; not more toadying, but more talent; not more base sycophancy, but more mighty manhood; not more mean fawning, but more sterling Godliness; not more servile adulation, but more of the terrible grandeur of the power of God resting upon us, so that we shall care for, and need no other power to bring to bay every enemy of God and man. [Amens.]

O, for twenty thousand men with the trumpets of Peter Cartwright and of Jesse Lee, with the heart of Francis Asbury and the fires of Benjamin Abbott, to bring up the Church to its highest heroism; that it may keep pace in its spiritual power, with the millionaires in the monetary power, that as the millions are rolled up from the soil by the industries and enterprises of our people, these millions may be rolled out to the mission field to carry the gospel to all the world. Step by step, *pari passu*, we are advancing with the State as the great heaven-sent Chieftainess, responsible for the instruction and inspiration of the masses, so that they may come up themselves, and then bring all they have to bring others up. I like the ring from Washington of ten millions for an American university; I would like the sound still better of ten millions being collected, and ten thousand heralds " going forth into all the world to preach the Gospel to every creature." Not merely to take a missionary excursion and education, and then return on furlough at the expense of the mis-

sionary treasury; but ten thousand men who mean
business as Paul meant it; ten thousand men who
will go out to live, and stay, and work, and preach,
and plead, and pray, and die, and be buried, and
sanctify the places they have saved by their graves.
I, for one, am sick of this missionary holiday business. And the thinking part of the Church is
getting tired of it. And it is to be feared the great
Head of the Church is getting weary of it. And
pretty soon the whole Church will revolt at it. It
is high time to stop it. It never should have been
begun. The man who is favored with a call to the
mission field, should feel so absorbed that he would
want no discharge. Let there be the spirit of
genuine apostolicity shown on the foreign field;
let the missionaries rise to the heroism of living
martyrs who glory in death for Christ's sake; let
it be known they go forth, to do and die gladly for
the salvation of this world; let it be seen that the
world is being saved by their sacrifices, and it
would be less troublesome, to raise ten millions for
ten thousand such heroes than it is now to raise
one million for one-tenth that number of comers
and goers. We have the money; we ought to have
the men. We have the commission; we have the
opened nations. The stress and grandeur of the
situation are upon us. O, for some missionary
eagle to swoop round the circles of the Church
with an eye that sees all the work, and a voice that

will be heard round the world, rousing the Church
to pour out its tens of millions, and stirring the
young, with such strokes from God, as shall make
them glad to go by thousands, and preach the
Gospel to the heathen, till they fall, and falling,
sweep up to glory from fields of victory. [Amens.]

Total suppression of the rum traffic and full enfranchisement of women, would contribute greatly
to this world's salvation, as would also free trade
among all nations. Reasons for this hereafter.
We should not now dwell so much, on conditions of
success as on gratitude for success. Nevertheless,
I have made this digression. If we have not made
all the progress we ought, this need not prevent us
from offering praise for the advance that has been
made. If there are some obstructions that block the
path, there are more inspirations that cheer the
way. If there are some things over which we
mourn and weep and pray, there are many things
over which we are glad, and rejoice and praise.
The pioneer of the cross has kept pace with the
pioneer of the plough; the rising, thickening villages have been blessed with the rising, growing churches; the aggregating towns have
been frequently supplied with able and aggressive preachers; and whilst, in some of our largest
cities, "the world, the flesh and the devil" have
been permitted to get ahead of us, chiefly through
the inundation of foreign people and practices,

nevertheless, on the whole, we have been enabled this year to present a larger percentage of population inside the Church than in any other year in our history. We have over ten million members in our Protestant Churches. Nearly one-half the people are either by person or proxy connected with the Church of Christ, and six millions more than one-half, if we include the Romanists, and I, for one, wish to include them. The Methodists constitute over one-third of the entire Protestant Church membership of the Republic. The past has been full of battles and successes; the future laden with conflicts of hope. The dawn has really come. Behind it is the rising sun. Phœbus, surrounded with the tripping angels of the morn, is about to appear. The world is ripening and the east is red. Our Master has not misled us. His is the only kingdom that seems about to come. Every evolution bespeaks the fulfillment of His promise and the proximity of His person. His Spirit fills our eyes with vision and our hearts with love. Myriads have safely gone, and myriads more crowd to the golden landing. [Hallelujahs.]

The Master and His love were never sung so sweetly by so many voices. The Gospel trumpet never had behind it so many hearts of feeling and minds of power. The Gospel tree never had in it so much vitality; nor on it so many leaves of promise; nor round it so many influences of heaven; nor under it such soil of culture; nor over

it such balm of blessing. Long through the lone
ages has it been preparing. But when ready it
will flush forth in a night. Then "shall a land be
born in one day." Then "shall a nation be brought
forth at once." The heavenly forces are all on our
side. The goal of the world is The Christ. The eyes
of the earth are examining the King. Every progression is radiant with promise. Every fulfillment
opens up a larger vista and a clearer view. Every
heart-beat feels the ecstasy and every mind-flight
thrills with joy. Closing in and over us is the
heavenly world; our life inhales the compressed
rapture, our being exhales the celestial radiance,
and so, amid this converging glory, gathering up
the streamers of this nation's standard, its physiographic, agricultural, financial, mechanical, educational, humanitarian, heraldic and religious, we
weave them all into a double garland of gratitude to
our loving, heavenly Father, and approaching reverently His glorious throne, we loyally lay it at
His feet, crying with the departed Hebrew saint:

$$\text{לֹא לָנוּ יְהוָה לֹא־לָנוּ כִּי־לְשִׁמְךָ תֵּן כָּבוֹד עַל־חַסְדְּךָ עַל־אֲמִתֶּךָ:}$$

"Not unto us, O Lord, not unto us, but unto
Thy name give glory, for Thy mercy, and for Thy
truth's sake." [Amens, Hallelujahs, Glories.]

www.ingramcontent.com/pod-product-compliance
Lightning Source LLC
Chambersburg PA
CBHW021119270326
41929CB00009B/955